CONTENTS

Published 2022. Little Brother Books Ltd, Ground Floor, 23 Southernhay East, Exeter, Devon EX1 1QL
books@littlebrotherbooks.co.uk | www.littlebrotherbooks.co.uk
Printed in the United Kingdom
The Little Brother Books trademark, email and website addresses, are the sole and exclusive properties of Little Brother Books Limited.

ONLINE ACTIVITIES

On some of the pages you will see QR codes. These QR codes take you to online Purple Mash activities which support learning from the relevant page.

To use the QR codes, scan the QR code with the camera on your web enabled tablet, click on the link and the activity will appear on screen.

Alternatively, QR readers are available on the app store for your device.

SCAN CODE

purple mash

PARTS OF A SENTENCE

In the Loud family, each sibling has their own special role to play, just like in a sentence where each word has a different role.

There are different parts of a sentence (also known as word classes). You will know them as **nouns**, **verbs**, **adjectives** etc. Each type of word in a sentence has a different role.

1

Match the type of word to its job.

noun	**a.** Describes a noun or a pronoun.
verb	**b.** Always used just before a noun that gives more information about it.
adjective	**c.** Joins phrases, clauses and sentences.
adverb	**d.** The name of a person, object, time or place.
conjunction	**e.** Shows more about the time, position or direction of the action.
pronoun	**f.** Describes an action, thought or state of being.
determiner	**g.** Mostly describes verbs but also adjectives and other adverbs.
preposition	**h.** Used to replace a noun to prevent repeating it over and over.

2

Look at the words below. Can you sort them into the correct word class?

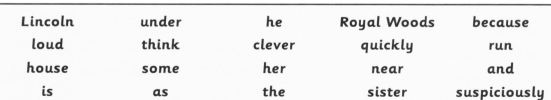

Lincoln	under	he	Royal Woods	because
loud	think	clever	quickly	run
house	some	her	near	and
is	as	the	sister	suspiciously

noun	verb	adjective	adverb

conjunction	pronoun	determiner	preposition

LINKING IDEAS WITHIN A PARAGRAPH

Lisa, the genius of the family, is getting a bit fed up with the family telling fibs to excuse their mischief. She has decided to write a report on how to get her family to be more honest. She knows she needs to make the facts flow better.

1

Here are the notes Lisa took during her experiment. Can you help her write the report by writing the steps into full sentences using the time conjunctions and phrases to help? Remember to put a comma after time conjunctions and phrases when they're at the start of a sentence.

Use time conjunctions and adverbial phrases from the boxes below to make the report flow better.

Time conjunctions:
next, later, after, then, first, finally, when, until, meanwhile, initially, immediately, eventually, afterwards.

Adverbial phrases:
once completed, at this point, after a while, to begin with, ten minutes later, soon after, a few minutes later.

LISA'S EXPERIMENT NOTES:

- Noticed that lots of people in house tell fibs – Lori said had to do homework rather than drive Lana to dump; Lincoln fibbed about how awful Leni's new haircut was; and everyone told Dad they liked his fish dinner when it was awful.

- Invented lie-detecting glasses and forced everyone to tell truth. Family hated telling truth and broke glasses.

- Activated lie-detecting cameras in house and continued forcing everyone to tell truth. Everyone got angry and went to their rooms.

- Helped family destroy the cameras - told as many fibs as possible to overload system.

USEFUL WORDS TO SPELL – PART 1

Twins Lana and Lola are used to seeing double! They have noticed that lots of words that they are learning have double letters, some even have two sets of double letters. Knowing how many double letters there are can help to learn the words.

1 Help Lana and Lola find and circle all the words that contain double letters.

accommodate	accompany	according	achieve
aggressive	amateur	ancient	apparent
appreciate	attached	available	average
awkward	bargain	bruise	category
cemetery	committee	communicate	community
competition	conscience	conscious	controversy
convenience	correspond	criticise	curiosity

2 Can you find the words with double letters in the wordsearch below?

w	c	c	x	l	u	z	k	a	d	a	a	s	q	c	a	i	a
d	o	a	n	m	x	w	m	p	i	p	c	i	c	o	y	a	k
l	m	c	q	d	c	a	d	p	y	p	c	k	o	r	z	g	y
p	m	c	p	c	j	c	a	r	s	a	o	y	m	r	r	g	r
c	u	o	n	m	l	c	t	e	n	r	m	q	m	e	f	r	y
e	n	r	y	y	l	o	t	c	i	e	m	a	u	s	m	e	e
x	i	d	x	b	j	m	a	i	w	n	o	f	n	p	w	s	p
o	c	i	i	w	d	p	c	a	s	t	d	f	i	o	x	s	q
t	a	n	l	h	m	a	h	t	k	s	a	u	t	n	u	i	w
r	t	g	k	c	s	n	e	e	a	x	t	i	y	d	c	v	x
v	e	a	i	o	r	y	d	y	w	z	e	f	x	i	t	e	b
g	z	t	a	u	f	b	a	c	o	m	m	i	t	t	e	e	s

COMMAS, BRACKETS AND DASHES

When adding extra details to sentences, you can use commas, brackets or dashes to mark where the words and phrases (known as parenthesis) have been added.

Brackets are used more for facts and figures and in formal writing. **Dashes** are often used more informally. One way of adding extra information is by including extra facts about the person, place or object.

1 Lincoln knows that a good plan needs to be detailed, so he's put lots of info into his plan for where to sit in Vanzilla. Fill in the gaps in Lincoln's plan using the information in the box below.

a. It is important to get the right seat, _____, to make long car journeys enjoyable.

b. Lynn (_____) is too active to sit beside for a long time.

c. Beware sitting next to Lola - _____ - or the whole journey could be a makeover session.

d. Lori (_____) gets carsick so don't sit in front of her.

e. It is best to sit next to Leni, _____, as she ends up in a daze.

> also known as the sweet spot
>
> always texting Bobby
>
> keen to practise martial arts
>
> the beauty pageant queen
>
> the second eldest sister

2 Lincoln has packed the sentences below full of information but has forgotten to use parenthesis. Choose whether to use commas, brackets or dashes for each sentence and mark where they should go.

a. Royal Woods founded in the 1600s is located just south of Saginaw Bay in Michigan.

b. It has a large population approximately 20,000 residents and has very little crime.

c. The two cities found nearby within a 60 mile radius are Huntington Oaks and Hazeltucky.

d. There are lots of restaurants including Aloha Comrade and Jean Juan's French Mex serving a wide range of cuisine.

SPEEDY READING

Lynn's reading a newspaper report about her favourite hockey team's latest match. She's in a hurry so is skim reading the text to quickly find the information she needs. Scan the report then see if you can complete the table below.

MICHIGAN MANIAC MASTERS GABA-GHOULS!

It was a dramatic night at the rink last night as the Royal Woods Jellyfish seized victory and reached the playoffs in the dying seconds against the New Jersey Gaba-Ghouls after a nail-biting match!

The enthusiastic crowd were right behind the home team in the first period as the puck zipped across the ice, chased by two teams determined to reach the playoffs.

Rowdy McQuads, as always, was the star of the Jellyfish show; his goal so forceful that the Gaba-Ghouls goalie fell over backwards trying to save it! McQuads, also fondly referred to as the Michigan Maniac, scored in the opening seconds of the second period. However, the Gaba-Ghouls fought back, matching the Jellyfishes' goal for goal.

There was huge excitement when McQuads scored his hat-trick, prompting the usual tossing of hats onto the ice by the home fans. By the end of the period, the Jersey team had pulled it back to a tie.

After some entertainment during the break - where a fan slid across the ice to high-five the Jellyfish players and was nicknamed 'the Penguin' - it was back to business! With just one minute remaining, New Jersey went up by one goal, much to the dismay of the home fans.

However, Rowdy McQuads should never be discounted, and he scored twice in the final seconds. The rink erupted with delight as the Royal Woods Jellyfish earned their spot in the playoffs!

1 Complete the table by deciding whether the statements below are true or false.

	TRUE	FALSE
a. The Gaba-Ghouls are from New Orleans.		
b. Rowdy McQuads scored the first goal.		
c. Fans throw their scarves on the ice when there is a hat-trick.		
d. New Jersey scored with just seconds to spare.		
e. Rowdy McQuads nickname is the Michigan Maniac.		

2 When did a fan slide across the ice? _____

ADDING SUFFIXES TO CREATE VERBS

Lucy loves dark and dramatic action words. She is writing a new spooky poem ready for Halloween and wants to use the very best words to create an eerie atmosphere.

You can create verbs from nouns and adjectives by adding **suffixes**. Remember that adding a **suffix** can cause the spelling of the root word to change.

1

Help Lucy create some spooky verbs in her poem by using the correct suffixes. Choose from the suffixes below. You may need to take off an existing word ending to add the suffix on.

| -ate | -en | -ify | -ise |

a. horror ➡ _____

b. threat ➡ _____

c. fright ➡ _____

d. terror ➡ _____

e. energy ➡ _____

f. irritation ➡ _____

g. Which word can create two verbs? _____

2

Lucy is changing these words using the same suffixes. Can you write the new word using the correct suffix from the ones above? You may need to remove a word ending before adding a new one.

beautiful _____

character _____

hard _____

active _____

electric _____

light _____

regular _____

equal _____

SUFFIXES -ABLE AND -ABLY

Ms Fix it, Lana, is great at mending things. She's writing an advert for her fix-it services and is trying to use the suffix -able and -ably as much as possible to describe herself.

To decide whether to use the suffixes **-able** or **-ible**, you can follow these rules: If there is a complete root word without the suffix then add **-able**. If there is not, it is spelt with **-ible**.

horror → horr → horrible   honor → honorable

↑ Not a full word   ↑ Is a full word

Words that end in: **-ation** use **-able**. Words that end in **-ce** and **-ge** keep the **e** before the suffix **-able**. This also applies to **-ably** and **-ibly**.

1

Write the correct **-able** or **-ably** word in the descriptions. Hint: There is one exception here that uses **-ible**. The first one has been done for you.

a. Lana is quite ___adorable___. (adoration)

b. She has _____ talents. (consider)

c. Her work is always _____. (depend)

d. The word 'perfection' is _____. (application)

e. You will view the work _____. (favour)

f. The whole experience will be _____. (enjoy)

g. She is always honest and _____. (rely)

h. She is very _____. (knowledge)

2

As usual, Lucy is taking the negative view on all this and has written her own anti-advert for Lana. She has used lots of words that end **-ce** and **-ge**, what is the rule for these?

a. Lana is also very _____. (change)

b. Her excess energy is barely _____. (manage)

c. The improvements are often not _____. (notice)

MAKING AN ACCOUNT FLOW ACROSS PARAGRAPHS

Luan is trying to write a funny story about the time she pranked Lincoln on April Fool's Day to cheer Lily up. She's made some notes to help her.

You can make a story flow by linking paragraphs using different methods:

Use **ellipses**: These are three dots in sequence at the end of a sentence like this …

Repeat words that you want to emphasise between paragraphs. For example, if you are trying to convey a feeling of beauty, you might use the word beauty several times across paragraphs adding suffixes when necessary for variety.

Repeat phrases the same way. For example, a spooky tale might repeat the phrase 'the darkest of nights,' several times.

1 Can you write her notes into sentences and add extra details? Make sure you use repeating words and phrases across the paragraphs and finish each paragraph on an ellipses.

NOTES:

Paragraph 1:
- April Fools' Day – Luan ready with lots of pranks
- Kitchen floor covered in grease – Lincoln slipped
- Was hit in the face with a punching bag

Paragraph 2:
- Went to bathroom – was covered in flour by falling flour bag.
- Luan watching
- Sprayed by the sink

Paragraph 3:
- Went to living room
- Was flung to ceiling and stuck on flypaper
- Exhausted – Lincoln called Clyde for help

SEMICOLONS, COLONS AND DASHES

Some twins finish each other's sentences. Lana and Lola have been known to do this, especially when finding a short cut to finishing their homework! Today, the twins are writing about their Scottish ancestors.

Colons join dependent clauses **:** The parts before and after the colon are full sentences on their own but the second part adds more detail to the first.

Semicolons extend a sentence by joining together two independent clauses **;** they do not need to be full sentences on their own.

If you want to emphasise a section **—** use **dashes —** this makes it stand out.

1

Can you match these related parts of a sentence together and write them below with a colon in the middle?

> a. Loch Loud is in Scotland.
>
> b. The current Loud family visited Loch Loud on a vacation.

> They were driven out after a resident called Aggie had enough of the noise!
>
> The Loud family ancestors lived there.

_____

_____

2

In this sentence, replace the underlined word with appropriate punctuation to join the two clauses.

> **Aggie was able to drive the Loud family out of Loch Loud <u>because</u> she controlled a dragon called Lolo.**

3

Separate the clauses in this sentence using dashes to see how this creates emphasis and drama.

> **Lincoln decided to make a name for himself in Loch Loud, he managed to fix many of the problems in the town, gaining him the support and respect of the residents.**

READING COMPREHENSION: INFERENCE PART 1

Luna is in the middle of reading a story about a space cowboy, a princess and a rock goddess. She is trying to use inference to understand more about the writer's meaning and why the characters behave the way they do. She knows that she needs to think about what the writer is hinting at and find evidence in the story to support her ideas.

Cautiously, Triton, Princess DeLola and Ribbon the frog picked their way along the forest path. Dark, shadowy trees surrounded them; only the starlit sky gave them light as they went searching for the next crystal shard. The hushed sounds of the forest were suddenly broken by the sound of someone jamming on an electric guitar.

Out of nowhere, a glowing figure appeared. The trio paused in shock as they stared up at the enormous, pink cloud holding the strange being who was playing the guitar and cackling loudly. It was a rock goddess: that much was evident from the pink Viking helmet, the numerous piercings in her ears and nose, and the sheer physical size of the creature. Her fingers flew across the huge strings at lightning speed as she picked and strummed with her other hand.

Triton, in all his years of travelling through space, had never seen anything like it before.

"Wow, she's incredible." He breathed, gazing up in awe and wonder.

Of more interest to one of the intrepid trio, however, was the source of the brilliant glow emitting from the goddess.

"Look at her guitar," the princess gasped, her eyes wide. "It's powered by a crystal shard! We have to get it from her."

1 Luna needs help answering these questions. Can you find hints in the text to help her answer them?

a. What suggests that the forest was peaceful before they met the rock goddess?

_____

b. Triton "breathed, gazing up in awe and wonder". What does this suggest about how he is feeling?

- [ ] He is surprised by what he sees.
- [ ] He is terrified by what he sees.
- [ ] He is amazed by what he sees.
- [ ] He is saddened by what he sees.

2 Luna is trying to find evidence in the text to answer these questions. Can you help her?

a. Find two pieces of evidence that suggest that the goddess is much larger than the other characters.

_____

_____

b. How does the princess feel when she notices the shard? How do you know?

_____

_____

ADDING PREFIXES

In the Loud House, there is always someone up to no good with their mischief changing the meaning of words...

Prefixes can be used to change the meaning of words. The prefixes below make many words have the opposite meaning.

dis-	de-	mis-	over-	re-	-un

Look at this example:

Appear is a verb; it means something comes into sight or becomes visible. For example, Lucy suddenly **appeared** in the basement.

Disappear means cease to be visible: The prefix **-dis** has changed the meaning of the verb. For example, Lucy seemed to **disappear** from the room.

1

This is Lisa's report card:
Perfect as usual...

However, Luan has seen an opportunity for mischief, she has intercepted the card by sneaking it out of Lisa's bag and is adding prefixes to make the words mean the opposite of what Lisa's teachers have written.

Insert some prefixes from the choices above to make Lisa's report card change in meaning.

Lisa always _____behaves. She usually _____agrees with everything that her teachers suggest to improve the quality of her work. I strongly _____approve of her _____obedience and her _____reaction to any suggestion. She is often recommended to Principal Huggins to allow him to have the opportunity to ____view the way Lisa ____acted when given a challenge. She is very ____respectful and makes other students feel very ____comfortable. I am sure that Mr and Mrs Loud will definitely _____like her latest report card.

2

Luckily nobody believed the fake report for even a moment! Luan's written a list of jobs she can do for the family to make up for causing such mischief.

Use the correct prefix either **re-** or **over-** so the list makes sense.

a. • _____take managing the washing up after dinner.

b. • _____build Lily's toy brick palace.

c. • _____write the report correctly... 100 times!

d. • Promise to _____look any pranking opportunities for the next two weeks.

e. • Give Lisa a foot massage to ____charge her damaged pride.

f. • _____make the family's beds every morning for a week.

SPELLINGS: EI WORDS PART 1

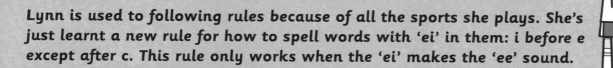

Lynn is used to following rules because of all the sports she plays. She's just learnt a new rule for how to spell words with 'ei' in them: i before e except after c. This rule only works when the 'ei' makes the 'ee' sound.

1 See how quickly you can reach the finish in this game. Roll a dice and move the number of spaces thrown. If you land on a word that's spelt incorrectly, go back to the start and try again.

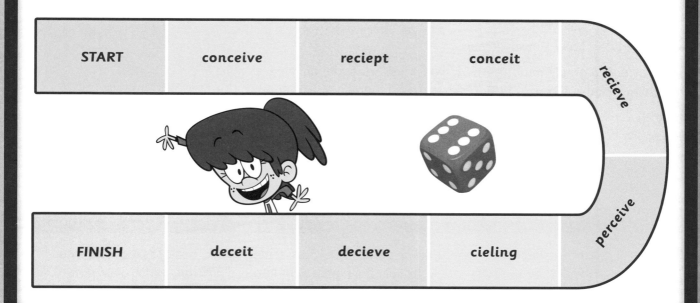

START	conceive	reciept	conceit	recieve
FINISH	deceit	decieve	cieling	perceive

2 Lynn wants to make a tricky version of the game above with some irregular **ei** and **ie** words, but first she needs to know how to spell them. Can you spot which of the words below follow the rule and which are exceptions? Finish spelling the words correctly.

	a. prot__n	ei / ie		d. f___ld	ei / ie
	b. shr__k	ei / ie		e. caff___ne	ei / ie
	c. s__ze	ei / ie		f. th__f	ei / ie

WRITING A PLAYSCRIPT

Lincoln loves writing comic strips and now he's learning how to turn his stories into playscripts.

A playscript should contain the following:
List of actors, setting, actor name followed by the line they say with a new line for each speaker, stage directions written on a new line and in brackets. Reading it should help you visualise the action in your head. Here is an example:

Actors: Lori (first born daughter of the Loud family, age 17) and Leni (a Loud sister, age 16, born fashionista)

Setting: The Loud House kitchen

Lori: (Looking pale and upset) Oh woe is me. I literally have never gone so long without a text from Bobby... my life is literally falling apart.

Leni: (Looking at herself in the mirror while holding lots of shopping bags) Hey sis, do what I do when I am sad... head for the mall!

(Leni holds the bags up in the air.)

(Lori drops her head onto the table in despair.)

1 Lincoln's latest comic strip starts after he's snuck the class spider, Frank, out of school and into his bedroom. Follow the rules above to turn the comic strip into a playscript. Write your script on a piece of paper.

WRITING A NEWSPAPER REPORT

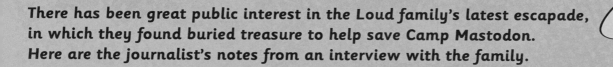

There has been great public interest in the Loud family's latest escapade, in which they found buried treasure to help save Camp Mastodon. Here are the journalist's notes from an interview with the family.

1 Use the notes to write a report. Think of a suitable headline and ensure that your writing captures the excitement of the event while including the facts. It should include:

- **Who? The Loud Family**
- **Where? Near Camp Mastodon**
- **When? Last week**
- **What? Saved the camp from closing**
- **How? Found buried treasure**

Write in the third person: like an outsider looking in, using pronouns like 'he', 'she', 'it' or 'they'.

Use time conjunctions such as 'firstly', 'meanwhile', 'later', 'finally' and 'eventually' to help create cohesion.

- Heard that the camp was closing.
- Went to visit one last time.
- Helped Mr Rinsler clear his office and found a treasure map.
- Followed the map to a treasure room.
- Realised the treasure was fake and got locked in the treasure room.
- Escaped treasure room to find real treasure room.
- Set off a trap and were nearly pushed off a cliff.
- Rescued by Leonard Loud, their grandfather.
- Took treasure back to the camp.
- The camp will be saved.
- Mr Rinsler will be retiring and the camp will be run by their grandfather.

RELATIVE CLAUSES

Luna has a gift for writing song lyrics and is working on her latest hit. Can you help her extend her sentences using relative clauses?

1 Relative clauses add more information about a noun in a sentence. Complete the song lyrics below by adding one of these relative pronouns in each gap:

which	where	when	whose	that

a. Dare you enter on Halloween night the corn maze, _____ has no end in sight?

b. There's a girl who hides below the ghostly moon, _____ glitters and gleams in the gathering gloom.

c. On Halloween, _____ the clock strikes one, there's a shadowy figure, _____ time has come!

d. So come on down to the creepy corn maze, _____ the monsters practise their wicked ways.

2 Luna wants to add some extra detail into this section of her song. Can you rewrite each sentence below and add a relative clause using a relative pronoun about the word in bold? Remember to put commas around the relative clause if it is in the middle of the sentence. The first one has been done for you.

a. Dancing, prancing in the spooky **maze**,

whose walls were higher than any gaze.

b. The **monsters** joining full of glee and song

_____

c. The shadowy figure returned later that **night**

_____

d. The whisps of wind chilled the **ground**

_____

SPELLINGS: EI WORDS PART 2

Lynn has been working hard on her tricky 'ei' spelling game, but baby Lily has just toddled past and spilt her juice all over the answer cards making some of the words dissolve.

1

Tick the cards that have the correct spelling. Put a cross on the cards that are spelt incorrectly and write the correct letters in the gaps. To help you, use the rule: i before e except after c. Remember, this rule only works when the 'ei' makes the sound 'ee'.

a.
Word shown:
perceive

Correct or incorrect

☐

Correct spelling:
pe_____e

b.
Word shown:
recieve

Correct or incorrect

☐

Correct spelling:
re_____e

c.
Word shown:
nieghbour

Correct or incorrect

☐

Correct spelling:
n_____bour

d.
Word shown:
field

Correct or incorrect

☐

Correct spelling:
f____d

e.
Word shown:
theif

Correct or incorrect

☐

Correct spelling:
th___f

f.
Word shown:
ancient

Correct or incorrect

☐

Correct spelling:
a_____nt

g.
Word shown:
reciept

Correct or incorrect

☐

Correct spelling:
re____pt

h.
Word shown:
leisure

Correct or incorrect

☐

Correct spelling:
l_____re

2

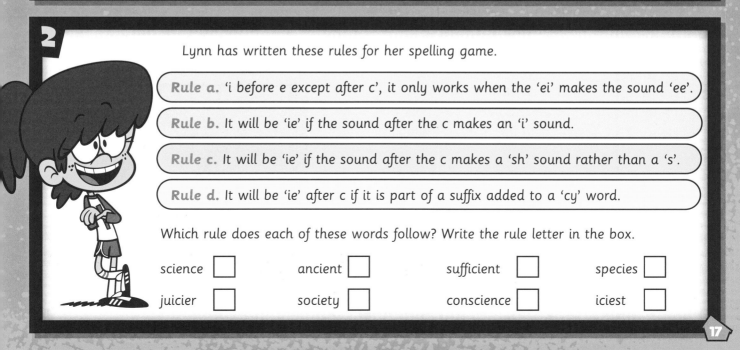

Lynn has written these rules for her spelling game.

Rule a. 'i before e except after c', it only works when the 'ei' makes the sound 'ee'.

Rule b. It will be 'ie' if the sound after the c makes an 'i' sound.

Rule c. It will be 'ie' if the sound after the c makes a 'sh' sound rather than a 's'.

Rule d. It will be 'ie' after c if it is part of a suffix added to a 'cy' word.

Which rule does each of these words follow? Write the rule letter in the box.

science ☐   ancient ☐   sufficient ☐   species ☐

juicier ☐   society ☐   conscience ☐   iciest ☐

COLONS AND SEMICOLONS IN LISTS

Lincoln is trying to be more organised so he's learning how to write lists correctly. He's found out he needs to use a colon at the start of a list and then commas or semicolons depending on the size of the item in the list.

> Example:
>
> **Short items**
> Items to pack in my schoolbag: pen, pencil, squirt ring, joke book, Mr Coconuts.
>
> **Long items**
> Ways to escape washing up: hide in Lisa's underground bunker; change Lily's diaper (yuck!); emergency trip to the bathroom; help Lola find another tiara; ask Lisa for a hypnotism potion.

1

Lincoln always has a plan to carry out. There is a science fair coming up at Royal Woods Middle school and he is determined to get top prize. He has made some lists to help him organise himself. The lists should use commas as the items are short. Punctuate his lists correctly.

a. People who could help me win Lisa Clyde Lana Luan.

b. Items to source are wood nails saw bicarbonate of soda cola paints.

c. Permissions required are Lisa Mom Dad Lily Principal Ramirez.

2

Lincoln is putting the finishing touches to his plan to secure the TV for watching his season finale. He needs to use semicolons between the items as they are longer and contain commas. Can you check he has included all the semicolons needed and add any that he has missed out?

To get the best spot and keep the sisters away, I need to: cause an argument with the twins using a tea set and frogs; tell Luan to get her camera to photograph the twins fighting; give Lisa milk, eggs, flour and sugar to experiment with give Lynn a helium-filled ball to play with; tell Leni she has a zit on her nose, even though she doesn't give Luna a glowing flashlight that creates a lightshow make sure Bobby phones Lori; and get Lily to fall asleep before the show starts.

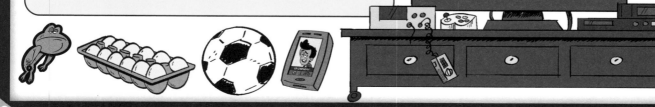

READING COMPREHENSION: VOCABULARY

Lisa is researching 24-hour sunlight in the Arctic Circle. She knows the importance of understanding scientific vocabulary so, if she's stuck on a word, she tries to use another word in its place. If the sentence still makes sense, she's found a word with the same meaning (synonym) to help her understand the text.

The Land of the Midnight Sun

Many countries in the Arctic Circle experience a phenomenon unique to the polar regions. During the summer months, the most northern parts of countries such as Alaska, Norway and Russia have endless days where the sun never sets. Conversely, in winter, these same areas will be plunged into three-month long darkness without a sunrise.

Why does this happen?

Due to the tilt of the earth's axis, running from pole to pole, the earth faces the sun at an angle. This tilt causes the seasons to occur. Seasons are fairly like each other near the equator with the differences between them becoming more extreme and noticeable the further away from the equator they get. In the polar regions, they have the most extreme seasons. In summer, the tilt means that the sun never dips low enough below the horizon to set. This causes 24-hour daylight. However, in winter, the tilt means that the sun never rises above the horizon causing endless night with the darkness fading to grey at the sun's peak.

1

Lisa is identifying some of the key vocabulary in the article. Can you help her by answering the following questions?

a. Find and copy a word that means a strange occurrence. _____

b. Find and copy a phrase that shows it is not all of the country that experiences 24-hour daylight.

_____

c. Find and copy a word that means obvious, easy to spot. _____

2

Lisa is having trouble understanding the end of the text. Can you help? Look at the final sentence. Which of these phrases is closest in meaning to 'peak'?

☐ Having a look   ☐ Lowest point

☐ Highest point   ☐ Mountain

3

Lisa is trying to explain what one of the words means. Can you help her write the answer? Look at the sentence beginning, 'Conversely, in winter, these…' What does the word conversely mean?

_____

ADVERBS TO INDICATE POSSIBILITY

Lynn would say her chances of winning any competitive event are a certainty. She feels she has no use for any other adverbs that describe how likely something is to happen!

1

Separate the adverbs in the box into those which show that Lynn is **certain** or *very* **likely** to win and those which show it **might** happen.

Certain or very likely	Might

certainly
definitely
maybe
possibly
clearly
perhaps
probably
obviously

2

Look at the sentences below. Circle the correct adverb to complete the sentences to help Lynn work out her chances in next week's football match.

a. As it is in December, the match is being held indoors so it will **maybe/clearly** stay dry.

b. The other team are excellent players so it will **definitely/possibly** be a challenging match.

c. Lynn is concerned that if one of her team's players gets injured, they might **certainly/perhaps** lose.

d. The other team are a bit taller than Lynn's so if the ball is in the air near the goal, they could **probably/obviously** score.

SPELLINGS: HOMOPHONES

Twins Lana and Lola know all too well that things can sound the same and look different! The trick is to know the meaning of each word to help know when to use it.

1 Lana is all about action! She's spotted that these homophones are spelt differently when they are a noun (the name) or a verb (the action). Nouns are spelt with a **c** and verbs are spelt with an **s**. Help her put the nouns and verbs in the correct column.

Noun	Verb

advice/advise

devise/device

license/licence

practice/practise

prophesy/prophecy

Complete these sentences with the correct homophone.

| advice/advise |
| devise/device |
| practice/practise |

a. Lynn asked coach Keck for _____ about being the best, coach Keck tried to _____ her that practice was important.

b. Lisa tried to _____ a _____ that made her sisters silent.

c. Luan was invited to do tricks at the medical _____ to cheer up the patients, she had to _____ every day to perfect her act.

2 Lola is trying to match these homophones to the correct definition. Can you help her match them correctly?

stationary	to abandon, a barren place
stationery	agreement, to agree
desert	to make something complete or more complete
dessert	paper, envelopes etc.
compliment	going up
complement	not moving
ascent	paper, envelopes etc.
assent	a sweet course after the main course of a meal

HANDWRITING PRACTICE 1

Lola always makes maximum effort to look good.
This even extends to the beauty of her handwriting!
She joins her letters and makes sure that the
spacing and sizing is always perfect.

1 Copy the sentences she has given Lincoln to practise.

Neat handwriting helps you make better plans.

Practise makes perfect with handwriting.

2 Lincoln has written a plan for Clyde. Can you copy it out neatly?

To win the camera, we will need to record lots of funny videos. We could hide quietly and film my sisters when they are not looking. We can then catch them doing something embarrassing and just put the clips together the next day.

CREATIVE WRITING: WRITING A PLOT

You now know so much about *The Loud House* you've been given the job of writing the plot for an episode! Remember to include the reactions of all the characters to a situation and think about what they would all do.

1

Use these ideas to get you started or use one of your own.

Lisa is always creating experiments and inventions to try to help her friends and family. In this episode, Lisa has decided to help one of her sisters with their problem by creating an experiment or an invention.
- Choose which problem you think she should solve.
- How could she solve it?
- What happens when she tells the sister she is going to help?
- How does the experiment or invention work? (Or maybe it doesn't work!)
- What happens after?
- Remember to include her sisters' reactions!

Lynn has a martial arts competition coming up, but no-one wants to practise with her as she hits too hard and they end up being hurt.

Leni is trying to create designs for new clothes but keeps forgetting what she was creating in the middle of each design.

Lori is cross because the batteries on her devices don't last long enough and keep dying when she's talking to Bobby.

_____
_____
_____
_____
_____
_____
_____
_____
_____
_____

VERB TENSES

Different tenses are used when describing something that happened either in the past, present or future.

The present perfect tense is a way to show that an action started in the past but not at a specific time. For example, Lori has texted Bobby 3256 times.

1

The Loud siblings have had a busy day. Write a sentence for each sister using the present perfect tense ('has') and the past tense of the verb. The first one has been done for you.

Run 5km.	Laugh the most.	Wait for Lola to get ready.	Walk into three walls.	Play a loud riff on her guitar.
a. Lynn	**b.** Lana	**c.** Luan	**d.** Lori	**e.** Luna
Lynn has run 5km.				

2

Leni is trying to convert these simple past tense sentences into past perfect tense sentences. Lisa has explained that she needs to add 'had' before the verb and check the verb is in the correct past tense form. Can you help her change the sentences to past perfect tense? The first one has been done for you.

a. Leni walked down the stairs. <u>Leni had walked down the stairs.</u>

b. She noticed Luan's banana skin. _____

c. She slipped on it anyway. _____

d. She fell down the stairs. _____

e. Leni went to the doctors. _____

USEFUL WORDS TO SPELL – PART 2

As the quietest Loud sibling, Lucy likes silence!

She has noticed that some of the words in the list below have silent letters or do not sound the way they are written. Sounding the words out and stressing the tricky parts the way they are written can help to learn these words, e.g. envi-RON-ment, de-FI-NITE.

1 Read through the words in the table then search for them in the word search. The words can be going downwards, left to right, or diagonal.

definite	desperate	determined	develop
dictionary	disastrous	embarrass	environment
equip	especially	explanation	exaggerate
excellent	existence	familiar	foreign
frequently	government	guarantee	hindrance

d	e	l	f	g	t	k	i	e	q	m	f	o	c	e	s	y	e
i	x	d	c	f	a	m	i	l	i	a	r	e	e	x	d	s	n
s	p	k	e	z	o	b	o	d	v	t	e	x	x	c	i	d	v
a	l	d	m	t	i	r	w	e	k	i	q	i	a	e	c	e	i
s	a	e	b	a	e	g	e	f	m	b	u	s	g	l	t	s	r
t	n	v	a	g	b	r	z	i	y	z	e	t	g	l	i	p	o
r	a	e	r	u	i	e	m	n	g	k	n	e	e	e	o	e	n
o	t	l	r	a	n	q	s	i	j	n	t	n	r	n	n	r	m
u	i	o	a	r	i	u	c	t	n	t	l	c	a	t	a	a	e
s	o	p	s	a	d	i	l	e	n	e	y	e	t	t	r	t	n
v	n	t	s	n	p	p	u	k	y	i	d	y	e	v	y	e	t
j	s	l	v	t	e	s	p	e	c	i	a	l	l	y	q	e	t
g	g	o	v	e	r	n	m	e	n	t	d	g	e	l	u	m	s
q	u	h	p	e	g	y	k	c	r	s	m	i	v	p	b	w	a
k	j	d	r	o	n	t	u	h	i	n	d	r	a	n	c	e	s

MODAL VERBS TO SHOW POSSIBILITY

Lynn is now learning how modal verbs can help her understand how likely it is that something will happen. Always helpful when she wants to win at all times!

*We **will** win the match today.*

One use of a modal verb is to show how likely something is to happen. The most used modal verbs for possibility are:

might	will	must	shall	can	would	should

1

Lynn is trying to decide if the sentences are showing possibility or certainty. Help her by ticking the correct box for each sentence.

		Shows certainty	Shows possibility
a.	It might rain in Royal Oaks tomorrow.		
b.	Lynn can play many sports.		
c.	Lily will try to escape her nappy.		
d.	Luna may be a rockstar when she's older.		

Modal verbs can also be used to describe:

- **Ability** e.g. could succeed... can run if they want to...
- **Obligation** e.g. should be happy.... should be grateful... it would be rude not to...
- **Permission** e.g. can climb the tree because they have claws to grip.

2

Lynn needs to identify the modal verb in each sentence. Can you circle the modal verb for her?

a. In the football match, Lynn could not score and passed the ball to Margo.

b. Margo was cheered by everyone and Lynn knew that she should be pleased for her.

c. Lynn knew she must score the winning goal in the next match to get the praise.

d. They agreed that they should be supportive of each other.

PREDICTING AND EXPLAINING

Lincoln has persuaded Lana to enter the Little Miss Prim and Perfect Pageant as he has his eyes on the prize. Read the text below then answer the questions about it.

He had to get Lana to behave better in the final round, the talent round! Otherwise, the chance to win those tickets to Dairyland would slip through his fingers.

"Lana, what is the problem?! We went over everything in Gil's book, and the companion DVD, and the podcast!" He growled, putting his hand on Lana's shoulder and nudging it. "How are you still not getting it?"

Gil Delily was a pageant expert whose book Lincoln had studied relentlessly in order to train Lana into becoming the perfect pageant queen.

Lana sighed and hung her head. "I'm sorry, Lincoln." She muttered. "No matter what I do, I can't be prim and perfect like these girls. Maybe there's something wrong with me."

Lincoln could see she was feeling bad about herself to the point where she would start to cry. As she turned to leave, Hops (her frog) jumped on top of her and looked at Lincoln. He too was clearly ashamed of his behaviour and shook his head. Lincoln felt a stab of guilt.

"Lana!" Lincoln cried, running to catch up to them and putting his hands around her shoulders.

"Wait. There's nothing wrong with you. I'm the one who messed up. I got so caught up in winning those tickets, I turned into Gil DeLily... who, when you stop to think about it, probably needs to get a life."

Lana snorted softly and nodded. She wasn't convinced though as she replied: "Yeah, but still, why can't I be like them?"

"Because you're you," Lincoln reassured her, smiling gently. "You're messy and muddy and keep a lot of reptiles in your pants. But that's what makes you awesome. And I was crazy to try and change you."

1

How did Lincoln's attitude to Lana change during the story? Tick one:

☐ He became more angry.

☐ He became more accepting.

☐ He became more ashamed.

☐ He became more attentive.

2

Can you use clues in the story to predict what might happen next and explain why you think this?

_____

_____

_____

_____

HYPHENS

Bobby, Lori's laid-back, absent-minded, pizza-delivering boyfriend, is finding out more about hyphens!

> Hyphens can join a prefix to a word and create compound words to make a sentence clearer. Although it looks like a dash, a hyphen is different; dashes join clauses while hyphens help create words.

1

Add the correct prefix **re-** or **co-** to the root words below.

a. ____ordinate	b ____enter	c. ____energise	d. ____operate
e. ____enact	f. ____elect	g. ____operation	h. ____equip

2

Can you explain how the hyphen helps make the meaning of the word clearer? Remember the prefix **re-** means again!

recover _____

re-cover _____

resign _____

re-sign _____

3

Can you add hyphens to join two or three words together so that the sentences make more sense?

a. If Lincoln goes to the aquarium, he might see a man eating shark!

_____

b. In the kindergarten class, Leni saw twenty two year olds painting pictures.

_____

c. This wall should be fine now as Lana used quick drying paint.

_____

WRITING A STORY FROM A PLAYSCRIPT

Lucy watched Lincoln's recording of what happened when the Loud siblings had to venture into the basement to turn the circuit breaker on. She thinks it will make a great spooky story for *ARGGH!*, Hunter Spector's TV show.

Lucy knows that great dialogue has all the correct speech punctuation, uses a variety of words for 'said' and adds information about how it is said. e.g. "The circuit breaker is... in the basement," Lincoln warned his sisters, folding his arms and gazing at each of them in turn.

1 Help Lucy turn the script below into a spooky story for ARGGH! Remember to make it dramatic by including lots of description with great adjectives to create a ghostly atmosphere! Describe how the siblings are speaking and what they are doing while talking, to really show their characters. Continue your story on a separate piece of paper if you run out of room.

[The kids arrive at the basement. Lori's silhouette peers over the basement's darkness.]
Lori: "Why am I the one who has to do this?"
Lori's Siblings: [at the same time angrily] "Because you're in charge!"
Lori: "All right, all right! Come on, Luan. Light the way."
Luan: "That's the brightest idea you've had all day!" [giggles. Lori pulls her from their siblings. After doing so, Luan's glow goes away. The rest of the siblings gasp.] "Oooh. I thought I was staying in tonight, but
I guess I'm going out!" [Luan giggles as the rest of her siblings sigh.]
Lori: "Lisa, give her another one of those cookies. We won't tell."
Lisa: [On her clipboard] "Negative. That was the only one. Prototype."
Lori: "Just great..." [hears a wooden creak and gasps in fear] "There's something in the basement! I'm not going down there!"
Lynn: [teasing Lori] "Ooh! You're scared of the dark!"
Lori: "I am not! You're the one who's scared."
Lynn: "I'm not afraid of anything."
Lucy: "Boo."
Lynn: "AAH!"
[While most of the girls start arguing, the twins start to tremble with fright.]
Twins: "THERE'S A GHOST IN THE BASEMENT!!!" [sobbing]

-OUGH WORDS

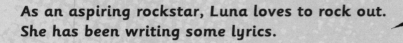

As an aspiring rockstar, Luna loves to rock out.
She has been writing some lyrics.

> Rocking out to a cheering crowd... hear them screaming Luna Loud,
> My favourite colours are platinum and gold... being a rockstar never gets old...
>
> She really wants to start perfecting her lyric writing skills but is a little unsure about some words as they have different sounds. Words with **–ough** in are the ones she needs help with.

1

Match these unusual **-ough** words to their pictures.

| bough |
| borough |
| dough |
| nought |
| plough |
| trough |

a.

b.

c.

d.

e.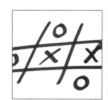

f.

2

There are seven sounds that **–ough** makes. Help Luna sort the **–ough** words below into the sounds they make so she can choose rhyming words for her song lyrics.

| although | borough | bough | bought | brought | cough | dough | enough |
| fought | rough | thorough | though | thought | throughout | trough |

off	oh	oo	or
		through	

ow	uff	uh	
plough	tough		

30

ADVERBIALS

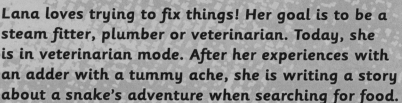

SCAN CODE

Lana loves trying to fix things! Her goal is to be a steam fitter, plumber or veterinarian. Today, she is in veterinarian mode. After her experiences with an adder with a tummy ache, she is writing a story about a snake's adventure when searching for food.

One way to make paragraphs flow properly is by using adverbials at the start of sentences and paragraphs to help them connect to the next or the previous sentence or paragraph. Here are some examples of adverbials:

after a while	finally	nearby	one day	under the stone

1

Lana wants to add time and place adverbials to the beginning of her paragraphs but can't decide which ones to use. Can you choose either a time or a place adverbial for each paragraph and write it in? Remember to include a comma afterwards.

a. _____ the snake went to look for some food.

b. _____ the snake still hadn't found anything, so he hid and waited.

c. _____ the snake was watching and coming up with a plan.

d. _____ the snake prepared to leap out and pounce.

e. _____ the snake had caught its prey! It was time to eat.

2

Look at these adverbials. Can you use some of them to write three sentences about a fun day you've had?

firstly	later	then	subsequently	as a result	after
finally	however	at the same time	during	next	

_____

_____

_____

_____

ALPHABETICAL ORDER

Lisa is working on her latest invention – a 'Gloweos' cookie that makes whoever eats it glow in the dark!

1 Lisa has written a list of things she needs for her Gloweos experiment. Can you help her put the list in alphabetical order?

beaker
test tube
Bunsen burner
funnel
milk
salt
tongs
water
fuel
sugar
pipette
eggs

2 Lisa is looking for a better word for '**heat**' in the thesaurus to include in her Gloweos report. She is currently on a page where the word at the top of the page is '**hole**'. Does she need to go **forwards** or **backwards** in the thesaurus to get to her word?

_____

3 Lincoln has written a list of his siblings in alphabetical order, but Lisa thinks he has made a mistake. Can you rewrite the siblings' names in the correct alphabetical order?

Lana   Leni   Lincoln   Lisa   Lily   Lucy   Lori   Lola   Lynn   Luan   Luna

_____

_____

_____

CREATIVE WRITING: WRITE A CHARACTER PROFILE

Lincoln and his sisters are always making new friends. They are able to describe both the personality and the appearance of their friends and can use descriptive phrases to help create a clear description.

1

Pick a sibling and describe a new friend they have made. Think about the friend's looks and personality. Draw a picture of the new friend and write some ideas about how their personality might match or clash with the sibling you've chosen.

Ideas for the new friend:

_____

_____

_____

Picture of the new friend:

2

The siblings are trying to describe the new friend using expanded noun phrases. They know they need to use two adjectives to describe the noun (e.g. long, dark hair) and can add more detail by adding a prepositional phrase at the end (e.g. long, dark hair with red highlights). Help them by picking three nouns and expanding them.

_____

_____

_____

3

Lincoln and his sisters are trying to describe their new friend to their parents. Can you write a character description using your expanded noun phrases to help them?

_____

_____

_____

SPELLINGS: -CIOUS OR -TIOUS

Luna is about to submit her latest song recording to America's Next Hit Maker. She dreams of opening a concert for Mick Swagger someday. Before she can submit the song, she wants to rehearse it one more time and check how catchy her rhyming lyrics are.

> When adding the suffixes **-cious** or **-tious** to create adjectives, you need to see if the root word ends in **-ce** or **-cacy**. If it does, add **-cious** but if it doesn't, add **-tious**.

1

After reviewing the lyrics, Luna wants to make some changes to key words. Help her decide whether to add **-cious** or **-tious** to these root words to create adjectives.

a. grace _____

b. ambition _____

c. caution _____

d. malice _____

e. infection _____

f. nutrition _____

g. delicacy _____

h. conscience _____

i. fiction _____

j. vice _____

2

Look at Luna's spelling practice. Can you spot any spelling mistakes in using **-cious** or **-tious**? Tick if the spelling is correct and rewrite it correctly if she has made a mistake. Watch out for the exception to the rule which uses **-xious**!

a. Spatious _____

b. nutricious _____

c. Precious _____

d. suspitious _____

e. Repetitious _____

f. ungracious _____

g. Ancious _____

h. ferotious _____

USING COMMAS TO CLARIFY MEANING

Pranking monster, Luan, always writes down her practical jokes when she's planning them. Because of this, she knows that a comma in the wrong place can sometimes lead to a very different meaning!

1

Look at the pairs of sentences. Help Luan explain how the comma changes the meaning of the sentence.

a. Let's eat Lincoln!
   Let's eat, Lincoln!

   _____

b. Lincoln's friends are his sisters, Clyde and Rusty.
   Lincoln's friends are his sisters, Clyde, and Rusty.

   _____

c. After leaving, Leni, Lori and Bobby played golf.
   After leaving Leni, Lori and Bobby played golf.

   _____

d. Bananas which come from hot countries are the best for practical jokes.
   Bananas, which come from hot countries, are the best for practical jokes.

   _____

2

Luan has been given a shopping list to take to the supermarket but some of the commas are in the wrong place. Rewrite the list so that Luan buys chocolate ice-cream, toffee apples and baby shampoo and definitely no chocolate chicken!

Things to buy at the supermarket:
bread, toffee, apples, milk, butter, baby, shampoo, chocolate chicken, ice, cream and oranges.

_____

_____

_____

_____

_____

USEFUL WORDS TO SPELL – PART 3

Leni wants nothing more than to be made employee of the month at Reininger's, the department store where she works. To improve her chances, she's studying the employee handbook to make sure she knows what all of the words in it mean.

1 Help Leni identify the different words and compete the crossword puzzle. The first letter has been given to you in the clues. Some of the other letters have been filled in to help you.

Crossword grid:
- 1 Down: L U L L (top right)
- 2 Across: I _ _ _ _ _ ; 3 Down: I ; U
- E ; G
- 4 Across: P _ O _ _ _ S _ ; I ;
- 5 Across: P _ _ S _ _ A _ I ; E
- A
- 6 Across: O _ _ 7 P _ _ _ N _
- 8 Across: M _ R _ _ L _ _ U _
- 9 Across: Q _ _ _ E
- A

Caption on image: SWEATERS

Across

2. A single person in a group. **(i)**
4. A paid job or occupation. **(p)**
5. Activity related to the body rather than the mind. **(p)**
6. A chance to make something possible. **(o)**
8. Extremely good or wonderful. **(m)**
9. A line of waiting people or vehicles. **(q)**

Down

1. Method of human communication through words or writing. **(l)**
2. When something happens instantly. **(i)**
3. The characteristics which make up a person. **(i)**
7. To make someone think or believe a certain thing. **(p)**

READING COMPREHENSION: INFERENCE PART 2

Lori is writing a story about a ghost who haunts a golf course. She has tried hard to use detail to build up a picture in the reader's mind. She has also tried to include a variety of facts and opinions - opinions being what someone thinks is true while facts are literally facts!

Behind the rusting, wrought-iron gates and the sign announcing in curled script that this is the Eternal Greens Cemetery, a legend lurks amongst the crumbling gravestones. In the midnight hours - when the few visitors that still come to pay their respects are no longer present - a luminescent figure can occasionally be seen endlessly replaying their eternal rounds of golf. Sparse trees cast long shadows on moonlit nights as their finger-like branches reach graspingly for signs of life.

On this night, tendrils of mist seep through the gates, covering the ground like a writhing blanket just waiting to wrap around unsuspecting ankles. The creaking of the gates alerts the few nocturnal residents that someone is entering their domain. The girl looks around. It is clear she is nervous; she feels she does not belong in this place, in this time. Cautiously, she edges forward, peering around the headstones celebrating the golfing heroes of yesteryear. A rustling sound catches her attention. She freezes. Eyes wide and darting, she slowly turns towards the sound. Her heart pounds as adrenaline races through her body. What can it be?

A dart of movement has her scrambling backwards. She shrieks. A small figure emerges from the mist and she heaves a deep sigh. There, in a patch of long grass and weeds, is a gopher. She does not know whether to feel relief or frustration. Her search for the golfing ghost continues...

1 What impression has Lori given of the cemetery? Find two adjectives that you feel describe the golf course and find evidence in Lori's story that support your ideas.

Impression	Evidence

2 Decide if these sentences are fact or whether they are Lori's opinion. Tick the correct box.

		Fact	Opinion
a.	The cemetery is for golfers.		
b.	The girl does not belong in the cemetery.		
c.	Few visitors come to the cemetery.		
d.	The cemetery is a scary place.		

SPELLINGS: WORDS WITH SILENT LETTERS

Lucy likes words with silent letters, particularly when they are spooky words! She has spotted several rules for knowing when there is a silent letter.

1 Help Lucy identify the silent letters in each word by circling them.

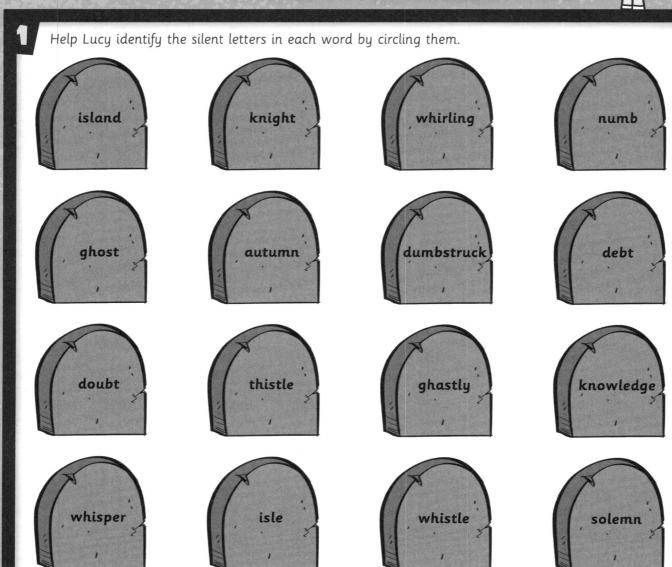

island

knight

whirling

numb

ghost

autumn

dumbstruck

debt

doubt

thistle

ghastly

knowledge

whisper

isle

whistle

solemn

2 Can you help Lucy complete her rules for silent letters?

a. Silent g or k is always before ___.

b. Silent n always comes after ___.

c. Silent ___ comes after w or g.

d. Silent s comes between ___ and ___.

e. Silent b comes either before ___ or after ___.

f. Silent ___ comes between s and l.

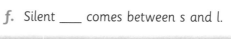

SYNONYMS AND ANTONYMS

Twins Lana and Lola know all too well about being similar and being opposite! They are learning that synonyms are words that have the same or a very similar meaning while antonyms are pairs of words that are opposites.

1

Look at the words below and help Lola to find four pairs of words that are synonyms and four pairs of words that are antonyms. The first ones have been done for you.

> before   cold   sell   loud   hot   buy   peaceful
> after   quiet   earlier   scorching   purchase

_____ before and earlier _____   _____ before and after _____

_____   _____

_____   _____

_____   _____

2

Lana is trying to think of some synonyms and antonyms for the words below. Can you help her find a suitable word for each?

Synonyms   **Antonyms**

big _____   night _____

small _____   true _____

fast _____   asleep _____

3

Lana and Lola need to find either a pair of antonyms or a pair of synonyms in each sentence. Can you underline the correct pair of words for them?

a. As the clock struck noon, the family gathered for a midday feast.

b. The valuable jewellery had all the stones stolen and became worthless.

c. Despite the rain, the younger children begged their sisters to take them to the kids' play park.

CREATIVE WRITING: WRITING A POSTCARD IN ROLE

"Bobby Boo Boo Bear" is away in Paris with Monica from his tour guide job and wants to send Lori a postcard so that she knows he is thinking of her. He knows that she will want lots of detail about what he is doing. He chooses to write informally so he can show how close they are.

1 Help Bobby change these phrases so that they're more informal.

Dear Miss Loud, _____

I have been visiting a wide variety of tourist sights. _____

_____

It has been a fantastic holiday _____

_____

I can not wait to see you again _____

2 Use the places that Bobby visited to help him write another postcard to Lori. Remember to keep it informal but still use proper punctuation.

Things to see in Paris:
• 'Mona Lisa' painting in the Louvre
• **Eiffel Tower** • **Notre Dame Cathedral**
• **Arc de Triomphe (monument)**

Lori Loud

1216 Franklin Avenue,

Royal Woods,

Michigan

_____

_____

_____

_____

_____

HANDWRITING PRACTICE 2

Lincoln's been set a poetry assignment at school and has asked Lucy for her help. He wants to make sure he presents his poem in his neatest handwriting.

1 Lucy has given Lincoln some sentences to copy in his best handwriting. Write them out in the handwriting grids below, remembering to keep the words consisitently sized and spaced.

Keep trying to make it even but go faster!

Can you zip through it and write quicker?

2 Lucy set Lincoln a challenge of writing a paragraph about his spooky sister as quickly as he could. Look at what he came up with! How quickly can you copy it out neatly?

Lucy is a gloomy and mysterious goth girl. She has an uncanny ability to seemingly teleport to different places, which often spooks her siblings, especially Lincoln! Occasionally, she can appear to be happy, like when she found out about Lincoln's romantic situation.

USEFUL WORDS TO SPELL – PART 4

Lana's pet snake, El Diablo, loves greeting guests by wrapping himself around them – often scaring them away! In his efforts to greet the Loud's latest guest, he's muddled up the words that Lana had been organising. Can you help her sort them out again?

1 Match the definition with the mixed-up word, then write the word correctly underneath. Each first letter has been given to you and the first match has been made for you.

a. A person's name written in a distinctive way. (s)

b. An organ in the body which plays a large role in digesting food. (s)

c. Something used to transport people or things across land. (v)

d. A large boat with sails. (y)

e. A person who serves in the army. (s)

f. The upper joint in a person's arm. (s)

g. A place where people can go to eat. (r)

ohsdurel _____

ehcvlie _____

unerstarat _____

isuerntga _signature_ _____

ayhtc _____

lodsire _____

chtmaso _____

2 Help Lana complete the spellings of these six words:

| rhythm | secretary | temperature | vegetable | rhyme | twelfth |

a. r _ _ _ _ m

b. r _ _ _ _

c. _ _ m _ _ _ _ _ _ _ e

d. v _ _ _ _ _ _ _ _

e. _ _ _ _ _ _ _ _ y

f. _ _ _ l _ _ _

ACTIVE AND PASSIVE SENTENCES

Luan is playing around with the order of words in her sentences to make the best jokes. To be able to do this, she needs to know what the subject and object is in each sentence. Then she can create active sentences – where the action is being done BY the subject – and passive sentences where the action is being done TO the subject.

Mr Coconuts hit Clyde.

This is an active sentence.

subject	object

Clyde was hit by Mr Coconuts.

This is a passive sentence.

1 Help Luan to circle the subject and underline the object in each sentence.

a. The monkey threw the banana skin.

b. The banana skin landed on the floor.

c. The man tripped on the slippery skin.

d. He fell on the floor and laughed.

2 Luan is turning her active sentences into passive sentences. She needs to change the order of the sentence, by swapping the **object** and the **subject**, and change the **verb**. She's finished the first sentence – can you complete the rest?

Active

a. The flower squirts water.

b. The ring gave an electric shock.

c. The whoopee cushion makes a loud noise.

d. The pie hit Lincoln in the face.

e. The rubber spider scares Leni.

f. Luan put snow in Lincoln's pants.

Passive

Water is squirted **by** the flower.

_____ was given **by** _____.

_____ is _____ **by** _____.

_____ was _____ in the face by _____.

_____.

_____.

BULLET POINTS AND NUMBERING

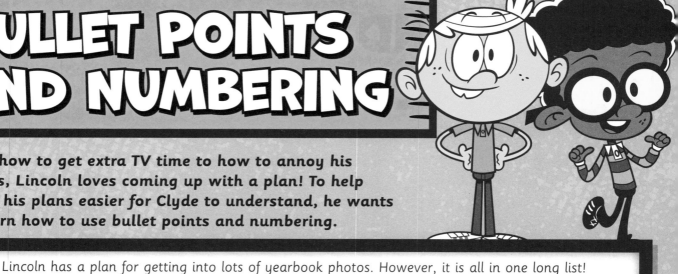

From how to get extra TV time to how to annoy his sisters, Lincoln loves coming up with a plan! To help make his plans easier for Clyde to understand, he wants to learn how to use bullet points and numbering.

1 Lincoln has a plan for getting into lots of yearbook photos. However, it is all in one long list! Can you separate the list into clear items and write each one against a bullet point?

Slide into the student council, carry a chess board into the chess club, wear some trunks for the swimming club, join the yearbook editing team, edit myself into all the photos, upload extra photos into the yearbook.

_____

_____

_____

_____

_____

2 Lincoln is trying to write instructions to get his sisters ready for school quickly but they're in the wrong order. Can you rewrite them in the correct order? Remember to use punctuation and be consistent with it.

1. **Get everyone in the van and off to school.**

2. **Make sure all the girls are dressed quickly.**

3. **Make sure everyone has their lunches.**

4. **Make breakfast so that they all have their favourite eggs.**

5. **Help get all the bags loaded in the van.**

_____

_____

_____

_____

_____

_____

SEQUENCING AND SUMMARISING

Lincoln is looking back in his diary and reminiscing about the time that he and his sisters sabotaged dinner in the Loud House in the hope of take away pizza! Read through his diary and answer the questions.

Thursday

Today, me and my sisters were determined to sabotage dinner! We were so fed up with Dad's boring food schedule and I knew that if the dinner plans were ruined, Dad would be forced to order pizza.

When he came home from the store, I distracted him while my sisters managed to confiscate the ingredients right under his nose! He had no idea. Annoyingly, he was going to go back to the store again but the steering wheel broke off the car - all thanks to Lana. He then began to cook tomorrow night's meal instead! This is NOT what we wanted.

We did everything we could to make take-away pizza the only option. We stole ingredients, moved utensils around the house, put racoons in the pot, even shut off the power! But nothing seemed to work. Then, out of nowhere, Dad tripped over Lily's rattle, the racoons raced in and ate the beans and FINALLY, Dad was left with no option other than to call for a pizza. When it arrived, we were all so excited. It tasted incredible, it honestly was the best dinner, ever!

Thursday (later on)

Well, we thought we had gotten away with it, but Dad has just found the meat in his slippers. Why Leni put the meat in his slippers, I have no idea! So, I had to come clean, but Mum got seriously mad. She said it's really difficult to cook for so many people and I understand what she means.

So, the new plan is that tomorrow night, us kids are going to cook. We are going to come up with a delicious new dinner, give Dad a break and show them how it's not hard to mix up the menu every once in a while. I can't wait to get cooking tomorrow, wish us luck!

---

1 Sequence these events in the order that they occurred. The first one has been done for you.

Dad tripped over Lily's rattle and the family ordered take-away pizza.	
Dad found the meat in his slippers and realised what the kids had been doing.	
The sisters stole ingredients from Lynn Snr.'s bag when he arrived home from the store.	1
Lincoln offered for himself and his siblings to cook dinner the next evening.	
The steering wheel broke off the car when Lynn Snr. was going back to the store to rebuy the ingredients.	

---

2 A summary is a brief recollection of the key points of a text. Can you summarise Lincoln's diary entry in two sentences only?

_____

_____

ANSWERS

Page 2: Parts of a sentence

1. **noun**: d   **conjunction**: c
   verb: f   **pronoun**: h
   adjective: a   **determiner**: b
   adverb: g   **preposition**: e
2. **noun**: Lincoln, Royal Woods, house, sister
   verb: run, think, is
   adjective: clever, loud
   adverb: quickly, suspiciously
   conjunction: because, and, as
   pronoun: he, her
   determiner: some, the
   preposition: under, near

Page 3: Linking ideas within a paragraph

1. The notes should be written into full sentences using the time conjunctions and adverbial phrases to join them together.

Page 4: Useful words to spell – Part 1

1. accommodate, according, accompany, aggressive, apparent, appreciate, attached, committee, communicate, community, correspond

2.

```
w c c x l u z k a d a a s q c a i a
d o a n m x w m p i p c i c o y a k
l m c q d c a d p y p c k o r z g y
p m c p c j c a r s a o y m r r g r
c u o n m l c t e n r m q m e f r y
e n r y y l o t c i e m a u s m e u
x i d x b j m a i w n o f n p w s p
o c i i w d p c a s t d f i o x s q
t a n l h m a h t k s a u t n u i w
r t g k c s n e e a x t i y d c v x
v e a i o r y d y w z e f x i t e b
g z t a u f b a c o m m i t t e e s
```

Page 5: Commas, brackets and dashes

1. a. also known as the sweet spot
   b. keen to practice martial arts
   c. the beauty pageant queen
   d. always texting Bobby
   e. the second eldest sister
2. Brackets, commas and dashes can be used to mark sentences a, c and d. Sentence b should only be marked with brackets.

Page 6: Speedy reading

1. a. False   c. False   e. True
   b. True   d. False
2. During the break between the second and third period.

Page 7: Adding suffixes to create verbs

1. a. horror - horrify
   b. threat - threaten
   c. fright - frighten
   d. terror - terrify or terrorise
   e. energy - energise
   f. irritation - irritate
   g. terror
2. **beautiful** - beautify
   character - characterise
   hard - harden
   active - activate
   electric - electrify
   light - lighten
   regular - regulate
   equal - equalise

Page 8: Suffixes -able and -ably

1. a. adorable   e. favourably
   b. considerable   f. enjoyable
   c. dependable   g. reliable
   d. applicable   h. knowledgeable
2. a. changeable   c. noticeable
   b. manageable

Page 9: Making an account flow across paragraphs

1. Three paragraphs should have been written telling the story. Each paragraph should finish on an ellipsis and have key words and phrases repeating through them.

Page 10: Semicolons, colons and dashes

1. a. Loch Loud is in Scotland: the Loud family ancestors lived there.
   b. The current Loud family visited Loch Loud on a vacation: they were driven out after a resident called Aggie had enough of the noise!
2. Aggie was able to drive the Loud family out of Loch Loud; she controlled a dragon called Lolo.
3. Lincoln decided to make a name for himself in Loch Loud - he managed to fix many of the problems in the town - gaining him the support and respect of the residents.

Page 11: Reading comprehension: inference - Part 1

1. a. hushed sounds in the forest / quiet broken by a guitar.
   b. amazed

2. a. **Any two of the following:**
   Sheer physical size / Huge strings / Enormous pink cloud
   b. The princess feels shocked or surprised as she gasps and her eyes widen.

Page 12: Adding prefixes

1. **mis**behaves, **dis**agrees, **dis**approve, **dis**obedience, **over**reaction, **re**view, **re**acted, **dis**respectful, **un**comfortable, **dis**like
2. a. **over**take   d. **over**look
   b. **re**build   e. **re**charge
   c. **re**write   f. **re**make

Page 13: Adding prefixes

2. a. prot**ei**n   d. f**ie**ld
   b. shr**ie**k   e. caff**ei**ne
   c. s**ei**ze   f. th**ie**f

Page 14: Writing a playscript

1. The playscript should have a new line for each speaker with stage directions written in brackets.

Page 15: Writing a newspaper report

1. The finished piece of writing should contain all the information outlined on the page and include an introduction, main paragraph and conclusion.

Page 16: Relative clauses

1. a. that/which   c. when and whose
   b. which/that   d. where
2. Any variations using relative pronouns to describe the bold word are acceptable, they do not have to rhyme.

Page 17: Spellings: ei words - Part 2

1. a. ✔   e. ✘ thief
   b. ✘ receive   f. ✔
   c. ✘ neighbour   g. ✘ receipt
   d. ✔   h. ✔
2. science: b   ancient: c
   sufficient: c   species: c
   juicier: d   society: b
   conscience: c   iciest: d

Page 18: Colons and semicolons in lists

1. a. People who could help me win: Lisa, Clyde, Lana, Lori.
   b. Items to source: wood, nails, saw, bicarbonate of soda, cola, paints
   c. Permissions requires are: Lisa, Mum, Dad, Lily, Principal Ramirez.

2. To get the best spot and keep the sisters away, I need to: cause an argument with the twins using a tea set and frogs; tell Luan to get her camera to photograph the twins fighting; give Lisa milk, eggs, flour and sugar to experiment with; give Lynn a helium-filled ball to play with; tell Leni she has a zit on her nose, even though she doesn't; give Luna a glowing flashlight that creates a lightshow; make sure Bobby phones Lori; and get Lily to fall asleep before the show starts.

Page 19: Reading comprehension: vocabulary

1. a. phenomenon
   b. the most northern parts
   c. noticeable

2. Highest point

3. Conversely means the opposite, the reverse.

Page 20: Adverbs to indicate possibility

1. **Certain or very likely:** certainly, definitely, clearly, obviously
   Might: maybe. possibly, perhaps, probably

2. a. clearly   c. perhaps
   b. definitely   d. probably

Page 21: Spellings: homophones

1. **Noun:** advice, device, licence, practice, prophecy
   Verb: advise, devise, license, practice, prophesy
   a. advice, advise   c. practice, practise
   b. devise, device

2. **stationary:** not moving.
   stationery: paper, envelopes etc
   desert: to abandon, a barren place
   dessert: a sweet course after the main course of a meal.
   compliment: to make nice remarks about someone
   complement: to make something complete or more complete
   ascent: going up
   assent: agreement, to agree

Page 22: Handwriting Practice 1

Handwriting should be joined, even and consistently sized and spaced.

Page 23: Creative writing: Writing a plot

The plot can be written in either present or past tense but should be written in full sentences and punctuated accurately.

Page 24: Verb tenses

1. a. Lynn has run 5km.
   b. Luan has laughed the most.
   c. Lana has waited for Lola to get ready.
   d. Lori has walked into 3 walls.
   e. Luna has played a loud rift on her guitar.

2. a. Leni had walked down the stairs.
   b. She had noticed Luan's banana skin.
   c. She had slipped on it anyway.
   d. She had fallen down the stairs.
   e. Leni had gone to the doctors.

Page 25: Useful words to spell – Part 2

1.

```
d e l f g t k i e q m f o c e s y e
i x d c f a m i l i a r e e x d s n
s p k e z o b o d v t e x x c i d v
a l d m t i r w e k i q i a e c e i
s a e b a e g e f m b u s g l t s r
t n v a g b r z i y z e t g l i p o
r a e r u i e m n g k n e e e o e n
o t l r a n q s i j n t n r n n r m
u i o a r i u c t n t l c a t a a e
s o p s a d i l e n e y e t t r t n
v n t s n p p u k y i d y e v y e t
j s l v t e s p e c i a l l y q e t
g g o v e r n m e n t d g e l u m s
q u h p e g y k c r s m i v p b w a
k j d r o n t u h i n d r a n c e s
```

Page 26: Modal verbs to show possibility

1. a. Shows possibility
   b. Shows certainty
   c. Shows certainty
   d. Shows possibility

2. a. could   c. must
   b. should   d. should

Page 27: Verb tenses

1. He became more accepting.

2. Answers could be related to the following clues in the text: Lana performing in the talent round, Lana either winning or losing the beauty pageant, Lana and Lincoln winning or losing the Dairyland tickets, a trip to Dairyland.

Page 28: Hyphens

1. a. **co**-ordinate   e. **re**-enact
   b. **re**-enter   f. **re**-elect
   c. **re**-energise   g. **co**-operation
   d. **co**-operate   h. **re**-equip

2. **recover:** This means to get better after something
   re-cover: This means to cover again
   resign: This means to quit your job
   re-sign: This means to sign again

3. a. man-eating
   b. two-year-olds
   c. quick-drying

Page 29: Writing a story from a playscript

1. The story should be in past tense and include a range of description in between the speech.

Page 30: -ough words

1. a. plough   d. trough
   b. borough   e. nought
   c. bough   f. dough

2. **off:** cough, trough
   oh: although, dough, though
   oh: through, throughout
   or: bought, brought, fought, thought
   ow: plough, bough
   uff: tough, enough, rough
   uh: borough, thorough

Page 31: Adverbials

1. a. One day,   d. Under the stone,
   b. After a while, e. Finally,
   c. Nearby,

2. Sentences should include some of the suggested words to describe a day.

Page 32: Alphabetical order

1. beaker, bunsen burner, eggs, fuel, funnel, milk, pipette, salt, sugar, test tube, tongs water

2. backwards

3. Lana, Leni, Lily, Lincoln, Lisa, Lola, Lori, Luan, Lucy, Luna, Lynn

Page 33: Creative writing: write a character profile

1. Multiple ideas correct.

2. Three expanded noun phrases should be written.

3. Character description needs to include the three expanded noun phrases planned and be written in full sentences.

Page 34: Spellings: -cious or -tious

1. a. gracious
   b. ambitious
   c. cautious
   d. malicious
   e. infectious
   f. nutritious
   g. delicious
   h. conscious
   i. fictitious
   j. vicious

2. a. spacious
   b. nutritious
   c. ✔
   d. suspicious
   e. ✔
   f. ✔
   g. anxious
   h. ferocious

Page 35: Using commas to clarify meaning

1. a. The first sentence says they're going to eat Lincoln and the second they're telling him to eat.
   b. The first sentence makes it sound like Clyde and Rusty are his sisters and the second shows it is a list.
   c. The first sentence shows all three are playing golf and the second only Bobby and Lori are.
   d. The first sentence makes it sound like the best bananas have to come from hot countries and in the second it is extra information that they come from hot countries.

2. Things to buy at the supermarket: bread, toffee apples, milk, butter, baby shampoo, chicken, chocolate ice-cream and oranges.

Page 36: Useful words to spell – Part 3

1. **Across:**
   2. individual
   4. profession
   5. physical
   6. opportunity
   8. marvellous
   9. queue
   Down:
   1. language
   2. immediately
   3. identity
   7. persuade

Page 37: Reading comprehension: inference - Part 2

1. **Impression:** Old
   Evidence: Rusting, crumbling gravestones, heroes of yesteryear.

   Impression: Run down
   Evidence: Rusting, crumbling gravestones, not many visitors, creaking gates, patch of long grass and weeds.

2. a. Fact
   b. Opinion
   c. Fact
   d. Opinion

Page 38: Spellings: Words with silent letters

1. island, knight, whirling, numb ghost, autumn, dumbstruck, debt doubt, thistle, ghastly, knowledge, whisper, isle, whistle, solemn

2. a. n
   b. m
   c. h
   d. m
   e. t or after m
   f. t

Page 39: Synonyms and antonyms

1. before and earlier
   before and after or earlier and after
   hot and scorching
   hot and cold or scorching and cold
   buy and purchase
   buy and sell or purchase and sell
   quiet and peaceful
   quiet and loud or peaceful and loud

2. **Synonyms**
   big e.g. large
   small e.g. tiny
   fast e.g. speedy

   Antonyms
   night e.g. day
   true e.g. false
   asleep e.g. awake

3. a. noon, midday
   b. valuable, worthless
   c. children, kids'

Page 40: Creative writing: writing a postcard in role

1. **For example:**
   Hey Lori!
   I've been to loads of tourist spots.
   It's been an awesome holiday.
   Can't wait to see you soon babe!

2. **For example:**
   Postcard should be written informally as per question 1.

Page 41: Handwriting practice 2

Handwriting should be joined, even and consistently sized and spaced.

Page 42: Useful words to spell – Part 4

1. a. signature
   b. stomach
   c. vehicle
   d. yacht
   e. solider
   f. shoulder
   g. restaurant

2. a. rhythm
   b. rhyme
   c. temperature
   d. vegetable
   e. secretary
   f. twelfth

Page 43: Active and passive sentences

1. a. The monkey the banana skin.
   b. The banana the floor.
   c. The man the slippery skin.
   d. He fell on the floor and laughed.

2. **Passive**
   a. Water is squirted by the flower.
   b. An electric shock was given by the ring.
   c. A loud noise is made by the whoopee cushion.
   d. Lincoln was hit in the face by the pie.
   e. Leni is scared by the rubber spider.
   f. Snow was put in Lincoln's pants by Luan.

Page 44: Bullet points and numbering

1. • Slide into the student council,
   • Carry a chess board into the chess club,
   • Wear some trunks for the swimming club,
   • Join the yearbook editing team,
   • Edit myself into all the photos,
   • Upload extra photos into the yearbook.

2. 1. Make sure all the girls are dressed quickly.
   2. Make breakfast so that they all have their favourite eggs.
   3. Make sure everyone has their lunches.
   4. Help get all the bags loaded in the van.
   5. Get everyone in the van and off to school.

Page 45: Sequencing and Summarising

1. 3, 4, 1, 5, 2

2. Accept any two sentences which summarise the main events of the diary. For example:

   Lincoln wanted take-away pizza for dinner so sabotaged his father cooking.

   His father worked out the plan so Lincoln and his sisters offered to cook dinner the next evening.

Hurricane MkXII BG974,
registered N96RW, flown by the
Lone Star Flight Museum at
Galveston, Texas, USA.
Luigino Caliaro

Contents

Hawker Hurricane Mk.Is
of 56 Squadron at RAF
North Weald.
Editor's collection

Editor: Tim Callaway
editor@aviationclassics.co.uk
Publisher: Dan Savage
Contributors: Luigino Caliaro, Keith Draycott,
Douglas C Dildy, Julian Humphries,
Maurice McElroy, Constance
Redgrave, David I Roberts,
Clive Rowley, Adam Tooby

Designer: Charlotte Pearson
Reprographics: Jonathan Schofield

Group production editor: Tim Hartley

Divisional advertising manager: Sandra Fisher
sfisher@mortons.co.uk
Advertising sales executive: Jamie Moulson
jmoulson@mortons.co.uk
01507 529465

Subscription manager: Paul Deacon
Newstrade manager: Steve O'Hara
Marketing manager: Charlotte Park
Production manager: Craig Lamb
Operations director: Dan Savage
Commercial director: Nigel Hole
Business development director: Terry Clark
Managing director: Brian Hill

Editorial address: Aviation Classics
Mortons Media Group Ltd
PO Box 99
Horncastle
Lincs LN9 6JR

Website: www.aviationclassics.co.uk

General queries 01507 529529
and back issues: (24 hour answerphone)
help@classicmagazines.co.uk
www.classicmagazines.co.uk

Archive enquiries: Jane Skayman
jskayman@mortons.co.uk
01507 529423

Subscription: Full subscription rates (but see page
129 for offer): (12 months 4 issues, inc
post and packing) – UK £20. Export
rates also available – see page 69
for more details. UK subscriptions are
zero-rated for the purposes of Value
Added Tax.

Distribution: COMAG
Tavistock Road, West Drayton,
Middlesex UB7 7QE
01895 433800

Printed: William Gibbons and Sons,
Wolverhampton

*Having trouble finding a copy
of this magazine? Why not
just ask your local newsagent
to reserve you a copy*

Just ask!

The pugnacious porpoise

How do you tell the story of a legend, a national icon and one of the most amazing flying machines ever built in a single page? Well, it's difficult. Like the Mosquito issue, this introduction has seen a few drafts to get to this stage.

To understand the Hurricane, you have to understand the urgency that created it. When the British Government finally admitted that another war in Europe was inevitable, the front line RAF fighters were open cockpit biplanes. Can you imagine the likely outcome of Bf 109Ds against Demons, Furys and Gauntlets? It would have been like fish in a barrel. So a huge expansion and rearmament programme began, to swell the ranks of the armed forces not just in size, but in capability, through more modern equipment.

Two designs were chosen as the new single seat fighters for the RAF. These were the Supermarine Spitfire, which became the most famous British fighter of the Second World War, and the Hawker Hurricane. The Hawker Hurricane was an amazing aircraft. It was cheap, easy to build and incredibly tough. It was built using the same methods as earlier biplane designs and had originally been known as the 'Monoplane Fury'. The frame of the aircraft constituted metal tubes and die stamped sheet metal parts, riveted and bolted together instead of welded, then covered in a predominantly fabric skin.

Hawker's chief designer, Sydney Camm, had broken the design down into simple tasks, which meant his factory workers, already familiar with the techniques, knew how to build the new fighter and could build it quickly. Given the simple nature of the sub-assemblies, new staff could be easily trained to expand production rapidly if needed. This was most important, as Britain would soon need as many modern fighters as possible.

The first Hurricane flew on November 6, 1935, its performance ensured the Government ordered 600 in 1936.

Over the next 10 years, 136 squadrons of the RAF, 16 of the Royal Navy and 48 other units were to be equipped with Hurricanes. Its inherent strength and ease of use endeared it to everyone associated with it.

The type was easily mastered by neophyte pilots and was deadly in the hands of experienced men. It saw action in every theatre of the war and was pitched against the Axis at a time when the opposition was in the ascendancy. Hurricanes held the line in the Mediterranean, the Far East and at sea for two years, because at the time it was all Britain had. By the time Spitfires and other types were available to enter a theatre in numbers, the Hurricane had already fought the enemy to a standstill. Time and again this happened, over Malta, in Egypt, in Burma, the Hurricane Squadrons dug in, held on and fought for their lives with little hope of relief.

It is often quoted that, during the Battle of Britain in 1940, Hurricane squadrons destroyed more enemy aircraft than all the other forms of defence put together. While this is true, what is a greater tribute is that the fighter accounted for just over 50% of all enemy aircraft shot down by British and Commonwealth forces throughout the entire war. This is amazing when one considers that the Hurricane had, by 1942, been relegated from front line fighter to ground attack aircraft.

It is no exaggeration to say that the Second World War may have had a very different outcome had the RAF not had such a robust aircraft available in such numbers. When compared with other fighters of its era, the Hurricane's conservative construction severely limited its potential for development. After the battles of 1940, both the Spitfire and the Bf 109 were progressively and extensively developed, while the Hurricane was only modestly improved. The final versions of the Spitfire hardly resemble the dainty fighter of 1937, but the Hurricane's appearance changed very little, retaining its hunchbacked, porpoise look, always appearing far more pugnacious a fighter than some other types.

Its ability to operate reliably from poorly equipped rough air strips in the desert and jungle, or from the pitching deck of a small 'Woolworth' aircraft carrier is an everlasting testimony to the robustness of the design.

Although some people have said that the Hurricane was obsolete at the beginning of the Second World War, it was to see service right up to the war's end, the airframe's versatility kept it at the forefront of the fighting overseas. Perhaps the best tribute to the Hurricane's toughness came from German fighter pilot and eventual General of Fighters Adolph Galland, who commented that you could shoot all your ammunition into a Hurricane and have big pieces fly off, but it would keep flying and fighting. Therefore it must have been made of lots of spare parts!

This issue of *Aviation Classics* is intended as a tribute to the men and women who designed and built the fighter, flew it into battle, and maintained it in difficult circumstances in every theatre of the Second World War. It is also a tribute to the 14,533 Hurricanes themselves, the tough little fighters that did many jobs, and kept flying and fighting when other aircraft could not.

All best,
Tim

How tough? Hurricanes could operate in conditions that would ground other types. This is a Hurricane IIC LE336, of 34 Squadron at Palel, Burma, in November 1944. **Editor's collection**

DEDICATED TO THOSE WHO LOVE FLIGHT, SPEED AND CHALLENGE

SQUADRATLANTICA

PASSION AND QUALITY

PRODOTTO IN ITALIA · VERONA · ROVIGO · TREVISO · DESENZANO

MAN SIZES: S/5XL
WOMAN SIZES: 2XS/XL

SA 002

Supermarine S6.B - Schneider Trophy Winner

SA 001
Macchi MC72
Speed World Record

SA 005
Jimmy Doolittle
1925 Schneider
Trophy Winner

MM 002C
First Italian
Postal Flight
Centenary

MM 002
Legionaria

MM 003
Brevetto

MM 001
Atlantica

Determination, courage & genius

Hawker Aircraft Ltd, Sir Thomas Sopwith, Harry Hawker, Sir Sydney Camm, Fred Sigrist and Roy Chaplin

I am indebted to one of Britain's greatest aviation historians, Francis K Mason, for pointing out a little considered fact about Hawker Aircraft Ltd, that is still true at time of writing in 2012. Since its formation, the Royal Air Force has never been without an aircraft designed and built at Kingston by Hawker or its forerunner, Sopwith. From the Camel of the First World War to the Hawk which entered service in 1976 and is still going strong, the effect Hawker Aircraft have had on British aviation is incalculable. Behind these remarkable achievements are some remarkable people, their story is summed up by the title of this article.

Thomas Octave Murdoch Sopwith, later Sir Thomas, CBE, Hon FRAeS. **Editor's Collection**

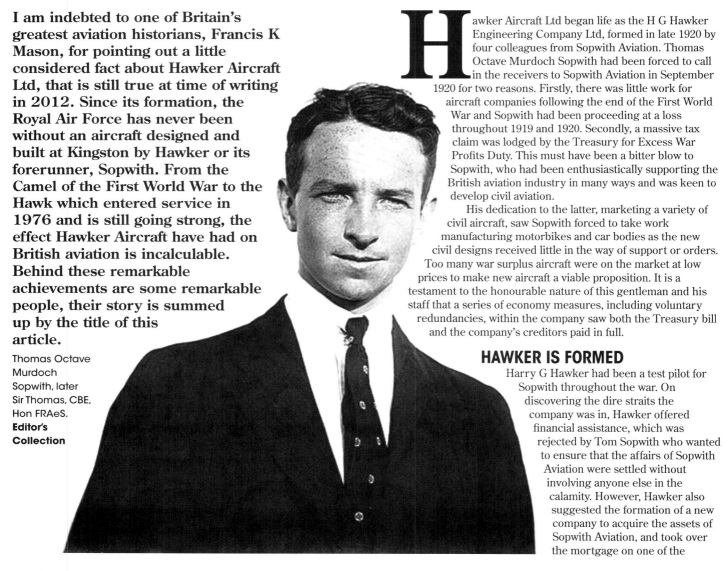

Hawker Aircraft Ltd began life as the H G Hawker Engineering Company Ltd, formed in late 1920 by four colleagues from Sopwith Aviation. Thomas Octave Murdoch Sopwith had been forced to call in the receivers to Sopwith Aviation in September 1920 for two reasons. Firstly, there was little work for aircraft companies following the end of the First World War and Sopwith had been proceeding at a loss throughout 1919 and 1920. Secondly, a massive tax claim was lodged by the Treasury for Excess War Profits Duty. This must have been a bitter blow to Sopwith, who had been enthusiastically supporting the British aviation industry in many ways and was keen to develop civil aviation.

His dedication to the latter, marketing a variety of civil aircraft, saw Sopwith forced to take work manufacturing motorbikes and car bodies as the new civil designs received little in the way of support or orders. Too many war surplus aircraft were on the market at low prices to make new aircraft a viable proposition. It is a testament to the honourable nature of this gentleman and his staff that a series of economy measures, including voluntary redundancies, within the company saw both the Treasury bill and the company's creditors paid in full.

HAWKER IS FORMED

Harry G Hawker had been a test pilot for Sopwith throughout the war. On discovering the dire straits the company was in, Hawker offered financial assistance, which was rejected by Tom Sopwith who wanted to ensure that the affairs of Sopwith Aviation were settled without involving anyone else in the calamity. However, Hawker also suggested the formation of a new company to acquire the assets of Sopwith Aviation, and took over the mortgage on one of the

The Hawker Cygnet, Sydney Camm's first design. This is a replica flying at the Shuttleworth Collection and bearing an appropriate registration. **Constance Redgrave**

Sopwith buildings, the office block on Canbury Park Road in Kingston upon Thames. Frederick 'Fred' Sigrist, who had been Sopwith's personal engineer in the early days of aviation and was now the works director at Kingston, along with engineers V W 'Bill' Eyre and new company secretary and works manager F I Bennett, founded H G Hawker Engineering together with Sopwith and Hawker as Sopwith Aviation was wound up. The new company was so named, according to Tom Sopwith, "to avoid any muddle" and in recognition of Hawker's contribution to the growth and success of Sopwith Aviation during the war.

The stated aim of Hawker Engineering was the manufacture of motorcycles and internal (spelt infernal in the official Company Notice, one likes to think not by accident!) combustion engines. However, given the directors of the new company and their collective history, it was obvious the direction the enterprise would take. By the time the official notice of the formation of the company was published, Hawker had already taken over most of the premises formerly occupied by Sopwith in Kingston, and almost immediately had won Government contracts to refurbish war-surplus aircraft.

Many of these were Sopwith Snipes, which was still the RAF's standard day fighter, but a number of other types, including de Havilland dH9A bombers were also to pass through the plant. Under the watchful eye of Hawker's now managing director, Fred Sigrist, these refurbishments were no mere wash and brush up. Each aircraft was dismantled down to its smallest components which were inspected and replaced if required, before being carefully

Harry George Hawker MBE, AFC.
Editor's Collection

reassembled. The build quality that made Sopwith-produced aircraft legendary was to continue in the new company.

On July 12, 1921, tragedy struck the company. The enthusiastic and likable Harry Hawker was killed in the crash of his Nieuport Goshawk at Hendon, which he was testing prior to entering the Aerial Derby. It was known he was suffering from spinal tuberculosis, but typical of his ebullient

Frederick 'Fred' Sigrist, MBE FRAeS, described by many as a natural engineer.
Editor's Collection

character, he would not allow this to interfere with his life. During a high G turn, the disease caused a haemorrhage. Critically ill, Hawker tried to land, but crashed in the process. Hawker had been a courageous and able pilot all his life. His innovative mind suggested all kinds of modifications and improvements to Sopwith aircraft throughout his test flying career, and his attempt to cross the Atlantic in May 1919 with Kenneth Mackenzie Grieve in the Sopwith Atlantic had made him a household name throughout Britain. ➤

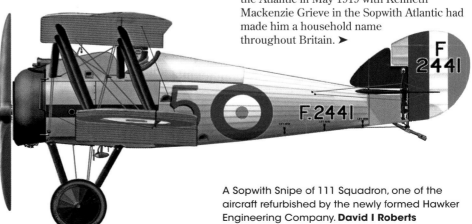

A Sopwith Snipe of 111 Squadron, one of the aircraft refurbished by the newly formed Hawker Engineering Company. **David I Roberts**

An industry – in which he was respected and liked by all, even his competitors – and a nation mourned the loss. King George V sent a message of condolence, stating simply that: "The nation had lost one of its most distinguished airmen." Through the new company he had founded, Harry Hawker's name was to live on to be associated with some of the most famous aircraft ever to be produced.

FIRST DESIGNS

Despite this terrible setback, the new company began to grow and indeed flourish. New draughtsmen and a new chief designer, Captain B Thomson, were hired, the intent obviously to begin the production of new aircraft designs again. By 1922 the British Government was beginning to realise the fallacy of the belief that the armed forces could continue to use refurbished First World War designs. Despite the tremendous cuts in service spending in the postwar period, tentative interest began to be shown in the development and acquisition of new aircraft. Specifications, albeit all too often badly written and vague ones produced by offices unfamiliar with aviation, began to be issued for bomber, reconnaissance and army co-operation aircraft and lastly, fighters.

Thomson produced two designs to meet these vague criteria emerging from Government. The first of these was to meet Specification D of R Type 3A, and became Hawker's first new aircraft design, a wooden, two seat, parasol-winged reconnaissance aircraft powered by a 389hp Bristol Jupiter IV radial engine. One was built, J6918, and oddly named the Duiker. To call this aircraft a disaster is doing it a kindness. It flew at Brooklands for the first time in July 1923 in the hands of test pilot Fred P Raynham. Brooklands was the home of Vickers aircraft but was used for Hawker test flying because there was no airfield at Kingston. Aircraft were disassembled and taken by road to the former Sopwith sheds at Brooklands, where they were reassembled and flown. This practice was to continue until Hawker acquired the lease of two hangars on the airfield at Dunsfold in 1950.

To return to the Duiker, it was delivered to Martlesham Heath, the centre for RAF test and development flying at the time, in late 1923. The list that was produced of things wrong with the aircraft was long and

Above left: Ernest Walter Hives, 1st Baron Hives CH MBE head of the Rolls-Royce Aero Engine division and chairman of Rolls-Royce Ltd, with Roy Chaplin, inventor of the dumbbell spar (right), during a visit to Hawker in 1944. **Rolls-Royce Heritage Trust**
Above right: Sydney Camm with one of his A frame models while a member of the Windsor Model Aeroplane Club. **Editor's Collection**

frightening, but included aileron flutter powerful enough to break the wing from the rear supporting struts that attached it to the fuselage, directional instability and a phugoid oscillation in pitch that developed whenever you closed the throttle. Repeated attempts by Hawker engineers to remedy these problems met with little success. The aircraft was then delivered to the Royal Aircraft Establishment at Farnborough on April 15, 1924. Suffice to say any comments are unrecorded. Three more Duikers had been ordered, only one of which was partially complete, when it was decided that the type was wholly unsuitable for service use and the project was dropped. Hawker legend has it that the partially complete Duiker was taken out of the shed at Brooklands and very quietly but very firmly buried in a far corner of the airfield!

Thomson's second Hawker design fared a little better. This was for a single seat day and

night interceptor powered by a 358hp Armstrong Siddeley Jaguar II radial engine and was designed to meet Air Ministry Specification 25/22. Called the Woodcock, it was to be Thomson's downfall. Every time a question arose regarding the design, Thomson would go and examine one of the Sopwith Snipes being refurbished in the Kingston factory, resulting in a new aeroplane that was little more than a rehashed First World War fighter.

The one and only Woodcock Mk.I, J6987, was test flown by Fred Raynham at Brooklands in July 1923 and displayed an alarming degree of wing flutter and a rudder which may as well have been left on the ground for all the good it was. Service trials at Martlesham Heath rejected the aircraft on the grounds of its lack of manoeuvrability, but noted that the view from the cockpit was excellent and the aircraft was deemed easy

The slim Hawker Hornbill proved to have a restricted cockpit, causing unfavourable comment. **Editor's Collection**

An early Hawker Woodcock II.
Editor's Collection

1. A second Hawker Cygnet replica at Shuttleworth. This aircraft was successful in the Royal Aero Club Light Aeroplane Trials of 1924, 5 and 6. **Editor's Collection**

2. The rear fuselage of a Hurricane shows how the tube boxes were built into a frame and braced with internal wires. **Julian Humphries**

3. The Hawker tubular method of construction is well illustrated in the sternpost of a Hawker Hurricane. Camm and Sigrist developed this method of tubes, flattened at the end, joined with bolts and rivets through pressed metal plates. **Julian Humphries**

to maintain, so Hawker was encouraged to persevere with it. Thomson left Kingston, and was replaced by George William Carter as chief designer. Carter had been chief draughtsman at Sopwith Aviation since 1916, and was well versed in aircraft design. His Woodcock Mk.II was re-engined with a Bristol Jupiter and had new single bay wings, replacing the original two bay layout, along with a much larger rudder. This transformed the aircraft and after more trials at Martlesham Heath, an order for 10 of the new fighters was received. With further modifications after continuing service trials, a total of 61 Hawker Woodcock Mk.IIs were delivered to the RAF, equipping three and 17 Squadrons in the day and night fighter role. After a shaky start, the service had its first Hawker fighter, the beginning of a long and illustrious line of successful aircraft.

COMETH THE HOUR, COMETH THE MAN

The Woodcock was followed by a number of other designs, including the Hedgehog, Hornbill, Heron, and an export version of the first Hawker fighter named Danecock for its Danish customer. While this military aircraft met with varying degrees of success and were built in small numbers throughout 1924 and 1925, a young designer was making a name for himself in the company.

Sydney Camm was born in Windsor on August 5, 1893. His love of aviation began at an early age, he joined the Windsor Model Aeroplane Club, constructing and flying a number of successful models of his own design before he and a number of other members constructed a man-carrying glider in 1912. In 1915, Camm joined the Martinsyde Aircraft Company where he initially worked as a carpenter's apprentice,

gaining valuable experience of aircraft factory techniques in the construction of wooden aircraft. He moved into design work, becoming a draughtsman, and in 1923 joined Hawker as a senior draughtsman. His talents and abilities to build strong light structures were obvious as he worked on the military aircraft then under development, so in late 1923, Carter gave Camm the design leadership of the Hawker Cygnet.

The Cygnet was a rare foray into civil light aircraft for Hawker, intended to enter the Royal Aero Club's Light Aeroplane Competition at Lympne in September 1924. The Air Ministry were offering £3000 in prizes for a variety of competitions such as longest range on a gallon of fuel, best take off performance and shortest landing. The Cygnet was a masterpiece of lightweight design weighing only 373lb (169kg) despite being a two seat aircraft. Cater had handed ➤

The developed Woodcock II with cylinder head covers to protect against high altitude icing. **Editor's Collection**

The Hawker Horsley torpedo bomber was the last all wooden aircraft to be built by the company. **Editor's Collection**

The Hawker Heron was the first aircraft to benefit from the new construction method. **Editor's Collection**

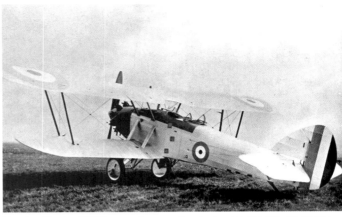

Hawker Harrier J8325 was also constructed using the new method. **Editor's Collection**

the project off to Camm as he said he "could not get used to thinking in ounces instead of pounds". Two Cygnets, G-EBMB and G-EBJH were entered, gaining third and fourth places, winning several of the competitions including the takeoff and short landing prizes. The following year, G-EBMB was entered again, winning the 100 mile international race and the 50 mile scratch race. It was flown by Flight Lieutenant P W S 'George' Bullman, a man who will feature again later in this magazine. Bullman also flew G-EBMB in the 1926 competition, and this time won the overall competition on September 26, taking the £3000 prize offered by the *Daily Mail* newspaper.

With such a success behind him, Camm was employed increasingly on the military aircraft, contributing to the Hornbill fighter and leading the design team behind the Danecock. His work on the Hornbill introduced Camm to metal construction techniques as the forward fuselage of the in-line engined biplane fighter was a metal-skinned metal frame. The close cowling of the engine and narrow fuselage made for a streamlined shape but a cramped cockpit, and although its high and low speed handling and performance made the aircraft very popular with service test pilots, it lost out in competition to the Armstrong Whitworth Siskin on this point and the Siskin's better service ceiling.

The failure of the design to achieve an order was a severe disappointment to Hawker – and to Sopwith and Camm in particular as they had put a great deal of time, work and money into it. The Hornbill did teach Camm one important lesson though. Test pilot George Bullman said of it that "the designer almost forgot that the pilot

is an important part of the design". It was a lesson he was never to forget.

CHIEF DESIGNER, METAL AND DUMBBELLS

In 1925, George Carter left Hawker to become chief designer at the Gloucestershire – later Gloster – Aircraft Company. The directors of the company, Bennett, Eyre, Sigrist, and Sopwith had been joined by Captain L F Peatty, Harry Hawker's brother-in-law, and all agreed that Sydney Camm was the man to lead the company forwards, despite his only being with the company for just under two years. At 32 years old, he was one of the youngest chief designers working anywhere in the world. He took over a number of ongoing projects, such as the Horsley torpedo bomber and Heron fighter. The Horsley design had started life under Carter and was

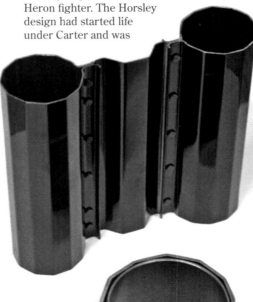

Roy Chaplin's innovative method of producing spars from rolled metal strips, known as the dumbbell spar, create main spars of great strength but light weight. **Editor's Collection**

The centre section main dumbbell spar of a Hawker Hurricane. **Julian Humphries**

the last all wooden construction aircraft built by Hawker. Conversely, the Heron was a redesign of the Woodcock fighter, and was the first all-metal framed aircraft built by the company. This was to feature not one but two of the great innovations that Hawker rightly became world famous for, both of which would be incorporated into the Hurricane.

CONSTRUCTION INNOVATION

As already mentioned, the Hornbill fighter had been partly metal framed and skinned. Fred Sigrist was a master welder and had provided a welding shop at the Canbury Park Road premises, which had encouraged Carter to use welded steel tubes to form the forward frame of the aircraft. On taking over as chief designer, Camm questioned the use of welding for a number of reasons, not least of which was the fact that very few qualified welders were working in engineering in the RAF. Any damaged aircraft would have to be returned to an aircraft park or depot as maintenance units were called then, in order for them to be repaired by specialists.

Despite his welding background, Sigrist was intrigued by the possibilities of weld free metal construction, and worked with Camm during 1925 to develop a simplified system for building airframes. This involved employing metal tubes flattened at the ends to allow them to be joined by simple flat metal plates, bolted and riveted together. From these, prefabricated box sections and formers could be built up, joined with longerons then have stringers and formers attached to cover with a ply, fabric or metal skin. Inside the box sections, cross bracing wires could be added, attached to the construction bolts, to give the boxes torsional rigidity. This was a construction technique that had two instant advantages for Hawkers.

The new frames could be built anywhere in the factory, not just in a specialist welding shop, and disassembly and reassembly of the aircraft was simplicity itself. For the customer, the new Hawker construction technique meant they did not need specialist engineers to keep their aircraft airworthy or repair them after an accident, major

The Hawker Tomtit, a delightful machine to fly. This is the only one left and flies regularly at the Shuttleworth Collection air displays.
Constance Redgrave

servicing and repair could now be undertaken by field units. As Fred Sigrist was often quoted as saying: "Give me a chippy with a spanner and we'll mend the aeroplane." Lastly, from a performance point of view, the new method resulted in incredibly light and very strong structures. This technique was to be so successful that it was used on all Hawker aircraft up to 1943, and was to have a major effect on the Battle of Britain. Hurricanes damaged in combat could be quickly and easily repaired at their home airfields. Badly damaged aircraft could be recovered to maintenance units for larger repairs, or rapidly stripped of their undamaged parts to form a readily available stock with which to repair other aircraft. Either way, damaged Hurricanes could be quickly returned to combat, a vital factor in the intense fighting of 1940.

To return to 1925, a second innovation that was to radically change the way Hawker built aircraft was also being developed. That year, a new draughtsman and designer had

arrived in the Hawker design office, Roland Henry 'Roy' Chaplin. Chaplin, like everyone at Hawker, was another engineer with a strong streak of practicality. He was eventually to become the chief designer at Hawkers in 1957, before which he worked as Camm's deputy on many Hawker aircraft. Again working with Sigrist, and intrigued by the new construction technique, Chaplin developed a complementary way of building light but incredibly strong main wing spars.

The technique called for two light steel strips to be rolled to form polygon section metal tubes, leaving a strip or flange sticking out on both sides of the slot, as the tubes were not completely closed while being rolled. These could be of any length or diameter, and by sliding tubes of decreasing diameter inside one another, could also be tapered, all without the use of welding. The two tubes were then connected by a sheet of metal called a web, riveted between the flanges on the tubes. The result of this was

that when you looked at it from the end, it looked like a dumbbell, so the dumbbell spar it became. To form a wing, pressed aluminium ribs could be attached fore and aft of the spar then skinned. This innovative method could be used to construct spars of any size or length, the only specialist equipment required was the machine to roll the tubes from sheet metal, otherwise, the tools needed could be operated by relatively untrained staff. It was so successful and produced spars of such strength and quality that Chaplin patented the design in 1926.

Like Camm and Sigrist's tubular construction technique, Chaplin's spar was to be used on many Hawker aircraft, including the Hurricane, and both were to have a vital effect on aircraft production. Both methods could be broken down into a series of simple tasks, so when time came to gear up for wartime production, inexperienced aircraft factory workers could be quickly trained to produce the sub-assemblies in large ➤

The first Squadron to operate the Hawker Hart was 33 in 1931. This is a 'B' Flight aircraft. **David I Roberts**

A small number of Harts were converted to two seat trainers and communications aircraft. This is a Hawker Hart (Communications) of 24 Squadron. **David I Roberts**

numbers, allowing for the rapid expansion of production that wartime demanded. This also meant that aircraft could be produced quickly and relatively cheaply. It took 10,300 man hours to produce a Hurricane, which sounds a lot, until you realise that a Spitfire required 15,200 to build.

The Heron, which possessed superb handling qualities and high performance but again, had failed to attract orders when test flown in 1925, was later fitted with a new wing with a dumbbell spar, the first Hawker aircraft to be so equipped. It also had a distinctive look to the redesigned tailplane, one which was to become almost a Camm trademark over the next 15 years. Even though the Heron failed, Hawker Aircraft was on a sound financial footing, its workshops were full of Woodcocks and Horsleys under construction. The Horsley was to be developed from an all wood aircraft to an all metal one during its production, be fitted with several different engines and become a significant export success, with aircraft being built for Greece and Denmark where it was known as the Dantorp. The Horsley, being a stable and reliable performer, was also used as a flying test bed for a variety of engines.

Most importantly these include the PV.12, the prototype of the Merlin, as well as the C, E, F, G and X versions of the engine, all of which made their first flights and gained certification fitted to a Horsley test bed. The Heron was followed by another single seat fighter design, the Hawfinch, which lost in evaluation against the Bristol Bulldog, and the Hawker Harrier, a large two seat biplane bomber which was a response to Air Ministry Specification 23/25. The Jupiter engine in the Harrier did not provide sufficient power to lift the required loads, so this too was dropped. Both of these designs first flew in 1927, and although seem like failures, both aircraft contributed experience and design elements to the Hawker aircraft that were just appearing on the drawing boards at Kingston. For Camm and Hawker, their innovations were about to bring them unqualified international success.

Before telling the story of the next generation of Hawker aircraft, mention must be made of the Hawker Tomtit of 1928, one of the most delightful-to-fly aircraft produced by

A late production Hawker Demon fighter of 64 Squadron. Skysport Engineering recently restored a Demon in these markings, which is a regular attraction at UK air displays. **David I Roberts**

A Rolls-Royce Kestrel V powered Hawker Demon of 608 Squadron in its colourful scheme. **David I Roberts**

A Hawker Hart of 'A' Flight of 600 Squadron in 1935. **David I Roberts**

anyone, anywhere. It was a two seat basic and advanced trainer of all metal construction, powered by a 150hp Armstrong Siddeley Mongoose radial engine. It was to replace the Avro 504 in RAF service and had some advanced features for a trainer, not least of which was the Reid and Sigrist blind flying panel that allowed full instrument flying training to take place. Only 24 were built for the RAF, which eventually decided on the Avro Tutor as its new trainer, these served with 3

Flying Training School and 24 Squadron. After disposal of the Tomtit began in 1933, a few were refurbished or re-engined for private owners. One still flies today with the Shuttleworth Collection at Old Warden in Bedfordshire.

ENTER THE HART

In May 1926 the Air Ministry issued Specification 12/26 for a light day bomber to enter service in five or six years, possessing the almost unheard of maximum speed of 160mph (257kph). The specification also suggested the use of the new Rolls-Royce Falcon 450hp inline engine. Hawker produced a tender to this requirement in December 1926, which was accepted in June the following year. Design work was aided by construction of a wooden mock up of the new aircraft, and a number of changes were incorporated into this, including a new undercarriage and the use of the new Rolls-Royce F.XI water-cooled V-12 engine, later named Kestrel. This was one of the engines that would lead to the famous Merlin. The prototype, J9052, began construction in late 1927 and in June the following year, George Bullman made the first flight at Brooklands.

The design, named the Hawker Hart, was a two seat light bomber that could carry 520lb (240kg) of bombs on racks under the wings. The pilot had a single fixed Vickers

Running in to display at the Empire Air Day at Hendon are these Hawker Demons of 41 Squadron. **Editor's Collection**

Hawker Demon fighters of 23 Squadron in formation.
Editor's Collection

A Hawker Audax of 'C' Flight of 2 Squadron. Note the retractable hook for retrieving messages from the ground. **David I Roberts**

A Hawker Hardy, the general purpose version of the aircraft, from 30 Squadron, the first to be equipped with the type in 1935. **David I Roberts**

A tropicalised and camouflaged Hawker Hardy of 237 Squadron, based in Eritrea in 1941. **David I Roberts**

machine gun mounted on the port side of the forward fuselage, the observer had a single drum fed Lewis machine gun on a ring mounting round the rear cockpit. To aim the bombs, he would lie on the floor under the pilot's seat, which had been a design feature of the cancelled Hawker Harrier, one which had met with much praise from the service trials of that aircraft.

On September 8, 1928, J9052 was delivered to the Aircraft and Armament Experimental Establishment (A&AEE) at Martlesham Heath for service trials where it was found to have a maximum speed in level flight of 176mph (283kph). The handling and performance of the new type impressed everyone, but what won the competition against the similarly capable Avro Antelope was the simplicity and low cost of maintenance, an important factor for the tight military budgets of the 1920s and complete vindication of the Camm and Sigrist construction technique.

In April 1929, the Hart was ordered into production, first equipping 33 Squadron in February 1930 followed by three more Squadrons in 1931. The speed with which Hawker aircraft could be built was another factor in its success, a total of 992 were built by four companies, primarily Hawkers but with Armstrong Whitworth, Gloster and Vickers as subcontractors, which made the Hart and its derivatives the most produced British aircraft of the inter-war years. Three major Hart variants were produced, the Hart India, which was a tropicalised version for service abroad, the Hart Special, another tropicalised variant with desert equipment and the Hart Trainer, a twin cockpit variant for pilot training. 114 Hart Trainers were built alongside 164 Hart bombers by Vickers at Weybridge, such was the demand for the aircraft. Two export versions of the Hart were also built, eight for Estonia and four for Sweden, the latter being powered by the Bristol Pegasus radial engine. The first four of these were delivered in 1934 and were followed by 42 more aircraft, licence built in Sweden.

HART FIGHTERS AND OTHER VARIANTS

The production Hart bomber was powered by a Rolls-Royce Kestrel IB of 525hp, which gave the aircraft an even higher maximum speed of 184mph (296kph). This proved to be both laudable and embarrassing for the RAF, as it was 30mph (48kph) faster than the Siskin fighters of the day. On air exercises the bombers frequently outran the fighters, and even if they were caught, such was the excellent handling of the Hart that they sometimes out manoeuvred their opponents. The Air Ministry solved this problem in the interim by ordering a fighter version of the Hart in 1930. Fitted with twin nose machine guns, this was initially known as the Hart ➤

Tropicalised Hawker Hardys on the airfield at Ramleh in Palestine. **Editor's Collection**

Fighter but later named the Demon. This too was built in large numbers for the time, with over 200 being delivered to the RAF, built by Hawkers with Boulton Paul Aircraft as a subcontractor. In addition to the RAF, 54 Demons and 10 Demon Trainers were built for the Royal Australian Air Force.

The next version of the Hart family was the Hawker Audax, an army co-operation aircraft of which over 700 were built for service with the RAF and eight other air forces which included those of Canada, Egypt, India, Rhodesia, South Africa, Iran and Iraq. First flying in 1931, the Audax was similar to the Hart, but had specialist equipment for the role, including a retractable hook to pick up messages from the ground. Four of the aircraft for South Africa were built in the UK before licence production in that country manufactured another 65 airframes. In South African service the aircraft was known as the Hawker Hartbees.

Alongside the development of the Audax came a navalised fighter reconnaissance version of the airframe with folding wings. Known as the Osprey, over 100 were built in four marks, serving with the Fleet Air Arm from 1932 to 1944. During the war they were used as pilot trainers for the Royal Navy. Ospreys were also exported to Sweden, Portugal and Spain.

A general purpose version of the Hart, capable of fulfilling the bomber and army co-operation roles but tropicalised for service in Iraq came next, first flying on September 7, 1934. Named the Hawker Hardy, 48 were built, entering service with 30 Squadron in January 1935. Probably the least known of the Hart family, they were to see more active service than any other of the variants. Hardys were used on operations against the Italians in Abyssinia as well as in other areas of North Africa up until 1941.

With the RAF expanding rapidly in the mid-1930s, the Air Ministry issued Specification G.7/34 for an improved version

A Hawker Hind of 15 Squadron. Note the tailwheel as opposed to the skid of earlier versions. The Shuttleworth Collection's Hind was recovered from Afghanistan and now flies in these colours. **David I Roberts**

The navalised version of the Hart family, a Hawker Osprey I of 803 Squadron when based aboard HMS Eagle. **David I Roberts**

A number of Hawker Demon fighters were converted to carry the Frazer Nash turret, such as the aircraft of 29 Squadron. **David I Roberts**

of the Hart in 1934. This was intended to replace the Hart and other types with an aircraft that could fulfil all the roles of the earlier variants until such time as the new monoplane bombers then under development were ready for service. This resulted in the Hawker Hind, first flown on September 12 1934, the speed of its development made possible through Hawker's experiences with producing all the other variants for home and overseas customers. Powered by a 640hp Rolls-Royce Kestrel V, 527 Hinds were delivered to the RAF from November 1935 onwards. The Hind was also heavily exported, serving in Switzerland, Yugoslavia, Afghanistan, Portugal, Iran and Latvia. In 1937, when the Hind began to be replaced by the Fairey Battle and Bristol Blenheim, ex-RAF aircraft were supplied to India, Ireland, Kenya, South Africa and New Zealand. When war broke out in September 1939,

613 Squadron was still operating the Hind, replacing it with the Hector in November. Many Hinds served as advanced trainers with the RAF during the war and a small number saw combat with the South African, Yugoslav and Iranian air forces.

The last version of the Hart family was an army co-operation variant of the Hind, intended to replace the Audax and differing from all earlier versions in two main ways. Firstly, it had no sweepback on the top wing and secondly, it was powered by the 24 cylinder 805hp Napier Dagger, which gave the nose of the aircraft a very 'squared off' look, because Rolls-Royce could not keep up with the demand for the Kestrel. The Hawker Hector made its first flight on February 14, 1936 in the hands of George Bullman. Since Hawker was so busy with other aircraft, all 178 production Hectors were built by Westland Aircraft at Yeovil.

Like the Hind, it was intended purely as an interim aircraft until Westland's own design, the Lysander, could be introduced. Hectors were to see action with 613 Squadron over northern France, attacking the advancing German army and losing two aircraft in fighting over Calais. Withdrawn from the front line, the Hector was used as a tug for Hotspur training gliders from 1940 onwards. These trained the glider pilots who later were to play such an important role in British airborne operations during the Second World War. Also in 1940, 13 airframes were supplied to Ireland for coastal patrol duties.

HAWKER SIDDELEY

Altogether over 2800 aircraft of the Hart family had been supplied to the RAF and Fleet Air Arm as well as 20 foreign air forces. They were built by eight major British aircraft companies and two overseas ones. T O M Sopwith had decided that the great good fortune Hawkers had created with the aircraft had best be shared among these companies to keep the aviation industry in the UK

The Shuttleworth Collection's Hawker Hind in flight. Wearing 15 Squadron markings, this aircraft is regularly displayed at Old Warden and is a surprisingly fast and nimble performer. **Constance Redgrave**

The two seat Hawker Demon fighter with the Shuttleworth Collection's Gloster Gladiator. The Gladiator was contemporary to the Hart family, and was to end the era of biplane fighters in RAF service. **Constance Redgrave**

flourishing at a time when work was scarce and the great depression was at its worst. During Hart family production, the company was officially renamed as Hawker Aircraft Ltd, in 1933. The following year, its strong financial position enabled Hawker to buy Gloster Aircraft Ltd, with its large factory, but 1935 saw Sopwith's masterstroke in ensuring a strong yet flexible aircraft industry grew in the UK in time for the conflict many industry leaders could clearly foresee.

He and the other directors formed Hawker Siddeley Aircraft, a powerful group comprising Hawkers, Gloster, Armstrong Siddeley, Armstrong Whitworth Aircraft and A V Roe and Company – better known as Avro. These companies had the security of operating within the umbrella of the group, yet remained autonomous as regards products and designs, often competing but always able to draw on the resources of the group as a whole. Hawker Aircraft was to remain just that until 1955, when the brand name was changed to Hawker Siddeley after the P.1127. This is why I regard Sir Thomas Sopwith (he was knighted in 1953) as one of the great figures of British aviation, throughout his career he selflessly worked for the betterment of the aviation industry, not just his company.

Even after Hawker Siddeley was nationalised he continued to work as a consultant up until 1980. Sir Thomas died on January 27, 1989 in Hampshire aged 101.

THE FURY

Alongside the development of the Hart family, Hawker was also considering the design of a new single seat fighter. This began with two designs in 1927, the aircraft produced to meet Specification F.20/27 and the Hoopoe, a land based and naval fighter respectively. Although neither of these designs attracted orders, much valuable experience and developmental flying was carried out with their prototypes, leading to the Hawker Hornet of March 1929. The single example built was evaluated by the RAF at A&AEE in 1930, as well as by Yugoslavia in 1931. Fitted with a Rolls-Royce F.XIS 420hp engine, the Hornet was capable of 205mph (330kph) and everyone who evaluated it was impressed with its superb handling and great structural strength. The Air Ministry, which had so far failed to find a suitable fighter for its earlier requirement, was so impressed it wrote a new Specification, F.13/30, around the Hornet design.

However, it didn't like the name, so this was changed to Fury and 21 of the new fighters were ordered in April 1930. The first flight of a production Fury took place at Brooklands on March 25, 1931 in the hands of P E G 'Gerry' Sayer, and it is testament to the new Hawker construction techniques that all 21 RAF aircraft and six Furies for Yugoslavia were completed and flown in just three weeks, despite a busy Hart production line. The first of three RAF Fury units, 43 ➤

The family resemblance between the Nimrod naval fighter, Demon fighter and Hurricane is obvious. The fuselages and tailplanes are very similar. **Keith Draycott**

Squadron based at Tangmere, received sixteen Fury Is in May 1931, followed by 1 and 25 Squadron. The Fury II was introduced into service in 1937 with 25 Squadron, replacing their Fury Is.

This had the more powerful Kestrel VI of 640hp which raised the maximum speed to 223mph (359kph). Despite its tremendous performance only 262 Furies were built, serving with the RAF and the air forces of Iran, Portugal, South Africa, Spain and Yugoslavia, the last three of which used their aircraft operationally in the Spanish Civil War and the Second World War. 92 examples of a naval fighter, the Nimrod, externally similar to the Fury but actually a development from the completely separate Hoopoe design, were also built for the Fleet Air Arm in two versions, entering service in 1934 and 1934. These were all replaced by the Gloster Sea Gladiator by 1939. A few were supplied overseas, one to Portugal, two to Denmark and oddly, one to Japan.

The main reasons for the relatively small numbers of the Fury and Nimrod was the fact that they were initially introduced at the height of the great depression, and by the time their more advanced versions were developed, both industry and their customers were more interested in the development and acquisition of monoplanes. Given the background and experience of producing these many and varied types, Sydney Camm and the Hawker design team began doing just that.

THE HURRICANE BEGINS

In 1933, with the popular high performance Fury in RAF service and the Hart family flying all around the world, Sydney Camm began considering the design of a new fighter, a monoplane that would become the Hurricane. Given the success of the Fury, it is not surprising that this aircraft was a starting point for the new design, indeed, if you place a Hind, a Fury and a Hurricane in a row it is impossible to escape their family resemblance, the fuselage and tailplane designs are incredibly similar.

Discussions with the Directorate of Technical Development at the Air Ministry led to a private venture design initially based around the Rolls-Royce Goshawk engine, but in January 1934 Rolls-Royce released details of the expected performance of its new P.V.12 engine, which would become the Merlin.

Despite the similarities, the Hawker Nimrod was not a navalised Fury, but was developed separately. **Julian Humphries**

A Hawker Fury I of 43 Squadron, the first RAF unit to operate the type in May 1931. This is the 'B' Flight commander's aircraft. **David I Roberts**

Camm took his first design, originally called the Fury Monoplane, and substituted the new engine, resulting in a new concept simply called the Interceptor Monoplane. In May 1934, detailed design work began and was completed along with a wooden mock up in August. This design was submitted to the Air Ministry, in response to which it issued Specification F.36/34 to Hawker on September 4, 1934. After the design and the mock up had been studied, a contract was issued to the company in February 1935 for "one High Speed Monoplane, K5083, to design submitted September 4, 1934, known as the F.36/34 Single Seat Fighter". The Hurricane was born, but still had some way to go as will be detailed later in this magazine.

SYDNEY CAMM

This aircraft marked a complete departure for Camm – his first monoplane, the first Hawker aircraft with a retractable undercarriage, its first single seat fighter with an enclosed cockpit, the first eight gun fighter. All of these radical departures from the earlier biplane designs had come about in just two short years, a quantum leap in

Sir Sydney Camm, CBE, FRAeS, who created most of the aircraft on these pages, in 1953. **Editor's Collection**

technology in a remarkably short time.

Camm's dedication and leadership was to provide the RAF with many of its most effective piston-engined fighters, from the Hurricane, through the Typhoon and Tempest. After the Second World War, there was still a world market for his next generation of fighters, the Fury and Sea Fury. The Furies had such high performance that several examples were heavily modified for the high octane sport of air racing, and are still winning today. In 1953 Sydney Camm was knighted for his services to aviation and in 1959 was appointed chief engineer of Hawker Aircraft Ltd. From this time he had been working exclusively on jet-engined designs such as the Sea Hawk naval fighter, a project begun in 1944.

The jet age brought new challenges, which he met with ground breaking designs.

The Hawker Hunter and Harrier are probably the most easily recognisable jet aircraft of the 1950s and 60s and Sydney Camm was heavily involved with both. The Hunter sold all over the world and was a very high performance fighter and fighter bomber. The Harrier was the world's first vertical take off and landing jet fighter and its developments are still in service with several air forces today. Never an easy man to work with, Sydney Camm demanded the highest standards of workmanship. He was renowned across the industry for his attention to detail and intolerance of incompetence. He died in 1966 and will always be remembered for his outstanding contribution to the defence of the British Isles. ■ *Words: Tim Callaway*

Skysport Engineering restored this immaculate Hawker Demon in 64 Squadron markings, seen here touching down at Old Warden. **Constance Redgrave**

The Battle of Britain Memorial Flight's Hurricane Mk IIC in the markings of Flying Officer Harold Bird-Wilson's P3878 of 17 Squadron at the time of the battle. **Luigino Caliaro**

Prototype, testing & production

With the design approved and a contract signed for the delivery of a single prototype, construction of the prototype began in August 1935. By October, the first Hurricane was ready to be fitted with its engine. This was the first of 14,533 examples of all versions of the Hurricane built, differing from later aircraft in a number of important respects. However, a number of problems had to be resolved before production could begin.

With the detail design work finished, construction of K5083, the Hurricane prototype, began at the Hawker factory in Kingston on Thames. The engine for the first aircraft was the Merlin type C with a single stage supercharger and a twin bladed, wooden, fixed pitch Watts propeller. Once completed, the impressive new fighter was taken by road to Brooklands, home of Vickers but where Hawker had a test facility, there being no airfield at Kingston. It was reassembled by October 23, 1935, with ground running and taxi trials by Hawker chief test pilot, Flight Lieutenant P W S 'George' Bullman.

Born in 1896, Paul Ward Spencer Bullman served in the Royal Artillery during the First World War. He transferred into the Royal Flying Corps and was awarded the Military Cross for his determined efforts strafing enemy positions in difficult weather conditions as the war came to a close.

Bullman commenced his test flying career at the Royal Aircraft Establishment at Farnborough in 1919. At the age of 29 he resigned his commission to become the chief test pilot at Hawker Aircraft Ltd where he undertook the maiden flights of many of the company's famous interwar designs including the Hart, Tomtit and Demon.

During the Second World War he was appointed to lead the British Air Commission to the United States and rose to the rank of Group Captain. He died in 1963, the nickname 'George' came from his habit of addressing others as George on account of his alleged inability to remember names.

UNIQUE PROTOTYPE FEATURES

The prototype differed in many details from later production Hurricanes. The engine covers were beautifully smooth polished metal, lacking the various bumps and shields fitted to later versions. The outer wing panels and the rear fuselage were fabric covered and finished in silver dope. The prototype's tail wheel was retractable, the ventral spine beneath the tail that distinguished all subsequent production versions of the Hurricane was absent. At Camm's insistence, the horizontal tail surfaces were supported by a single strengthening strut on either side. This was later found to be unnecessary as the tail had been designed with sufficient internal integrity to carry the loads imposed.

Initially, no guns were carried in the expansive bays in each wing, but to simulate the weight of the eight weapons and their ammunition, ballast was installed. K5083's wings had straight leading edges, lacking the rearward sweep of the outer panels featured on all production versions. This modification was found to be necessary to maintain the aircraft's centre of gravity when full military equipment was installed.

The exhaust gases were simply ejected from six ports on either side of the engine, no exhaust pipes were fitted. The sliding portion

The prototype Hurricane, K5083. Note the folding doors at the base of the main undercarriage doors, the simple canopy and the tailplane struts, all features discontinued on later Hurricanes. **Editor's collection**

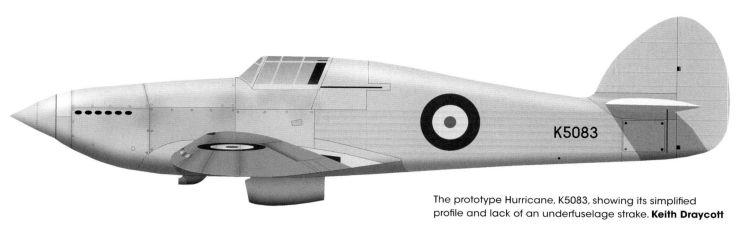

The prototype Hurricane, K5083, showing its simplified profile and lack of an underfuselage strake. **Keith Draycott**

Fairey Battles in formation. The light bomber had the entire production of the Rolls-Royce Merlin I earmarked for it by Government, meaning the Spitfire and Hurricane had to wait for the Merlin II. **Editor's collection**

Flight Lieutenant Richard Reynell, one of the test pilots on the Hurricane. Reynell was to be killed in action while guest flying Hurricane Mk.I V7257 with 43 Squadron on September 7, 1940, during the first major raids on London in the Battle of Britain. **Editor's collection**

of the canopy lacked the heavy bars of the production variant, the windscreen and fairing was much simpler and was not fitted with the armoured glass centre section. The upper decking of the prototype's rear fuselage swept gently rearwards towards the fin, lacking the flat portion directly behind the cockpit which characterised all later Hurricanes.

Another prominent feature carried only by the prototype was the semi-circular hinged wheel doors that were attached along the bottom edge of the main undercarriage doors. Flush rivets were used throughout K5083's construction, but these were difficult and more time consuming to fit than the mushroom headed examples used in later examples.

TESTING TIMES

Hurricane trials began with taxi runs at various speeds to establish the new type's ground handling characteristics. The Merlin performed well enough initially, however, the engineers at Rolls-Royce discovered a serious and perplexing flaw in the unit. After 40 hours of running, the engine demonstrated a significant and worrying drop in power. This alarming trait was only cured in subsequent versions of the engine with revised cylinder heads and valve gears.

While this issue was being resolved, it was decided not to delay the flight testing and the new fighter made her maiden flight on November 6, 1935. The undercarriage was not retracted on this first flight which lasted 30 minutes. Bullman found, probably to some surprise, that the high performance machine had docile handling characteristics across its speed range. The low position of the thick wing and the large flap area gave the type a

relatively low landing speed, which in turn endowed the Hurricane with another desirable trait, its landing run was much shorter than had been anticipated. Even with undercarriage and flaps up, the type could be flown close to its stalling speed of 70mph (112kph). Spins were easily recovered from provided there was sufficient altitude. These features, among others, would endear the Hurricane to pilots familiar with the biplane types of the day and would inspire great confidence in the new monoplane.

During the early flights, the three-piece flaps were found to have an undesirable effect as the large centre flap blanked off the exit to the central radiator and oil cooler. As a result, engine temperatures rose alarmingly during the landing phase with a severe risk of overheating. The central section of the flaps was locked closed for all subsequent test flights and modified for the production version of the Hurricane. However, overheating problems persisted until a new larger radiator cowling was designed to optimise the entry and flow of cooling air through the radiator core. Designed to be no larger than was absolutely necessary, the radiator had no cooling fan and only the movement of air through the matrix dispersed the considerable heat generated by the engine. In common with most water-cooled piston engine fighters of the time there was a limit to the amount of ground running that could be undertaken before the pilot had to either take off or shut down the engine.

Bullman made a further nine flights over the next two months. Not all were incident free. During a high speed run the sliding portion of the canopy broke away. Bullman

landed the aircraft without mishap and the replacement canopy strengthened with additional bars that formed an arched frame.

The Merlin C was still an imperfect machine, the first eight flights were made with engine number 11 but further company testing was completed with engine 15. The airframe, however, performed very well and the company was satisfied it was ready for service acceptance.

In February, 1936, K5083 was delivered to the Aeroplane and Armament Experimental Establishment (A&AEE) at Martlesham Heath for extensive service testing for the RAF. The staff at A&AEE found the Hurricane to be a "pleasant and stable" aircraft. It received favourable reports, especially for its good ground handling and ease of maintenance, refuelling and rearming. It was considered to be suitable for service pilots to convert on to and had benign stall characteristics. Criticism was levelled at the stiffness of the rudder and ailerons in high speed flight and violent manoeuvres. The Merlin C remained troublesome and engine numbers 17 and 19 were installed at various stages of the trials. A&AEE pilots took the new machine to 34,500ft (10,520m) and achieved a respectable 312mph (501kph) at 16,500ft (5030m). ➤

IMPROVING THE DESIGN

Several modifications were carried out to the prototype as a result of the trials. The hinged outer wheel doors were deleted as it was found they fouled easily when the aircraft was operated on rough ground. Ejector exhaust stubs were fitted which directed the exhaust gases rearwards. Despite the additional weight and drag of these units, the thrust generated by the exhaust added approximately 5mph (8kmh) to the top speed. The first stubs were kidney shaped and were retained on the first batches of production Hurricane Mk.Is. Later versions had improved Rolls-Royce units, frequently referred to as 'fishtail' stubs.

K5083 was fitted with two batteries of four Browning .303 machine guns in August 1936. The full complement of eight guns and associated fittings including ammunition chutes weighing 221lb (100kg); the 2660 rounds of ammunitions and their respective boxes added an additional 202lb (91.6kg).

RAF radio equipment was also fitted and a radio mast appeared behind the cockpit, with the wire antenna anchored between it and the top of the fin. The rudder had a small trim tab fitted to ease directional control in the cruise. During spinning trials, it was found that the aircraft was more easily recovered with the tail wheel down, therefore the unit was locked down and all subsequent Hurricanes had a fixed tail wheel. To further aid spin recovery, a ventral spine was fitted below the rear fuselage, fore and aft of the tail wheel. This modification increased the area of the vertical tail surfaces without involving a major redesign of the fin and rudder.

So great was the confidence in the new fighter, the board of directors at Hawker Aircraft Ltd issued instructions to prepare the factory for the assembly of 1000 Hurricanes. This required new tools, jigs and the drawing up of detailed plans to manage the whole process. If there were any nerves within the company at this bold move, they were quickly settled when official orders for 600 Hurricanes were received on June 3, 1936.

At Rolls-Royce, development of the Merlin continued and the improved F version was selected for production as the Merlin I. Production of the Hurricane began far more smoothly than the more complicated Spitfire, the two new fighters were both single-seat eight-gun fighters powered by the same

The ease of rearming a Hurricane and maintaining its eight guns scored highly on the tests at A&AEE, and was a popular feature with RAF armourers. **Editor's collection**

engine, but their construction was entirely different. At Hawker the Hurricane simply followed the company's familiar patented method of construction, at Supermarine the elegant curves of the Spitfire's monocoque structure took longer to master. The British public got its first official view of the new monoplane fighter in July 1936 when K5085 appeared at the Hendon Air Pageant.

The work of the prototype was not yet over; in August 1936 K5083 took to the air for the first time with the guns installed. Later it was equipped with a TR9B radio and a G22 gun camera to record the effectiveness of the armament. During firing trials it was found that at high altitude the guns were prone to stoppages after short bursts or failed to fire altogether. To resolve this, hot air was channelled from the engine into the gun bays to prevent the effects of the freezing air entering through the leading edge gun ports.

As production Hurricane Mk.Is became available for testing and development, the first Hurricane was placed into storage at No 6 Maintenance Unit at Cardington. During the Battle of Britain a Hawker test pilot brought down a German bomber over south east England in K5083. Later, the airframe was used as an instructional aid, bearing the serial number 1211M. Sadly for posterity, no historic significance was placed on K5083 and she was scrapped before the end of the war.

PRODUCTION BEGINS, AND GROWS

The first production Hurricane, L1547, first flew on October 12, 1937, at Brooklands, in the hands of Bullman's assistant test pilot, Flight Lieutenant Philip Lucas. Lucas would later become the chief test pilot for Hawker, flying aircraft such as the Typhoon.

L1547 closely resembled all other production Hurricanes regardless of mark, except that it lacked the ventral strake under the tail which would feature on all production aircraft from February 1938. The decision to allocate the Merlin I engine to the Fairey Battle light bomber had been taken in 1937, but its replacement, the Merlin II, was earmarked solely for the two new single seat fighters. This new engine featured inclined valve rocker boxes on top of the cylinder banks, which would not fit in the nose of the prototype Hurricane, necessitating a complete redesign of the upper engine panel. The most obvious change was two small teardrop shaped bulges, one on each side of the top engine panel, not far behind the propeller spinner, to accommodate the new engine.

It took Hawker's team four months to complete the redesign and tool up the new panels for production. Fortuitously, the delay

A side view of K5083 showing the lack of the flat section just aft of the cockpit that became a feature of all later Hurricanes to allow the fitting of service radio equipment. **Editor's collection**

Paul Ward Spencer 'George' Bullman flying an early production Hurricane Mk.I. Note the fabric covered outer wings, ejector exhausts and early tube style radio mast. **Editor's collection**

Hurricanes under construction at the new factory at Langley. Note the stocks of outer wing panels nearest the camera. **Editor's collection**

caused by the change of engine coincided with an interruption in supply, as Rolls-Royce worked up production of the Merlin II. Once this interruption was overcome, the flow of Hurricanes increased dramatically.

Additional test pilots were engaged to assist Bullman as Hurricanes poured out of the factory. Among the newcomers were Flight Lieutenant Richard Reynell and Johnny Hindmarsh, a famous racing driver who won the 24 hour Le Mans race with Luis Fontes in 1935. Hindmarsh was killed on September 6, 1938, while conducting a test flight of Hurricane L1652; his aircraft entered a vertical dive and exploded on impact with the ground. Although never confirmed, it was suspected that he had been overcome by exhaust fumes entering the cockpit.

Once the difficulties with the Merlin II engine were resolved, Hurricane production continued without further interruption. Hawker was able to complete 40 Hurricane Mk.Is in the first three months of full-scale production, the first of which were delivered to the RAF in late December 1937.

The development of the Hurricane did not stop once the Mk.I was in production. The fabric covered outer wings were not sufficiently resilient and were susceptible to damage at high speed. Even before production had commenced, Camm had planned to replace them. The Hurricane's wing was effectively in three parts, so the new outer panels were easily introduced without interrupting production. On April 28, 1939, Hurricane L1877 flew with the all metal wing and from early 1939 they were fitted to production aircraft. Initial production of the new metal wing was slow, so as there were existing stocks of the older type, the last Hurricane with fabric wings did not leave Brooklands until March 1940. Remarkably, considering its rarity, a sole surviving fabric winged Hurricane, L1592, is displayed at the Science Museum in South Kensington, London.

The new metal wing incorporated better access panels for the gun bays. The guns were completely enclosed within the thick wing, the two inner pairs on each side were fed from two ammunition boxes inboard of

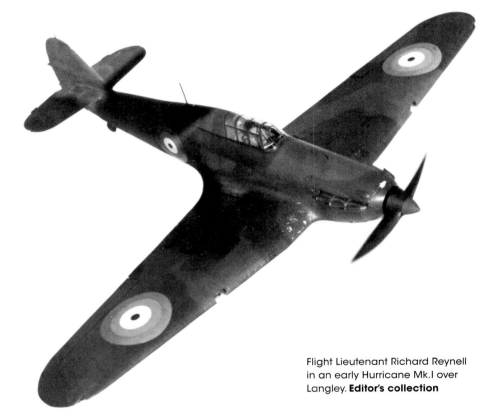

Flight Lieutenant Richard Reynell in an early Hurricane Mk.I over Langley. **Editor's collection**

their respective bays. The outer pairs received their ammunition from the opposite side. Hurricanes were popular with armourers, as easy access could be obtained to all the guns by the removal of the six quick release panels. The closely grouped guns produced a dense cone of fire and the harmonisation point could be adjusted simply at the rear mounting of each gun. So capacious was the Hurricane's wing that it would later carry an unprecedented 12 machine guns without major modification.

Further factory space became available during the latter half of 1938 with the completion of the Parlaunt Park Farm facility at Langley in Buckinghamshire. This was fortunate as the Government placed orders for a further 1000 Hurricanes in November of that year; 81 squadrons of the RAF were eventually to be equipped with the Hurricane

Mk.I, including eight Polish, two Czech, two Canadian, one Greek and one New Zealand squadron of Fighter Command. Four squadrons of the Fleet Air Arm were also so equipped, 748, 760, 803 and 806 Squadron. A total of 4224 was produced; 1994 Mk.I aircraft were built by parent company, Hawker Aircraft Ltd, at its Kingston upon Thames, Brooklands and Langley sites. A further 1850 aircraft were built by the Gloster Aircraft Co under contract and 380 by the Canadian Car and Foundry Company, Canada.

The high speed mass production of the Hurricane Mk.I was timely to say the least. The Munich Crisis of September 1938 did more to encourage Hitler's aggression than appease it. Germany invaded the whole of Czechoslovakia in March 1939 and another European War now seemed inevitable. ∎
Words: Tim Callaway and Julian Humphries

Into service

The first squadrons and the Hurricane Mk.I

As the production lines began to get into their stride and Hurricanes began to be delivered in numbers, the first RAF unit to receive them was 111 Squadron in late December 1937. However, a number of changes were to occur as a result of the ongoing test flying programme that would see the Hurricane made ready for war.

An early Hurricane Mk.I fitted with the de Havilland variable pitch propeller. Note the pointed spinner of this type. **Editor's collection**

The Hurricane was clearly a sound design but its performance was inhibited by the fixed pitch Watts propeller. Testing of a de Havilland three-bladed variable pitch propeller began as soon as it was available. Based on the American Hamilton Standard design, each blade could twist between 30.5 degrees pitch, the 'fine' setting, and 42.4 degrees, the 'coarse'.

Hurricane L1562, the 16th production example, first flew with the new unit on August 29, 1938. Being made of metal the new propeller installation was some 300lb (136kg) heavier, but despite this endowed the Hurricane with a dramatically improved climb and cruise performance. The new propeller was introduced at the factory from airframe L1780 onwards.

Good as it was, the de Havilland unit was not a fully developed variable pitch propeller. Rolls-Royce and Bristol developed a more advanced system under the name Rotol Limited, a combination of the names of the companies. To test the Rotol propeller and its

hydraulic operating system, Hawker purchased Hurricane L1606 back from the Air Ministry, an aircraft that had previously been issued to 56 Squadron.

The Merlin II engine required a modification to fit either propeller as they required different drive shafts. The next development of the Merlin, the Merlin III, would accept either manufacturer's propeller on a universal shaft. This engine was installed, along with a Rotol propeller, in L1606. Now resplendent in silver paint and bearing the civil registration G-AFXX, L1606 took off to test the new engine and propeller combination on January 24, 1939.

Careful measurements revealed a marked improvement in climb performance and an altitude of 20,000ft (6096m) was now achieved in 9.8 minutes compared to 11.7 minutes with the fixed propeller. The maximum speed was less dramatically improved from 318mph (512kph) to 324mph (521kph), but the other benefits were sufficient to drop the Watts propeller and either the de Havilland or the Rotol unit was fitted as standard at the factory from that time forward.

INTO SERVICE

The honour of accepting the first modern monoplane fighter into RAF service went to 111 Squadron, then equipped with open cockpit Gloster Gauntlet biplanes and based at RAF Northolt in Middlesex. Initially, there were insufficient machines to equip the whole squadron, so it was issued Hurricanes L1550, L1551, L1552 and L1553 to form a single flight in late December 1937.

First to convert onto the Hurricane was the squadron's commanding officer, Squadron Leader John Gillan.

As more Hurricanes were delivered, the last of their Gauntlets were withdrawn and the squadron's pilots were steadily rotated through a carefully constructed training program to get them used to the differences in handling their new mounts.

On their first flight, each pilot was instructed to leave the undercarriage in the down position and to keep the canopy locked open.

The more advanced Rotol propeller had a more bulbous spinner giving it a distinctive look, as evident on this 85 Squadron Hurricane Mk.I. **Editor's collection**

A close up of the nose of a Hurricane Mk.I with the Volkes sand filter fitted. Used widely in the Mediterranean and Far East, this filter was first tested as early as May 1939. **Editor's collection**

The first 111 Squadron Hurricanes carried only the basic national markings with a small squadron badge on the fin. The aircraft serial number was repeated under the wings. **Keith Draycott**

Two early production Hurricane Mk.Is with the fixed pitch two bladed Watts wooden propeller. **Editor's collection**

Although they would have been familiar with flying from an open cockpit, the Hurricane was considerably faster and much nosier than anything they had previously experienced. Many pilots noted the vibration made by the Merlin engine in comparison with the smooth running Bristol radial they were accustomed to. On their second or third flight, pilots were allowed to raise the undercarriage and close the canopy. Circuits and bumps were carried out during short flights of 30 minutes, each landing being closely observed and critiqued. There was a great deal more to think about in the new aircraft, with deployable flaps, undercarriage and radiator controls. Aerobatics were strictly forbidden, but doubtless a few were unable resist a loop and roll or two.

By spring 1938, deliveries were being made directly from the Hawker factories and 111 Squadron finally received its full complement of new aeroplanes. The Hurricane hit the headlines in Britain on February 10, 1938, when Sqn Ldr Gillan flew L1551 from Northolt to Drem airfield near Edinburgh and back in the same day.

During the outbound flight he faced strong headwinds, but these aided his return trip, which was accomplished in the incredible time of 48 minutes at an average speed of 408.75mph (658kph). It demonstrated the potential of the Hurricane, but said more about the navigational skills, determination and airmanship of the pilot. Gillan had made the flight at an altitude of 17,000ft (5180m), without oxygen and in dangerous icy conditions. Naturally the nation's press made a great deal of this flight, although they neglected to state the aircraft's true still air speed. Within the RAF this feat earned the commanding officer of 111 the nickname of 'Downwind' Gillan.

During the summer of 1938, 3 and 56 Squadrons were next to take delivery of the Hurricane. By the end of the year Fighter Command could boast 11 Hurricane units, as 1, 32, 43, 73, 79, 85, 87 and 151 Squadrons also converted. Not every squadron was fully operational, but an incredible transformation in the RAF's fighter capability had occurred in a very short period. Fighter Command was not the only branch of the RAF to be so modernised, as Bomber Command was also

taking delivery of two major new types, the twin engined Bristol Blenhiem and the Vickers Wellington heavy bomber. Naturally, 111 Squadron became the most experienced Hurricane squadron and liaised closely with Hawker and Rolls-Royce personnel. There were teething problems with the engine and several in-flight failures were experienced.

There were also several accidents, as pilots unfamiliar with complex aeroplanes learned to master the type and its systems. Inevitably, 111 Squadron also suffered the first Hurricane casualty, when Flying Officer Mervyn Seymour Bocquet lost control of his aircraft during an exercise and crashed.

NIGHT AND DAY

From March 1938, 111 Squadron were the first to undertake night flying training on the Hurricane, where they quickly found that the glare from the exhaust stacks obliterated their night vision. Pilots had to carefully concentrate on their instruments to remain orientated and avoid staring at the glare. Thin metal plates were later fitted, sticking out from either side of the upper fuselage panel immediately ahead of the cockpit. These blocked any direct view of the exhausts from the cockpit and protected the pilot's eyes from the bright glow.

Despite this, no serious limitations were identified in operating the Hurricane at night, something which could not be said of the Spitfire. The Hurricane's wide track undercarriage and easy ground handling were great advantages over the Supermarine fighter in this role. Gun firing trials were also conducted in the dark without undue problems, the muzzle flashes being mostly

contained within the gun tubes in the wing. As well as the night flying trials, 111 also exercised in the daylight interception of attacking bomber formations, dutifully simulated by Bomber Command Wellingtons and Whitleys.

When not engaged in practicing for war, the squadron's pilots prepared for their breathtaking displays of formation flying and aerobatics at the Empire Air Day displays of 1938. At home, Sqn Ldr Gillan and his men were kept busy entertaining foreign dignitaries anxious to examine the new aircraft, including a contingent of Luftwaffe personnel. In July, nine Hurricanes were dispatched to take part in the Fete de L'Air display at Villacoublay near Paris, where they enjoyed their hosts' hospitality for five days.

At this time, the RAF concentrated a great deal of its efforts on precision formation flying which, while impressive to the general public, would prove to be of no tactical value. Each pilot was too busy maintaining his position within the formation, effectively reducing the number of eyes scanning the sky for enemy aircraft to just those of the leader. This fascination with formation flying came from the 'Fighting Area Attacks', a series of fighter manoeuvres formulated in the 1930s then laid down in the RAF Manual of Air Tactics of 1938. In these attacks, a squadron would manoeuvre around an enemy bomber force, making precision attacks in differing formations as the situation required. Each type of attack and formation was given a number, the formation leader calling which attack he wanted to perform to his pilots, such as "Fighting Area Attack number three… go!" ➤

> THE HONOUR OF ACCEPTING THE FIRST MODERN MONOPLANE FIGHTER INTO RAF SERVICE WENT TO 111 SQUADRON

This rare flying example of a Hurricane Mk.I shows the development of the type with the metal wings, gun camera, streamlined radio mast and ejector exhausts all evident. The Hurricane was ready for war. **Constance Redgrave**

Of course, this assumed that there were no enemy fighters to break up the attack, and that the enemy formation would continue flying in a predictable manner, i.e. straight and level. The RAF would learn the error of its rigid tactics very quickly, adopting looser and more flexible formations as combat taught its bitter lessons. The last words many an early Hurricane pilot heard were "Fighting Area Attack X… go!", usually just before the Bf 109s they hadn't seen bounced them.

The first Spitfire unit, 19 Squadron at Duxford, began to take delivery of its new machines from August 4, 1938. It is worthy of note that by the time this squadron was fully operational, the RAF was in possession of nearly 200 Hurricanes, justifying Camm's choice of construction techniques and his company's decision to prepare for production before firm orders had been placed.

READYING FOR WAR

Further developments of the Hurricane continued as war became increasingly likely. Serious consideration was now given to protecting the pilot and vital aircraft systems from enemy fire. Armour plate was planned for the seat and cockpit, while bulletproof glass was thought necessary for the windscreen. Self-sealing fuel tanks were also investigated, the rubber lining of the tanks sealing after the passage of a bullet, preventing fuel leaks and more importantly, fire. These features were gradually introduced on the production line along with an improved radio.

An investigation of the potential problems of operating current British fighter types overseas was made in early 1939. The limited numbers of Spitfires available had already been earmarked only for home defence, therefore the more robust but slower Hurricane was the only logical choice. Experience of operating earlier aircraft in hot and sandy conditions led Hawker to collaborate with C G Volkes Ltd to develop a suitable engine air filter.

The new filter changed the contours of the lower engine panel dramatically and had a

When 111 Squadron converted to the Hurricane, it was flying the Gloster Gauntlet two-bay open cockpit biplane. This is a 19 Squadron aircraft. **Editor's collection**

slightly detrimental effect on performance, but without it, abrasive sand and dust could enter the engine via the carburetor air intake and very quickly cause serious damage. The filter system was tested on Hurricane L1669, which was first flown by Flight Lieutenant Philip Lucas on May 17, 1939. Even at this early stage, the Hurricane was demonstrating its adaptability.

The looming war also had other effects on Hawker and Hurricane production. By September 1939, the three Hawker factories at Kingston, Langley and Brooklands could boast 4000 employees, mostly involved in building the new fighter. Hurricanes were also being built under licence by the Gloster Aircraft Company at Hucclecote, near Gloucester. As a result of this rapid expansion, nearly 500 Hurricanes were in the hands of RAF squadrons, maintenance or conversion units. Production had reached sufficient levels that Hawker was permitted to consider orders from friendly nations.

The British Government had been approached by several countries with a view to obtaining Hurricanes to bolster their fighter forces. All of the machines delivered

abroad were standard Hurricane Mk.Is, differing only in armament and radio installation as specified by the customer and will be discussed later in this magazine. Hawker had also been developing two other two seat machines, the ill fated Hotspur and Henley. Both had varying degrees of commonality with the Hurricane, but would only be built in very small numbers while the company concentrated on the fighter.

Despite the rapid build up of home grown fighters, the RAF was still in desperate need of modern combat aircraft. Britain's aircraft industry was placed under enormous pressure to reach the targets drawn up by the Air Ministry for both fighter and bomber types. Moves were also being made to purchase suitable aircraft from American manufacturers. Some of the aircraft procured from this source, such as the Brewster Buffalo, were found to be woefully unsuitable for use in the European theatre and only deployed in the Far East. The stage was set for war, and on September 1, 1939, the Germans invaded Poland. The Hurricane was about to be tested in battle. ■ *Words: Tim Callaway and Julian Humphries*

Over France in 1940:

The Hawker Hurricane meets the Luftwaffe, the First Time

At the time of the Munich Crisis in September 1938, the RAF had a fighter force predominantly equipped with Gloster and Hawker biplanes[*1], augmented by four squadrons of Hurricane Mk.Is and one of Spitfires. Neville Chamberlain's "peace in our time", the RAF leadership knew, would not last long. Spurred by this certainty, one year later Fighter Command fielded 18 squadrons of Hurricanes and was gaining an additional two, on average, every month when Hitler's forces invaded Poland.

PHONEY WAR

"Peace in our time" ended on September 3, 1939, when the British and French governments declared war on Nazi Germany. As previously agreed, the two nations mobilised their armed forces and the 10 division strong British Expeditionary Force (BEF) began its deployment into northern France, opposite the Belgian border. To provide air defence for the BEF, four Hurricane units (1, 73, 85 and 87 Squadrons) followed, eventually being based at Lille-Seclin and Merville.

The parlous state of the Armée de l'Air's (AdA) bomber force – and the ranges involved – led the RAF to establish the Advanced Air Striking Force (AASF) intended for the strategic bombing of Germany, moving No. 1 (Bomber) Group's 10 squadrons of hideously slow, under-armed and highly vulnerable Fairey Battle single-engine light bombers to French bases around Reims.

By the end of the month this type's deficiencies were made glaringly obvious in three deadly encounters with Messerschmitt Bf 109Es and Bf 110Cs, the most dramatic being when four of five Battles from 150 Squadron were shot down outright and the fifth crash landed at its base, while conducting a photo-reconnaissance of the Saarbrücken area.

After that, Battles were prohibited from approaching the front without fighter escort and the BEF's two most experienced squadrons (1 and 73) were transferred to the AASF to provide it. Their replacements in the BEF's Air Component (AC) were a pair of Gladiator units (607 and 615 Squadrons) whose mission was to protect the even slower and more vulnerable Westland Lysander army co-operation aircraft.

During the eight months known as the 'Phoney War' the Hurricanes of the BEF(AC) and AASF clashed sporadically with Luftwaffe fighters along the frontier and intercepted a number of Dornier and Heinkel twin engined long-range reconnaissance bombers. The Hurricane pilots claimed some 60 German aircraft shot down, although the actual tally was 35 destroyed and 14 damaged, and lost eight of their number in these early engagements. ➤

Hurricane Mk.Is of 73 Squadron on patrol in April 1940. **Editor's collection**

DURING THE EIGHT MONTHS KNOWN AS THE 'PHONEY WAR' THE HURRICANES OF THE BEF(AC) AND AASF CLASHED SPORADICALLY WITH LUFTWAFFE FIGHTERS ALONG THE FRONTIER AND INTERCEPTED A NUMBER OF DORNIER AND HEINKEL RECONNAISSANCE BOMBERS.

*1 The air order of battle of RAF Fighter Command in September 1938 included 13 squadrons of Gloster Gauntlets and Gladiators and 12 squadrons of Hawker Fury IIs and Demons. At this time, 3, 32, 56, and 111 Squadrons were equipped with Hurricanes and 19 Squadron with Spitfires.

To simulate a gas attack for training purposes, smoke bombs were used near these Hurricanes of 87 Squadron at Lille-Seclin aerodrome in March 1940. **Editor's collection**

THE BALLOON GOES UP

Following one of the harshest winters on record, and after numerous cancellations, Hitler launched Aufmarschanweisung No. 1, Fall Gelb (Deployment Directive No. 1, Case Yellow, commonly called 'Fall Gelb'), the long anticipated invasion of France and the Low Countries. Luftwaffe doctrine called for the initial bombardment of enemy airfields to gain air superiority, and that happened – but the bombing by He 111s of Luftflotte 2 and 3 was inaccurate and only three Hurricanes were lost on the nine RAF bases targeted.

As the BEF began its move into Belgium to meet Generaloberst Walter von Reichenau's Sixth Army, three more Hurricane squadrons (3, 79, and 504 Squadrons) joined its Air Component while a fourth (501 Squadron) joined the AASF further south. In the north the BEF(AC)'s 72 Hurricanes – along with AdA 25e Groupement's 88 serviceable fighters*[2] – faced the 612 Bf 109Es (456 of them serviceable) of Luftflotte 2's fighter command (Jagdfliegerführrer 2 or Jafü 2) and struggled defiantly to cover that part of the front.

At first the battle was in the north, with BEF(AC) Hurricanes intercepting numerous He 111 raids escorted by Jafü 2's 102 twin-engined Bf 110C Zerstörers. But as the Allied armies clashed with the Germans at Gembloux and along the Dyle River, the Hurricane finally met the aggressively-flown Bf 109E in swarms on May 12. It was a stunning introduction to modern fighter combat.

Nine Hurricanes were lost to 10 'Emils' claimed, but only two were actually shot down (it must be remembered that in reality victory claims rarely reflect the enemy's actual losses, only the intensity of the combat).

Then the battle shifted – as did the strength of the German Jagdwaffe ('fighter arm') – to the south as General der Panzertruppen Heinz Guderian drove his three armoured divisions across the Meuse River at Sedan on May 13, breaching the French defensive line. Supporting the assaults was Generalmajor Wolfram von Richthofen's VIII. Fliegerkorps, which flew 270 Stuka dive bombing sorties shielded by Jagdfliegerfürhrer 3's (Jafü 3's) fighters.

While the RAF fighters claimed 15 Ju 87Bs shot down, only three were actually destroyed. In this and other battles, six Hurricanes were lost to another two Bf 109Es destroyed.

To try and make good the mounting losses – in the first three days 43 Hurricanes were lost – 32 replacements drawn from various UK-based squadrons were flown to the battered units of the British Air Forces in France (BAFF). But the numerical reinforcement was largely neutralised because the sourced squadrons sent their dregs – some lacking gunsights and armour, having fabric wings and two-blade propellers, and plagued with inoperative radios – flown by the newest pilots to the units, fresh out of training schools.

The next day the RAF attempted to disrupt the crossings by bombing the pontoon bridges thrown across the Meuse, AASF Battles and Blenheim twin engined light bombers flying 81 tactical bombing sorties, supplemented by 28 Blenheims from the UK-based No. 2 Group, covered by its three Hurricane squadrons.

They were reinforced by fighter sweeps flown by BEF(AC) units. Jafü 3 mounted a maelstrom of a defence, flying 814 Bf 109E sorties*[3]. It was the bloodiest day in RAF history so far: AASF's Battle force was decimated, losing 33 aircraft, with 14 Blenheims also falling in flames. Two dozen Hurricanes were lost – 15

The winter of 1939 was one of the worst on record, so life outside for the Hurricane crews must have been unbearable. The cab of this 87 Squadron bowser offered scant warmth. **Editor's collection**

pilots being killed – half of them to Bf 109Es. From this point on AASF bombers were relegated – with rare, desperate exceptions – to night operations, relieving the Hurricanes to mount defensive operations only.

The French IIe Armée recoiled to the south-west, blocking the route to Paris, and accordingly the AASF retired its squadrons south to airfields around Troyes. Abandoning eight Hurricanes on their evacuated airfields, 1 and 73 Squadrons had only nine aircraft remaining between them. The Battle units were reformed into six squadrons but there was no fuel or bombs at their new airfields for days.

Desperate, the French appealed to Prime Minister Winston Churchill for 10 more fighter squadrons. Fighter Command's Air Chief Marshal Sir Hugh Dowding objected, stating before the War Cabinet: "If the present rate of wastage continues for another fortnight, we shall not have a single Hurricane left in France… or in this country." By dusk that day the RAF had lost 76 Hurricanes, 48 of them from the original BAFF squadrons.

Photographed at their mess at Neuville-sur-Omain are the officers of 1 Squadron, taken in April 1940 a few weeks before the 'balloon went up'.
Editor's collection

HAWKER HURRICANE IN THE SERVICE OF THE BELGIAN AÉRONAUTIQUE MILITAIRE 1939-40

When the BEF drove across the Belgian frontier to man its positions along the Dyle Line, it would be standing 'shoulder to shoulder' with the 20 division strong Belgian Army. Its Aéronautique Militaire (AéM) was very much a biplane-based army cooperation air force, the most modern fighters being 23 Fiat CR.42s, 15 Gloster Gladiators, and 11 Hawker Hurricanes.

Frantically trying to modernise its fighter inventory to enforce its staunch neutrality, the Belgian government contracted for the purchase of a score of Hurricane Mk.Is in April 1939 to replace its ancient, and patently obsolete, Fairey Firefly biplanes, the 2e Escadrille/Ier Groupe/2e Regiment (abbreviated 2/I/2. Aé) accepting the first three examples on May 1939. Once 'the balloon went up' in September, the last five deliveries were retained by the RAF, initially limiting the AéM to 15 examples.

However, the RAF inadvertently contributed another four Hurricanes when three 87 Squadron and one 1 Squadron pilots wound up landing in neutral Belgium in November and December, respectively.

These proved useful in compensating for the loss of two of the modern fighters in landing accidents and a third in intercepting an overflying German aircraft.

In the latter case three unarmed (no ammunition) Hurricanes were scrambled to intercept a Dornier Do 17P (1.(F)/22) reconnaissance aircraft over the Ardennes. As the fighters closed to usher the Dornier out of Belgian airspace, the rear gunner opened fire, shooting down S/Lt Xavier Henrard, who was killed in the crash of his aircraft north of Bastogne.

Warned by their Berlin military attaché on the evening of May 9 that the long feared Nazi invasion would begin the next morning, 2/I/2. Aé at Schaffen-Diest – and the rest of the AéM – went on alert at 3.30am with orders to deploy to their aérodrôme campagne ('campaign airfields') at first light. The visiting Fairey Fox VIIIs of 5/III/2. Aé took off first while the locally-based (14) Gladiators and 11 Hurricanes sat, parked in rows facing their hangars, warming up their engines. Fog began forming as the fighters of I/2. Aé prepared to take off, delaying their departure.

At 4.30am, aircraft were seen approaching, so the Gladiators of 1/I/2. Aé scrambled in three-ship 'platoons', the first three formations getting airborne as four Bf 110Cs roared in, strafing the parked and taxiing fighters. One Gladiator was riddled, the wounded pilot unable to control his damaged biplane as one tyre burst and it careened into the Hurricane of 2/I/2. Aé commander, Captain M Charlier, setting them both on fire.

These strafing attacks – and a staffel of Do 17Z (KG 77) bombers roaring in at low-level dropping SC50 110lb bombs – destroyed another Gladiator and three Hurricanes, badly damaging five more and wounding four pilots. Captain Alix van den Hove took off with one wingman and engaged He 111s (KG 27) near Brussels-Evere airfield, and landed – his aircraft damaged by return fire – safely at Le Culot airfield with Corporal Jacobs. Later that day, at Schaffen, one Hurricane was repaired and joined his platoon that afternoon.

However, the next morning the Luftwaffe repeated its paralysing airfield attacks and the last three Belgian Hurricanes were destroyed when a swarm of Bf 109Es (I./JG 1) roared in at dawn, strafing, followed by another bombing attack.

At Charleroi the Avions Fairey S.A. factory, which had been contracted to produce 80 Hurricanes under license, was bombed, destroying the three completed examples and ending the Aéronautique Militaire's experience with the first great British fighter of the Second World War.

Hurricane Mk.I H-21 of the Belgian Air Force 2nd Squadron, 'Thistles'. **Thjis Postma Collection**

The Hurricane Mk.Is of the Belgian Air Force 2nd Squadron, 'Thistles', lined up at Schaffen airfield. **Thjis Postma Collection**

FIGHTING THE LOST CAUSE

The next day (May 16), in Paris, Churchill was badgered by the French leaders clamouring for more RAF fighters to save the day. Confronted with the enormity, certainty, and gravity of the impending defeat, he acquiesced, ordering six more Hurricane squadrons to France "at once". Back in London, Chief of the Air Staff ACM Cyril Newall convinced the Cabinet to compromise since the dwindling number of airfields in northern France could only accept three more squadrons anyway.

These would be formed by marrying one flight each from six squadrons to form three 'composite' units. The rationale was that if any flight was lost in France there would be a core remaining in England from which to rebuild the squadron.

The source squadrons gathered in south east England and it was planned that the composite units would fly out in the mornings, fight, refuel/rearm, fight, and return, spending the night in the safety of the UK. Tactically, however, the composite squadron concept was a really bad idea: attempting to forge halves of different squadrons into single units in the midst of combat was foolhardy, and the resulting formations either failed to rendezvous and individually were too small to

survive clashing with the group-strength enemy, or fell apart upon the first encounter. Losses soared immediately: 28 Hurricanes falling on May 16-17.

This initiative was soon supplemented – in defiance of Dowding's famous but ultimately ineffective stand – with the deployment of three full squadrons (17, 32, and 151 Squadrons), but the Luftwaffe caught on quickly, bombing the main refuelling/rearming base at Vitry-en-Artois while two squadrons were in their 'combat turnaround', destroying four Hurricanes on the ground. In the air the RAF lost another 26 shot down. The 'wastage' continued unabated.

With the ground situation rapidly deteriorating from desperate to doomed – 20 enemy divisions, 10 of them armoured and another four motorised were pouring in behind the Allied armies – the chronically vulnerable Lysandrôs began withdrawing to England and BEF(AC) Hurricanes had to be used for visual reconnaissance. Spotting Nazi concentrations near Rethel, the AASF launched one of its last daylight Battle raids, sending a formation escorted by 26 of its Hurricanes.

Five Battles were lost and another two were badly damaged, and in another battle five AASF Hurricanes were lost to Ju 88 and

He 111 defensive gunners. The BEF(AC) and Fighter Command units lost an additional 29 Hurricanes. In this chaotic period 20 Hurricane pilots were killed, eight captured (becoming prisoners of war) and another 11 wounded. The next day – after losing another 16 Hurricanes and six pilots – the BEF(AC)'s fighters were ordered home lest they be overrun on their own airfields. That night Guderian's panzers reached the French coast, slamming shut the steel ring that trapped the British, Belgian, and French armies. ➤

---

*2 25e Groupement was responsible for covering the two French armies accompanying the BEF into Belgium and consisted of four Groupes de Chasse (GC): GC III/1 and III/2 had 64 Morane-Saulnier MS 406s/48 of them serviceable, GC I/4 had 30 Curtiss Hawk 75As/29 serviceable, and GC II/8 had 19 Bloch MB 152s/11 serviceable.

*3 For perspective, it is instructive to realize that BAFF fighter units flew 832 sorties in five days, May 11-15.

THE NORWEGIAN CAMPAIGN

Eighteen Hurricanes were also sent to help stem the German invasion of Norway, when 46 Squadron was put aboard the carrier HMS Glorious by crane in May 1940. Despite not being equipped for carrier operations, the take off proved no problem as the engineers of HMS Glorious managed to achieve 30 knots, giving the Hurricanes sufficient wind over the deck to get airborne safely.

Along with the Gloster Gladiators of 263 Squadron, the Hurricanes began operations from Bardufoss on May 26, providing patrols over the Allied forces at the port of Narvik. Fierce combats against daily raids were the order of the day, with some 14 German aircraft being shot down, but faced with the German advance they were ordered to evacuate on June 7 after just 13 days.

The remaining eight Hurricanes and 10 Gladiators flew back to HMS Glorious, where, despite being land aircraft without arrester hooks, they landed safely. Sadly, the aircraft carrier and her two escorting destroyers encountered the German battleships Scharnhorst and Gneisenau, all three ships being sunk with a loss of over 1500 men. Only two of the Hurricane pilots survived, the OC of 46 Squadron, Squadron Leader Kenneth 'Bing' Cross and Flight Lieutenant 'Jamie' Jameson.

A rare photograph of a 46 Squadron Hurricane Mk I, which has been lowered onto a barge at Abbotsinch to be taken out to HMS Glorious. **Editor's collection**

85 Squadron armourers prepare .303 ammunition belts for their Hurricanes in May 1940. Note the limited facilities and equipment the crews worked with. **Editor's collection**

In 11 days of hard fighting, the BEF(AC) had lost 75 aircraft in combat, but was forced to abandon another 128 – 74 of them Hurricanes – on their bombed damaged airfields because they could not fly out. Operations over northern France were continued by Fighter Command, launching from its stations in south east England, but the battle in the north was lost. The BEF was in retreat to Dunkirk, and the Royal Navy was organising their evacuation under the codename Operation Dynamo.

THE AASF FIGHTERS FIGHT ON

By May 25, when Hitler and his Wehrmacht staff issued the plan for Fall Rot ('Case Red', the final phase of the conquest of France) the AASF was down to 65 "night bombers" and two dozen Hurricanes. The renewed German offensive crossed the Somme and Aisne Rivers on a broad front on June 5. The Jagdwaffe roamed the skies with 250 Bf 109Es and the AdA fighter force, having recovered its strength during the two-week reprieve, met them with 487 sorties, claiming 23 kills for the loss of 19 aircraft.

The three AASF Hurricane squadrons – now down to 18 aircraft between them – patrolled the Rouen sector of the lower Seine River, flying cover for the last remaining BEF unit, the 51st (Highland) Division, which had been stationed with the French IIIe Armée behind the Maginot Line during the initial Nazi onslaught.

Patrolling with Bloch MB 152s of GC II/10, the mixed formations intercepted two raids attacking Rouen, the Hurricanes losing four fighters and two pilots to escorting Messerschmitts. The Blochs shot down three He 111s (I./KG 27) and the Hurricanes got two more, the two units sharing in the destruction of two Ju 88As (III./LG 1) in the later raid.

Two days later, as the French front crumbled again, the AASF units withdrew to the west, the Hurricane squadrons alighting at Le Mans. Sadly, taking off to fly "one more beat up, me lads", before departing for Le Mans, the RAF's hero of the Phoney War, Flying Officer E J 'Cobber' Kain (17 confirmed kills, plus two damaged), was killed while performing low altitude aerobatics at 73 Squadron's former base.

The next day two of the emaciated AASF fighter squadrons (1 and 501 Squadrons) escorted two 12-ship formations of Battles attacking German columns approaching Rouen, losing one of their number to Bf 109Es. Reinforcing these exhausted units, 17 and 242 Squadrons arrived to help provide cover for the next evacuation port, Le Harve, losing five Hurricanes – and shooting down one Bf 109E – in the next two days.

Unable to make it to Le Harve, on June 12 the 51st (Highland) Division surrendered at St-Valéry-en-Caux while Operation Cycle's 207 vessels evacuated 24,000 troops, shipping them to Cherbourg where the BEF was being reconstituted. The two newly arrived squadrons teamed up to shoot down three He 111s attacking Le Harve.

In the face of the approaching panzers, the French declared Paris an 'open city' and began negotiations for an armistice, the German 9. Infanterie Division parading down the Champs Elysées on June 14. With the French ground defence having collapsed completely, the AdA withdrew south of Orléans, and the AASF – five fighter and six Battle squadrons – began retreating west, fighting as they went. In valiant attacks against approaching enemy columns, another score of Battles were lost, as well as three more Hurricanes, during those desperate two days.

The following day (June 15) the AASF was finally ordered to begin evacuating to England – the shattered remnants of the six Battle squadrons departing in the next two days. The Hurricanes were retained to provide air cover for the evacuation ports and British shipping, with 1, 73, and 242 Squadrons moving to Nantes to cover the Brittany ports while 17 and 501 flew to Dinard, then to the Channel Islands, to defend the Normandy ones.

From these ports Operation Aerial evacuated 191,870 British and Allied servicemen to England. But the exhausted pilots and weary Hurricanes at Nantes were unable to prevent Luftwaffe interference with the embarkation at St Nazaire, He 111s and Ju 88As raiding the port three times on June 17. In the Loire Estuary, one of several Ju 88As (from 3./KG 30 or 4./LG 1) put two bombs into the 16,243 ton ocean liner RMS Lancastria. The stricken ship heeled over and sank in less than 30 minutes with a great loss of life – 2823 dead, according to the Admiralty.

While much publicity was made of the

The AASF bomber force was largely composed of Fairey Battles, like those of 105 Squadron pictured here. **Editor's collection**

1 Squadron pilot who "shot down the Heinkel He 111 that sunk the Lancastria" that Junkers Ju 88A was only damaged (and later repaired) in what was hailed as "the last RAF victory of the battle of France". Somehow this sad episode epitomises the RAF's initial combat experience: while naïvely optimistic expectations produced inflated claims, the Hurricane force was outclassed by its Messerschmitt-flying adversaries – outnumbered and outfought by them – resulting in ruinous losses and depressingly disappointing results.

THE LAST RETREAT – BULWARK BRITANNIA

Of 452 Hurricanes sent to battle in France, only 66 returned. Almost all the units' ground equipment was lost there. Far more seriously, 56 pilots had been killed, 18 were now POWs, and 36 had been wounded. While some 500 victories had been claimed, German records reveal 299 losses attributable to BAFF Hurricanes, comparing favourably (if only just) to the 215 of the latter lost in aerial combat.

As costly as this brutal initiation was, it is fortunate that from this sad experience, the survivors of the Fighter Command's Hurricane squadrons that went to war in France in 1940

87 Squadron practice a scramble at Lille-Seclin. Note the mixture of metal and fabric wings, two and three bladed propellers and the fact some aircraft have the armoured windscreen fitted. **Editor's collection**

came home having learned the harshest of lessons, imprinted upon them in the crucible of combat. This experience enabled them to adapt their tactics to match their determination and would permit them to persevere and eventually emerge victorious – against the very same enemy – in the skies over southern England in just a few weeks' time. ■

Words: Douglas C Dildy

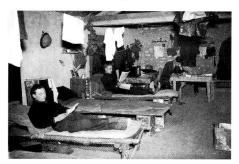

73 Squadron air and ground crew in their accommodation at Rouvres in France. **Editor's collection**

Refuelling had to be done quickly. This 501 Squadron Hurricane is topped up by a bowser at Bethenville on May 11, 1940. **Editor's collection**

The Battle of Britain
Phase One and Two

The Battle of Britain was one of the Hawker Hurricane's finest hours. The historic events of the summer of 1940 have been broken down into their four distinct phases, which are my interpretation of the differing parts of the battle, and may not tally with other official histories. The battle has previously been dealt with in even greater depth in *Aviation Classics* Issue Six.

With the fall of France, Britain now stood alone against the might of the German forces, which were rapidly consolidating their positions in the newly captured territories. In order to invade Britain, the Germans had to establish absolute control in the air over the English Channel, otherwise the RAF and the Royal Navy would have been able to destroy much of their invasion force before it reached the coast.

It has been postulated by many naval experts that due to the type of flat-bottomed barge built by the Germans, simply running a destroyer squadron at full speed through their ranks would have caused many to capsize in the ships' wake. The troops would have suffered heavy casualties, large quantities of equipment would have been lost and the invasion effectively stopped with little or no gunfire. The Luftwaffe's command of the air was therefore vital to any plan for an invasion fleet to successfully cross the channel, to prevent British sea or air forces from interfering with the operation.

The German navy, army and air force each had their own plans and ideas as to how and where the invasion should be launched. There seems to have been little co-operation between the German armed forces, and despite the impressive build up of barges and other equipment in the channel ports, the actual detailed planning for the invasion operation, code-named Sea Lion, was never really thrashed out. All depended on the success of the Luftwaffe it would appear, before the invasion was to be taken seriously.

In order to achieve this air superiority, three Luftflotte (air fleets) were established, arranged from France to Norway. The most powerful of these was Luftflotte II in the Netherlands, Belgium and northern France, commanded by Generalfeldmarschall Albert Kesselring from his headquarters in Brussels. Kesselring had already proved himself an able leader in the attacks on Poland and the Low Countries and was given command of the air forces closest to Britain because of this. Luftflotte II comprised 23 bomber groups, two dive bomber groups and four heavy fighter groups flying the Messerschmitt Bf 110. There were also 13 fighter groups of short range Messerschmitt Bf 109 fighters in the fleet, because if its proximity to the UK. Luftflotte II was to bear the brunt of the fighting.

South of Luftflotte II, Luftflotte III established its headquarters at Villacoublay, Paris, and covered the front from Le Harve to Brest in France. It was commanded by Generalfeldmarschall Hugo Sperrle and comprised 15 bomber groups flying the He 111, Do 17 and Ju 88, nine fighter groups, seven dive bomber groups and four heavy fighter groups. The two Luftflotte commanders had divided the UK in two – east and west of a line running through the Isle of Wight, to Oxford and Manchester then north to Edinburgh, to define their areas of operation, although these were not always strictly adhered too. Luftflotte V in Norway was the smallest of the fleets, with two bomber groups, two fighter groups and sundry support units, but its presence forced the RAF to defend the whole of the eastern coast line against the possibility of its attacks.

Air Chief Marshal Sir Hugh Dowding, Air Officer Commanding-in-Chief of Fighter Command and architect of the successful defence of the UK. **Editor's collection**

Facing this force of more than 2600 bombers and fighters at the beginning of July 1940 were just over 640 RAF fighters, mostly Hurricanes. These numbers had been built up after the losses in France during the two months of delay while the German forces consolidated their positions. The fighters were deployed in four groups, 10 Group covered the south west of England and southern Wales, 11 Group covered south east England and London. Central England was covered by 12 Group and 13 Group had responsibility for the rest of the country and Scotland on a line north of Liverpool. The strongest of the four groups was 11 Group as it was closest to the main enemy threat.

From Fighter Command Headquarters at Bentley Priory, Air Chief Marshal Sir Hugh Dowding, Air Officer Commanding-in-Chief of Fighter Command, had established an efficient command and control system which combined long range radar detection with the eyes of the Observer Corps to provide accurate raid information. This system meant that the thinly spread RAF fighter force could be deployed with maximum efficiency, responding to each threat as it developed and not wasting resources on costly patrols. ➤

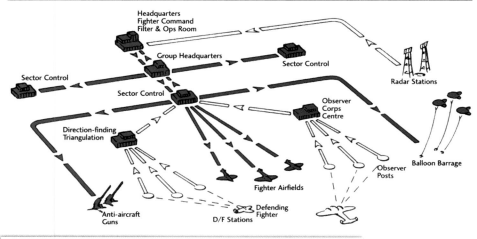
The RAF Battle of Britain fighter control system in diagram form, showing the way the information flowed to the controllers and pilots. **Editor**

The filter room at Fighter Command Headquarters at RAF Bentley Priory took information from the radar stations and forwarded it to the Group and Sector control rooms. **Editor's collection**

With the fall of France, the attack on England was inevitable. All over the UK, young men waited near their aircraft for the order to 'scramble'. Here, a Hurricane pilot adjusts his equipment at RAF Exeter. **Editor's collection**

Hurricane numbers increased dramatically with the establishment of sub-contractor production lines, such as the Gloster factory seen here during a visit by King George VI. **Crown Copyright**

HURRICANE SQUADRONS AT THE BEGINNING OF THE BATTLE OF BRITAIN.

10 GROUP – AIR VICE-MARSHALL BRAND

Squadron	Airfield	Commanding Officer
87	Exeter, Devon	Sqn Ldr J Dewar
213	Exeter, Devon	Sqn Ldr H McGregor
238	Middle Wallop, Hampshire	Sqn Ldr H Fenton

10 Group's remaining three fighter squadrons, 92, 234 and 609, operated Spitfires.

11 GROUP – AIR VICE-MARSHALL PARK

Squadron	Airfield	Commanding Officer
1	Northolt, West London	Sqn Ldr D Pemberton
17	Debden, Essex	Sqn Ldr R McDougal
32	Biggin Hill, Kent	Sqn Ldr J Worrall
43	Tangmere, Sussex	Sqn Ldr J Badger
56	North Weald, Essex	Sqn Ldr M Manton
85	Martlesham, Suffolk	Sqn Ldr P Townsend
111	Croydon, South London	Sqn Ldr J Thompson
145	Tangmere, Sussex	Sqn Ldr J Peel
151	North Weald, Essex	Sqn Ldr E Donaldson
257	Hendon, North London	Sqn Ldr H Harkness
501	Croydon, South London	Sqn Ldr H Hogan
601	Debden, Essex	Sqn Ldr M Aiken
615	Kenley, London	Sqn Ldr J Kayall

Of 11 Group's remaining 11 fighter squadrons, 54, 74, 64, 65 and 610 operated Spitfires, 25, 600 and 604 flew Blenheims, and the last, 141, was equipped with Defiants.

12 GROUP – AIR VICE-MARSHALL LEIGH-MALLORY

Squadron	Airfield	Commanding Officer
46	Digby, Lincolnshire	Flt Lt A. Murray
229	Wittering, Cambridgeshire	Sqn Ldr H. McQuire
242	Coltishall, Norfolk	Sqn Ldr D. Bader

Of 12 Group's remaining eight fighter squadrons, 19, 66, 222, 266 and 611 operated Spitfires, 23 and 29 flew Blenheims and the remaining unit, 264, was equipped with Defiants.

13 GROUP – AIR VICE-MARSHALL SAUL

Squadron	Airfield	Commanding Officer
3	Wick, Scotland	Sqn Ldr S Godden
73	Church Fenton, North Yorkshire	Sqn Ldr J More
79	Turnhouse, Scotland	Sqn Ldr H Heyworth
245	Turnhouse, Scotland	Sqn Ldr F Whitley
249	Leconfield, Yorkshire	Sqn Ldr J Grandy
253	Turnhouse, Scotland	Sqn Ldr T Gleave
263	Grangemouth, Scotland	Sqn Ldr H Eeles
504	Castletown, Scotland	Sqn Ldr J Sample
605	Drem, Scotland	Sqn Ldr W Churchill
607	Usworth, Co Durham	Sqn Ldr J Vick

Of 13 Group's remaining seven fighter squadrons, 41, 72, 152, 602, 603 and 616 operated Spitfires, the last, 219, flying Blenheims.

Because of the dire need for new fighters, the Ministry of Aircraft Production (MAP) led by Lord Beaverbrook set challenging delivery targets to industry. Hawker actually exceeded its target figure of 1045 new Hurricanes by 328 deliveries in just seven months. No other manufacturer was able to boast such a feat, which was made possible by streamlining the production process and sub-contracts being agreed with other companies. The MAP also set up centres around the UK to repair damaged fighters and return them to service as quickly as possible. A myth regarding the Battle of Britain is that the RAF ran short of fighters, but in fact, the MAP repair system and the herculean efforts of the manufacturers meant that the number of fighters available to Fighter Command actually increased throughout the battle. These new Hurricanes replaced the last of the biplane fighters in RAF service, and so the stage was set for the first battle to be decided in the air alone.

PHASE ONE – JULY 10 TO AUGUST 9, 1940

The first day of the Battle of Britain is widely recognised as July 10, 1940, and on this day a convoy code named 'Bread' was making its way through the English Channel. Earlier in the day Spitfires of 74 Squadron had scrambled to intercept a reconnaissance Do 17 with a heavy fighter escort shadowing the vessels. The Dornier was damaged but managed to return to its base. By early afternoon radar was reporting the massing of enemy aircraft over Calais.

The convoy was now being escorted by two flights of three Hurricanes from 32 Squadron and soon came under attack by a force of 26 bombers with an escort of more than 60 Bf 110s and 109s. The call for assistance was met by another Hurricane unit, 111 Squadron, which made a dramatic head on attack in squadron formation. Further RAF squadrons were scrambled as the controllers realised that this was a major enemy effort.

The battle raged above the convoy and only one ship was struck by the many bombs dropped. Four German aircraft were destroyed but many more were damaged for

the loss of a Hurricane to a mid air collision. The system Dowding had implemented was now proven in action. The radar had given sufficient warning to allow the deployment of defending fighters and the controllers were able to direct them to a position and altitude to intercept the enemy accurately.

The remainder of July followed in similar fashion, Fighter Command could not allow the enemy to harass the convoys and was forced into maintaining wasteful defensive patrols over the channel. Given the effectiveness of the attacks against the convoys, the Admiralty withdrew them in early August and sent the south coast cargoes by rail. The Luftwaffe also attacked several coastal ports, including Weymouth and Portland in Dorset, spreading the attacks along the south coast.

At this stage of the battle, the Luftwaffe was in effect probing the British defences, looking for weaknesses before a major assault could be launched to exploit them. The British fighters were doing well against the Luftwaffe, inflicting losses without excessive casualties. It is another myth that the number of RAF fighter pilots reached critical levels during the Battle of Britain, in fact, the numbers available actually increased through July to November of 1940, and although many of the newly trained pilots had relatively few hours and no experience, the RAF's replacement pilot situation was far superior to that of the Luftwaffe.

The advantages of the Hurricane's construction came to the fore as the fighting intensified, because it was easier to repair and return to action after battle damage than the Spitfire. Its qualities as a gun platform and the firepower of the close grouped gun batteries was also proving effective in many combats. This period of the battle enabled Fighter Command to hone its procedures and resolve problems with the communications system. After all, this was the first time an integrated network of radar sites, observers and fighters had been controlled from a remote operations room.

The resolute commander of 11 Group, Air Vice Marshall Keith Park, himself an ace of the First World War, adopted a policy of

deploying the minimum number of his fighters while maintaining a creditable reserve. Although these tactics meant that his fighters were almost always outnumbered, it did preserve the Group's capability and contributed to the enemy misjudging the true state of British fighter strength. Dowding began a system of regular rest periods for squadrons to further maintain the fighting effectiveness of his force. At the squadron level, units began to abandon the rigid formations practiced so vigorously before the war and adopted the more flexible formations and tactics that served the Luftwaffe fighter units so well. This testing period readied Fighter Command for the major attacks that were about to begin.

PHASE TWO – AUGUST 10 TO SEPTEMBER 6, 1940

Given the success of the attacks on the convoys and coastal towns, the next stage of the Luftwaffe's plan was to directly attack the RAF defensive system. Its commanders recognised the importance of the British radar masts and attacked four stations on the south coast on August 12, damaging some of them, but only putting them out of action for hours at a time rather than days. Even the hard hit Ventnor radar station on the Isle of Wight continued to transmit radar signals, even though it was badly damaged and unable to receive.

This ruse helped the Luftwaffe to believe that the radar equipment was far hardier than it actually was, so the attacks against these stations were discontinued by mid-August. The other major targets of this second phase were the RAF fighter airfields and the fighter aircraft factories, the aim being to so cripple Fighter Command that it could no longer mount an effective defence, clearing the way for the planned invasion.

The initial attacks on the RAF had been planned for August 10, but were delayed by bad weather. On August 13, known as Adlertag, or Eagle Day, heavy attacks by high and low level formations were aimed at airfields in the South East. Hurricanes of 111 and 145 Squadron met the first of these,

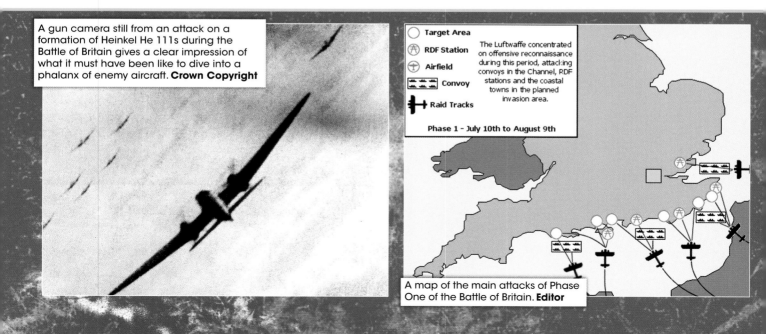

A gun camera still from an attack on a formation of Heinkel He 111s during the Battle of Britain gives a clear impression of what it must have been like to dive into a phalanx of enemy aircraft. **Crown Copyright**

Target Area
RDF Station
Airfield
Convoy
Raid Tracks

The Luftwaffe concentrated on offensive reconnaissance during this period, attacking convoys in the Channel, RDF stations and the coastal towns in the planned invasion area.

Phase 1 – July 10th to August 9th

A map of the main attacks of Phase One of the Battle of Britain. **Editor**

Three Hurricanes of 247 Squadron return to land between sorties in the battle. **Editors collection**

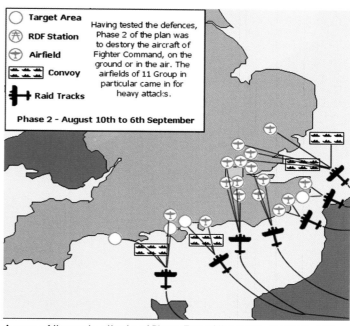

A map of the main attacks of Phase Two of the Battle of Britain. **Editor**

Do 17s of KG2 that had bombed RAF Eastchurch in Kent. In the face of these heavy attacks, trials to increase the firepower of RAF fighters were conducted. One of the 46 Squadron Hurricanes, flown by Flt Lt A Rabagliati, was fitted with 20mm cannons with which he managed to damage two aircraft on this day. This experimental installation was considered unsatisfactory due to jamming and the weight of the guns and ammunition, so it was not until the Hurricane Mk.IIC came into production that the Hispano 20mm cannons became standard armament. After a number of airfield attacks during the day, the Supermarine factory at Castle Bromwich and the Shorts factory at Belfast were both badly damaged by night bombing raids.

The airfield and radar station attacks of August 15 were the largest of the battle to that date, with Luftflotte V also mounting raids from Norway, the belief being that the RAF fighter defences were concentrated in the south. Inadequately escorted, these raids against the north of England suffered heavy losses and were not repeated on the same scale again. On August 16, Flight Lieutenant James Brindley Nicolson flying Hurricane P3576 on his first combat sortie became the only member of Fighter Command to be awarded the Victoria Cross.

Wounded when his Hurricane was 'bounced' by Bf 110s, and with his aircraft well alight, Nicolson stayed with his burning Hurricane to shoot down one of his attackers when it overshot his fighter. August 18 saw another day of heavy raids, with the largest losses of aircraft being suffered by both sides. RAF Kenley, Biggin Hill, West Malling and North Weald were attacked by large bomber formations, while dive bombers struck at the radar stations on the south coast and RAF Ford and Thorney Island and RNAS Gosport.

Flight Lieutenant James Brindley Nicolson, the only member of Fighter Command to be awarded the Victoria Cross. **Editors collection**

However, RAF fighters inflicted such losses on the Ju 87 Stukas that they were withdrawn from the Battle of Britain from that point onwards. Luftflotte III was ordered to concentrate on night bombing and most of its Bf 109 units were transferred to Luftflotte II to provide stronger escorts for the bombers. The 'Frei Jagd' or free hunting fighter sweeps were cut back in favour of stronger escorts by order of Reichsmarschall Hermann Goering, Commander in Chief of the Luftwaffe. This was to prove a tactical mistake, as the German fighters no longer had the ability to intercept British fighters before they reached the bomber raids, something the Bf 109 pilots had achieved great success with.

Despite the size of the attacks on the airfields, relatively little serious damage was done. Biggin Hill was the only Sector airfield to be closed, and that was only for two hours while unexploded munitions were dealt with. The grass airfields were easily repaired, and while refueling, rearming and maintenance became more difficult within the bomb damaged facilities, none of these activities were ever stopped. The raids on airfields continued, but less continuously as the weather began to worsen as August wore on.

During this crucial period, Fighter Command actually grew in strength. On August 18, 551 Hurricanes and 275 Spitfires were available. A further 77 machines, of which 52 were Hurricanes, were anticipated to be available in 12 hours as the ground crews and repair centres worked throughout the night. Damage that wrote a Spitfire off was not always fatal to a Hurricane. New wings or a replacement tail section could easily be exchanged and the fuselage framework did

Pilots from all over the Commonwealth and occupied Europe swelled the ranks of Fighter Command during the battle. These are a group of Polish pilots from 303 (Polish) Squadron, led by Squadron Leader Johnny Kent, a Canadian, second from left. **Editors collection**

not require welding. Adding to the numbers were new squadrons being formed and introduced to the battle, including many manned by pilots from the Commonwealth and occupied Europe. During this period the development of the Hurricane continued in the light of combat experience. Self sealing fuel tanks, armoured windscreens and more armour plating, over 100lb (45 kg) of it, were added, the armour mostly behind the pilot's seat. Despite the modifications to the Merlin III it wasn't until more than 5600 engines had been completed that they were fitted with a truly universal output shaft that could accommodate either a Rotol or de Havilland propeller. In service the Rotol unit was found to be marginally superior and became the most common propeller fitted to Hurricanes.

Since British cities and port facilities such as Portsmouth, Bristol and London had been attacked by Luftflotte III's night raids, the latter reportedly by mistake, RAF Bomber Command began a series of retaliatory raids on Berlin on August 25. This led to Hitler threatening to destroy British cities and withdrawing his directive that banned raids on London. The next phase of the Battle of Britain began on September 7, and will be described later in this magazine. ■ *Words: Tim Callaway and Julian Humphries*

HURRICANE FORCE

Based at RAF Exeter, Flight Lieutenant Ian 'Widge' Gleed in his Hurricane Mk.I LK-A P2798 of 87 Squadron is seen attacking a Messerschmitt Bf 110C of II./ZG76 on August 15, 1940 at the height of the Battle of Britain. Flt Lt Gleed shot down two of the eight Bf 110C's lost that day and claimed one of the escorting Bf109s as a 'probable'

The Battle of Britain
Phase Three and Four

During the first stages of the battle, the Luftwaffe had probed the British defences then launched all out attacks to cripple the fighter control system and the aircraft manufacturers. The attacks on civilian targets, some of which were unintentional and punished by Luftwaffe command, prompted a response against German cities from Bomber Command, which in turn caused the Luftwaffe to change its strategy. The first raid of the new policy took place on September 7, and the next phase of the battle had begun.

PHASE THREE – SEPTEMBER 7 TO OCTOBER 5 1940

Some of the airfield raids in the second half of August had been extremely heavy, with hundreds of aircraft committed to them. These airfield attacks were interspersed with raids on harbours and aircraft factories as the Luftwaffe split its forces to keep the defence network guessing as to its true target. Luftflotte III had gone over to mostly night raids, with strategic targets being attacked in cities around the UK.

Toward the end of August, fighters were encountered in smaller numbers by some of the raids due to the RAF's new tactic of splitting its defences. This, along with erroneous and contradictory data from the ineffective German intelligence services gave Goering cause to believe that Fighter Command was nearly destroyed.

Reports indicated that the RAF may be down to its last 100 fighters, a figure far from the truth. With the encouragement of Hitler's directive to attack cities, issued on September 5, in retaliation for Bomber Command's continuing raids on Berlin, Goering planned to begin a daily campaign of attacks on London.

Additional pressure to successfully establish air superiority over the Channel came from Hitler, the German Army and the German Navy, who had begun to build up the necessary barges and other craft required to transport the 12 divisions of Army Group A to the south coast of England. The potential for invasion had to be taken seriously by the British, so Bomber Command mounted a series of raids on the ports containing the concentrations of vessels.

However, major divisions in opinion still existed between the three forces as to the detailed plans for the invasion. Indeed, the German Navy considered it impossible with the resources available. With this background, the change in the Luftwaffe's attack had three main aims; to draw the remaining RAF fighters into combat to defend the cities, to achieve the required air superiority by this means, and lastly to crush British morale with a view to forcing either a surrender or a negotiated peace.

September 7 saw this momentous change in the battle. The day began very quietly, but by late afternoon more than 1000 Luftwaffe aircraft, over 600 of them fighters, were forming up in layers up to 20,000ft (6000m). Watching this huge armada assemble, the RAF controllers were unaware of the enemy's intentions and feared further raids on the already damaged airfields.

Every available fighter in 11 Group was scrambled to patrol in the vicinity of the airfields and factories that had previously been the Luftwaffe's objectives. Both 10 and 12 Groups were brought to standby as this unprecedented number of enemy aircraft made unpredictable direction changes with the intention of confusing the defenders.

When it became apparent that London was the target, few fighters were in position to prevent the bombing. Hurricanes of 1, 303, 501 and 507 Squadrons were directed from their patrol over the Thames estuary to intercept the tidal wave of enemy aircraft. The Poles of 303 Squadron carried out a devastating attack on a formation of Dornier Do 17s and claimed 10 destroyed for the loss of two of their own.

Elsewhere the enemy fighters were more successful in protecting their charges, six Hurricanes of 249 Squadron were shot down

Based at Gravesend, Hurricanes of 501 Squadron take off on August 16, 1940 to intercept a raid. **Editor's collection**

At the height of the Battle of Britain, September 15, 1940, ground crew of 310 Czech Squadron work to rapidly rearm a Hurricane at Duxford in Cambridgeshire. **Editor's collection**

Radio communications were a vital part of the fighter control system. Here technicians service a Hurricane's radio, a task made simpler by its open frame construction. **Editor's collection**

The Battle of Britain was won by groundcrews who kept the aircraft in the air as much as by the pilots who flew them. Here a 601 Squadron Hurricane Mk1 is worked on at Exeter. **Editor's collection**

FIGHTER COMMAND HURRICANE SQUADRONS ON SEPTEMBER 1 1940

10 GROUP		
Squadron	**Airfield**	**Commanding Officer**
No 87	Exeter	Sqn Ldr Mills
No 213	Exeter	Sqn Ldr Mcgregor
No 238	St Eval	Sqn Ldr Fenton
No 249	Boscombe Down	Sqn Ldr Grandy
11 GROUP		
Squadron	**Airfield**	**Commanding Officer**
No 1	Northolt	Sqn Ldr Pemberton
No 17	Tangmere	Sqn Ldr Miller
No 43	Tangmere	Sqn Ldr Hill
No 56	North Weald	Unit awaiting replacement CO
No 85	Croydon	Sqn Ldr Townsend
No 79	Biggin Hill	Sqn Ldr Heyworth
No 111	Debden	Sqn Ldr Thompson
No 151	Stapleford	Unit awaiting replacement CO
No 253	Kenley	Unit awaiting replacement CO
No 257	Debden	Sqn Ldr Harkness
No 303	Northolt	Sqn Ldrs Kellet & Kransnodesbski
No 501	Gravesend	Sqn Ldr Hogan
No 601	Debden	Sqn Ldr Sir Archibald Hope
No 1 (RCAF)	Northolt	Sqn Ldr McNab
12 GROUP		
Squadron	**Airfield**	**Commanding Officer**
No 46	Digby	Sqn Ldr Murray
No 229	Bircham Newton	Sqn Ldr McQuire
No 242	Coltishall	Sqn Ldr Bader
No 310	Duxford	Sqn Ldr Blackwood
13 GROUP		
Squadron	**Airfield**	**Commanding Officer**
No 3	Wick	Sqn Ldr Godden
No 32	Acklington	Sqn Ldr Crossley
No 73	Church Fenton	Sqn Ldr Robinson
No 145	Dyce	Sqn Ldr Pugh
No 263	Grangemouth	Sqn Ldr Eeles
No 302	Leconfield	Sqn Ldr Satchell
No 504	Castletown	Sqn Ldr Sample
No 605	Drem	Sqn Ldr Churchill
No 607	Usworth	Sqn Ldr Vick

by Bf 109s before they could reach the bombers. Bombs began falling on the East London docks at about 5pm, the bombers maintaining orderly formation, for the moment only troubled by anti-aircraft fire as Fighter Command redirected its Squadrons into position. A huge battle raged over the capital as successive waves of bombers attacked until about 6.30pm. Vast areas of the docks were now alight from end to end, warehouses filled with timber, sugar and other combustible materials fuelled the fires.

The bombers returned that night to stoke the fires set in the day, the first of 57 consecutive night raids. East London was now one massive beacon despite the efforts of fire crews, who fought valiantly to extinguish the flames among the falling bombs. The raids continued in this fashion of afternoon and night attacks against London until bad weather on September 12 caused a brief respite during the day.

On the morning of September 15, the Luftwaffe launched two waves of bombers against the London rail network and dockyards. The first raid of 25 Do 17s missed its rendezvous with its fighter escort and was met by a force of 12 Squadrons as they approached London, over 130 Spitfires and Hurricanes, which must have come as a shock to the German bomber crews. Five more squadrons arrived from 12 Group as they bombed, then harried the raiders all the way to the coast. ➤

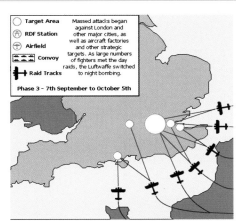

A map of the main attacks of Phase Three of the Battle of Britain. **Editor**

The second raid was much larger, with a force of 110 Heinkel He 111s and Do 17s heavily escorted by Bf 109s. British Prime Minister Winston Churchill was visiting 11 Group's operations room at RAF Uxbridge that day, and watched as Air Vice Marshal Keith Park deployed his squadrons to meet the raids. All 21 Squadrons of 11 Group were scrambled to meet the second raid, along with three more from 10 Group and five from 12 Group. Churchill asked Park what reserves were available, and received the rather sobering reply: "None, sir".

The bombers did reach London, but were attacked continually, even out to sea. That afternoon the Luftwaffe returned, again in force, with over 500 aircraft heading for London. Park was able to get eight squadrons airborne and in position 15 minutes before the raid crossed the coast, and again the bombers were under attack all the way to and from their target. Secondary attacks were also made on Portland harbour and the Supermarine factory at Southampton, both of which were met by a strong fighter defence. The claims of both sides for aircraft lost this day were greatly inflated, largely caused by the size and confusion of the battles, but the truth of the matter is that 56 German aircraft were shot down, as were 26 Spitfires and Hurricanes, with many more damaged on both sides.

This loss rate was unsustainable for the Luftwaffe. Experienced crews were now in short supply and the personnel replacement situation was becoming critical. At the time the Luftwaffe training system was simply not geared to support a long campaign of attrition and the aircraft manufacturers were only just getting into their stride. The myth that Fighter Command was on its knees was finally dispelled and the defeat of September 15 caused Hitler to postpone the invasion for a month, two days later. Because of these events and the size of the attacks, September 15 is now known as Battle of Britain day.

Pilots of 310 Czech Squadron are briefed during the Battle of Britain. **Editor's collection**

The change of plan to attack cities was a mistake for a number of reasons. It gave 11 Group a chance to repair its airfields and radar sites, so the defences became fully operational again. The German Bf 109 fighter could only carry enough fuel for 20 minutes flight over Britain, so London was on the edge of its limited range. Finally, the German raids now came within the range of 12 Group, and its large formation tactics known as 'Big Wings'.

Much has been written about the different tactics employed by 11 and 12 Groups and their commanders, and the supposed disagreements these differences caused. Suffice to say that 11 Group's fast response tactic – using whatever was available and meeting the enemy formations as far from their targets as possible – was best suited to its geographical proximity to the German bases.

Squadrons of 11 Group simply did not have the time to assemble. They had to get airborne and climb to height as quickly as possible or miss intercepting the raid altogether. Being further north, 12 Group had somewhat more time for a large formation of fighters to assemble and climb to meet the oncoming attacks, tactics that suited their circumstances. Dowding, as befits a true leader, allowed his group commanders to run their organisations as they saw fit, the detail work being done at group level while he dealt with the overall picture.

The life of an 11 Group pilot was difficult, but Park understood the true situation of his command, and employed his Squadrons with brilliant effectiveness. In the light of the outcome of the Battle, and the fact that for many days he had the fate of a nation resting on his shoulders alone, Park must be considered alongside Dowding as an architect of the RAF's success.

Knowing the targets to be London and the industrial centres, the British controllers now had time to assemble a large number of fighters to attack the German formations and break them up before they could bomb. By changing tactics and targets, the Germans had actually helped Fighter Command to deal with raids. For the people living in the cities, the Blitz had begun, as night raids followed daytime raids and gave the civilians little rest and casualties mounted rapidly.

Everybody was in the front line, and there was little the RAF could do to stop the night raids. Airborne radar was in its infancy, but there were some successes for the Blenheim, Defiant and early Beaufighter night fighter squadrons. Some of the Hurricane and Spitfire day fighter squadrons also took part in the night defences, but relied largely on luck to make an interception.

Over the next few days there were few daylight raids, the Luftwaffe continuing the night attacks in large numbers. Daylight attacks on aircraft factories were then stepped up again with the realisation of how badly the

The fighter team. Hurricane MkIs of 1 Squadron with Spitfire MkIs of 266 Squadron based at Wittering in October 1940. It was intended that the Spitfire units would attack and draw off the escorts, allowing the Hurricanes to deal with the bombers during the Battle of Britain, but this rarely worked out in practice. **Editor's collection**

Hurricane MkIs of 85 Squadron in formation on October 5, 1940. **Editor's collection**

German commanders had underestimated the size and strength of Fighter Command. Supermarine's factory at Southampton was bombed on September 24 and 26, the latter heavy raid stopping Spitfire production.

Fighter-bomber raids of Bf 110 and Bf 109s were made alongside the bomber raids, in an attempt to draw more RAF fighters into costly battles against pure fighter opposition. The German fighters now operated at much higher altitudes and the Hurricane MkI was unable to make interceptions at heights in excess of 25,000ft (7500m). The Spitfire and Bf 109 were both markedly superior to the Hurricane at these altitudes, an early indication that the Hurricane's days as a pure fighter were coming to an end in the European theatre.

Renewed heavy daylight attacks on September 28 and 30 caused mixed results for the Luftwaffe. On the 28th the new tactics proved successful, with the RAF's losses exceeding those of the Luftwaffe, but the 30th saw 50 more German aircraft shot down as the RAF adapted to the new threats. By October 5, the daylight bomber raids ceased as in the face of these losses, with the bomber force concentrating on night attacks.

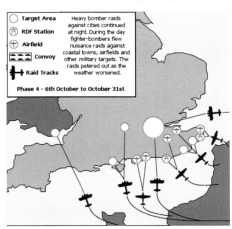

A map of the main attacks of Phase Four of the Battle of Britain. **Editor**

Hurricane MkI P3059, SD-N of 501 Squadron. This aircraft was lost on August 18, 1940, when Pilot Officer Kenneth Norman Thomson Lee was 'bounced' by Bf 109s over Canterbury. Lee bailed out and was admitted to hospital. **Keith Draycott**

PHASE FOUR – OCTOBER 6 TO OCTOBER 31 1940

As the long, hot summer ran into October, the German raids continued. During the day, German fighters, mostly Bf 109s but occasionally Bf 110s, were sent over carrying bombs in small and large scale Jagd-bomber or "Jabo" fighter-bomber raids. Largely, these nuisance raiders were aimed at engaging the RAF fighters and disrupting defensive operations over the South-East. Defenders, tired from the night attacks, were stretched still further by these raids. They flew fast and high and were difficult to intercept. The radar warning was not far enough in advance to allow a Spitfire to climb to this height from the ground, so the RAF had regular patrols between 15,000 and 20,000ft. This was a costly and inefficient use of the aircraft and pilots, exactly the situation the control system had helped to avoid during the earlier phases of the Battle, but German losses began to increase.

The weather also began to worsen and the raids stopped in late October. On October 13, Hitler again postponed the invasion until the following spring, then as preparations for the invasion of Russia commenced, cancelled it altogether. The Battle of Britain was over. Strangely, for such a ground breaking battle, the first to be decided purely in the air and the first real test of air power as a defensive and offensive weapon, it did not really end, so much as petered out.

Throughout the winter of 1940/1 the Luftwaffe concentrated its bombing effort on British cities under the cover of darkness. On October 18, Fighter Command could, despite the loss of over 1150 aircraft since May 10, boast 512 Hurricanes and 285 Spitfires. This amazing feat was achieved through dispersion of production and the Luftwaffe's failure to identify and attack key sites.

Attacks against Hawker facilities were mostly inconsequential, despite the Brooklands and Langley factories being within easy range of the Luftwaffe bases in France. Later, in 1941, some damage was caused at Langley during a night raid. The production of Hurricanes averaged just over 62 per week between June 1 and November 1, 1940. A total of 1367 were built over that period in comparison to the 724 Spitfires which were completed at an average of 33 per week.

Large numbers of damaged Hurricanes were returned to the squadrons from the hard working RAF Maintenance Units and various civilian companies engaged in this vital work. The Luftwaffe's tactics were often misguided and with the benefit of hindsight are sometimes difficult to understand. There is no doubt that the Hurricane and the men that flew and maintained it deserve their place in history as the true victors of the Battle of Britain. ■
Words: Tim Callaway and Julian Humphries

The Hurricane Squadrons of the Battle of Britain

Here are representative aircraft from all the RAF Squadrons that flew the Hurricane during the Battle of Britain. Along with the aircraft, there is a list of stations the Squadrons were based at during the period of the battle, July to October 1940.

1 SQUADRON

Stations
Tangmere, June 23, 1940
Northolt, August 1, 1940
Wittering, September 9, 1940

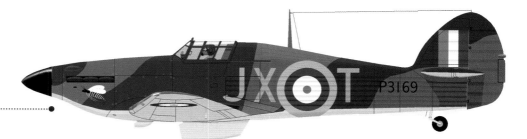

3 SQUADRON

Stations
Wick, May 23, 1940
Castletown, September 2, 1940
Turnhouse, September 14, 1940
Dyce, October 9, 1940
Castletown, October 12, 1940

17 SQUADRON

Stations
Debden, June 19, 1940
Tangmere, August 19, 1940
Debden, September 2, 1940
Martlesham Heath,
October 8, 1940

32 SQUADRON

Stations
Biggin Hill, June 4, 1940
Acklington, August 28, 1940

43 SQUADRON

Stations
Tangmere, May 31, 1940
Northolt (D) July 23, 1940, to
August 1, 1940
Usworth, September 8, 1940

46 SQUADRON

Stations
Digby, June 13, 1940
Duxford, August 18, 1940
Digby, August 19, 1940
Stapleford Tawney,
September 1, 1940

56 SQUADRON

Stations
North Weald, June 4, 1940
Boscombe Down,
September 1, 1940

73 SQUADRON

Stations
Church Fenton, June 18, 1940
Castle Camps, September 5, 1940

79 SQUADRON

Stations
Biggin Hill, June 5, 1940
Hawkinge, July 2, 1940
Sealand, July 11, 1940
Acklington, July 13, 1940
Biggin Hill, August 27, 1940
Pembrey, September 8, 1940

85 SQUADRON

Stations
Debden, May 22, 1940
Croydon, August 19, 1940
Castle Camps, September 3, 1940
Church Fenton, September 5, 1940
Kirton-in-Lindsey, October 23, 1940

87 SQUADRON

Stations
Church Fenton, May 26, 1940
Exeter, July 5, 1940

111 SQUADRON

Stations
Croydon, June 4, 1940
Debden, August 19, 1940
Croydon, September 3, 1940
Drem, September 8, 1940

145 SQUADRON

Stations
Tangmere, May 10, 1940
Westhampnett, July 31, 1940
Drem, August 14, 1940
Dyce, August 31, 1940
Tangmere, October 9, 1940

151 SQUADRON

Stations
North Weald, May 20, 1940
Stapleford Tawney,
August 29, 1940
Digby, September 1, 1940

213 SQUADRON

Stations
Exeter, June 18, 1940
Tangmere, September 7, 1940

229 SQUADRON

Stations
Wittering, June 26, 1940
Northolt, September 9, 1940

232 SQUADRON

Stations
Sumburgh, July 17, 1940
Castletown, September 18, 1940
Skitten, October 13, 1940
Drem, October 24, 1940

238 SQUADRON

Stations
Middle Wallop, June 20, 1940
St Eval, August 14, 1940
Middle Wallop, September 10, 1940
Chilbolton, September 30, 1940

242 SQUADRON

Stations
Coltishall, June 18, 1940
Duxford, October 26, 1940

245 SQUADRON

Stations
Aldergrove, July 20, 1940

249 SQUADRON

Stations
Leconfield, May 18, 1940
Church Fenton, July 8, 1940
Boscombe Down, August 14, 1940
North Weald, September 1, 1940

253 SQUADRON

Stations
Kirton-in-Lindsey, May 24, 1940
Turnhouse, July 21, 1940
Prestwick, August 23, 1940
Kenley (A), August 29, 1940
Kenley (G), September 16, 1940

257 SQUADRON

Stations
Hendon, May 17, 1940
Northolt, July 4, 1940
Debden, August 15, 1940
Martlesham Heath,
September 5, 1940
North Weald, October 8, 1940

263 SQUADRON

Stations
Grangemouth, June 28, 1940
Drem, September 2, 1940

302 SQUADRON

Stations
Leconfield, July 13, 1940
Northolt, October 11, 1940

303 SQUADRON

Stations
Northolt, July 22, 1940
Leconfield, October 11, 1940

310 SQUADRON

Stations
Duxford, July 10, 1940

312 SQUADRON

Stations
Duxford, August 29, 1940
Speke, September 26, 1940

401 SQUADRON

Stations
Middle Wallop, June 21, 1940
Croydon, July, 1940
Northolt, Mid-August, 1940
Prestwick, October 11, 1940

501 SQUADRON

Stations
Croydon, June 21, 1940
Middle Wallop, July 4, 1940
Gravesend, July 25, 1940
Kenley, September 10, 1940

504 SQUADRON

Stations
Castletown, June 21, 1940
Catterick, September 1, 1940
Hendon, September 5, 1940
Filton, September 26, 1940

601 SQUADRON

Stations
Tangmere, June 17, 1940
Debden, August 19, 1940
Tangmere, September 2, 1940
Exeter, September 7, 1940

605 SQUADRON

Stations
Drem, May 28, 1940
Croydon, September 7, 1940

607 SQUADRON

Stations
Usworth, June 5, 1940
Tangmere, September 1, 1940
Turnhouse, October 10, 1940

615 SQUADRON

Stations
Kenley, May 20, 1940
Prestwick, August 29, 1940
Northolt, October 10, 1940

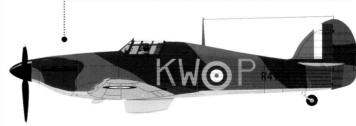

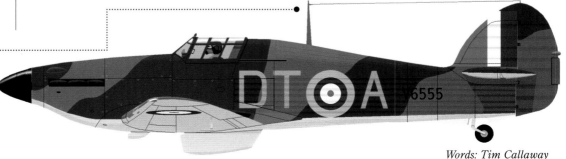

Words: Tim Callaway

The Sea Hurricane
Storm at sea

The Hawker Hurricane first flew from British aircraft carriers without any conversion for naval operations. This happened due to necessity, it was the only way to retrieve the aircraft of 46 Squadron stranded in Norway, and later, was the only way to reinforce the island of Malta. The success of these missions, and the fact there was only a biplane fighter on British carriers at the time, led Hawker Aircraft to develop the Sea Hurricane, the first modern single seat fighter to serve in the role with the Royal Navy.

During the late 1930s the Royal Navy was entirely dependent on navalised versions of the Gloster Gladiator to fulfil the single seat fighter role. Based on the Gladiator II, the Sea Gladiator could only be considered an interim type, bridging the gap between what was immediately available and future monoplane fighters.

They were complemented by the two-seat Blackburn Roc, the four gun armament of which was grouped in a turret behind the cockpit in the same fashion as the Defiant. Burdened by the unwieldy and heavy turret, it was 30mph (48kmh) slower than the Gladiator and was found to be of such limited value as a fighter that it was quickly relegated to secondary duties ashore.

The unhappy experience that befell 46 Squadron in Norway, as described earlier, at least highlighted the Hurricane's potential as a naval aircraft; its wide track undercarriage and docile handling characteristics allowed unmodified aircraft to alight on the deck of carriers at sea. But the loss of the carriers HMS Courageous in September 1939 and HMS Glorious during this abortive campaign was a serious blow, leaving a gaping hole in the Navy's ability to defend vital merchant shipping beyond the range of land based aircraft.

To provide some kind of interim capability, serious consideration was given to mounting a fighter on floats. A pair of floats from a Blackburn Roc were supplied to Hawker, where they were test fitted to the centre section of a Hurricane. The two floats were attached at the undercarriage pick up points at the extreme ends of the centre section by 'N' shaped struts and braced with a single strut between them.

However, the installation was never flown, the Roc on floats could not even achieve 200mph and the anticipated reduction to the performance of a floatplane Hurricane brought an end to the experiment. Later in the war, several modified Spitfires were flown with floats but never used operationally; the only country to achieve any success with this arrangement was Japan in the Pacific campaign.

The situation in the mid Atlantic was turning seriously against Britain. As an island her economy and indeed the entire war effort was dependent on the uninterrupted supply of food and raw material from overseas. The Germans recognised this and employed long range reconnaissance bombers, converted from Focke-Wulf civil airliners, to harass the convoys and direct U-boat attacks. Known as the Condor, the Fw 200 was an elegant but frail four engined machine that had an endurance of over 12 hours.

These aircraft posed a deadly threat as they worked in concert with the enemy's submarines and attacked isolated vessels with bombs and cannon fire themselves. An emergency measure was needed. There was no

Hawker Sea Hurricane MkIA, KE-M Z4936, of the Merchant Ship Fighter Unit launching from the training catapult at Speke airport, Liverpool. The full power of the cordite rockets is evident in this shot. **Editor's collection**

A Hawker Sea Hurricane MkIA launches from the training catapult at Speke, showing the flaps lowered to 25 degrees. The undercarriage was only left down on training launches. **Editor's collection**

time to wait for new carriers to counter the enemy long range aircraft, whose actions, unchecked, would bring the country to its knees by cutting the vital sea lanes.

The operation of aircraft from naval vessels was a well established practice. Using a launching rail, capital ships were able to catapult spotter aircraft as large as the Supermarine Walrus, which was of similar weight to a Hurricane MkI. In October 1940, Hawker was approached to investigate the possibility of adapting the standard Hurricane for naval use, both on carriers and launching catapults.

A repaired Hurricane was supplied to Hawker to build a prototype for trials. The modifications were not extensive and involved considerable strengthening of the rear fuselage, which would have to absorb the energy of being accelerated

to flying speed within a very short distance. Catapult attachment points were fitted to the rear of the centre section and lower rear fuselage to carry the aircraft on the launch rail. A 'V' shaped arrester hook was installed and was attached to the existing frames at the ground handling point about midway between the trailing edge of the wing and the tail plane.

It swung forward from this point and was attached just ahead of the tail wheel fairing, necessitating the removal of a portion of it to allow the frame and hook to lay flush with the lower fuselage. The frame was fitted with a damping system to prevent it bouncing over the arrestor wires when it made contact with the carrier deck.

Arrestor hooks were unnecessary for Hurricanes destined for catapult use and were never fitted. To enable the aircraft to be

lifted on board ship, shackle points were provided on the upper surface of the centre section. To secure it on the catapult, lashing points were installed in the lower surface of the wing.

Since the aircraft would be carried exposed on the decks of ships without the benefit of a hangar, clamps were provided to lock the rudder, ailerons and elevators to prevent them being damaged in high winds. These were removed before flight and when fitted passed over the movable surfaces of the wing and tail.

The armament of the standard Hurricane was retained and at this stage there was no provision for under wing stores. Lastly, the cockpit instrumentation was changed, the air speed indicator reading in knots not miles per hour. Once complete, the trials aircraft was delivered to Farnborough for testing. ➤

The bow mounted catapult on a CAM ship with a Sea Hurricane loaded. **Editor's collection**

Such was the urgent need for effective fighter cover over the convoys, 50 navalised Hurricanes, to be converted from repaired and stored aircraft, were ordered before the trials were even concluded.

The weight added by the conversion and the age of some of the stored airframes had a detrimental effect on the Sea Hurricane's performance, but it was thought it would be unlikely to encounter an enemy single seat fighter far out at sea.

The first Sea Hurricanes were converted by General Aircraft Ltd and were intended as catapult launched aircraft. Although visually similar to the RAF's Hurricane MkI, they were fitted with TR.1147 radios as used by the Royal Navy and featured the modifications listed above. A special headrest was also installed to prevent whiplash injuries as the rapid, rocket assisted acceleration exerted about 3.5G, putting great strain on the pilot's neck.

The aircraft was carried along the launching rail on a trolley that fell into the sea after the launch. During the very short trip down the rails, the pilot had to input sufficient pressure on the rudder to counter the Hurricane's natural urge to swing to port on take-off. The flaps were set at about 25 degrees to provide greater lift for the climb away from sea level.

Even with the engine at full throttle and with rocket assistance, the Hurricane was propelled into the air dangerously close to its stalling speed and every launch was a dramatic affair. Over 30 Merchant Navy vessels were fitted with a single launch rail slightly offset to starboard on the bow. They were capable of carrying a pair of Hurricanes but had no weather protection for them other than tarpaulin covers.

There was no way to recover the aircraft once launched and this was the major disadvantage of the system. It essentially meant each Sea Hurricane could be used just once and if the aircraft was out of range of land the pilot was forced to either ditch into the sea or bail out in the hope of being rescued.

The 35 converted civilian vessels were known as Catapult Aircraft Merchantmen, or CAM ships, and were crewed by Merchant Marine and RAF personnel. Another five Naval Auxiliary vessels were also converted, but were known as Fighter Catapult Ships and crewed by Royal Navy and Fleet Air Arm personnel.

A rare colour shot of the firing of a CAM ship catapult, the cordite rockets accelerated the Sea Hurricane MkIA at about 3.5G. **Editor's collection**

The converted Hurricanes were unofficially referred to as 'Hurricats' and the first sea trials were conducted from the Empire Rainbow early in 1941. One of the CAM ships, the Micheal E, was torpedoed by a submarine in May, its unused Sea Hurricane being lost with the ship before it could be launched.

On June 18, 1941, HMS Maplin, one of the Fighter Catapult Ships, deployed her Hurricane against a Condor prowling at the edges of a convoy she was protecting. Unfortunately for the fighter pilot, the enemy aircraft was brought down by naval gunfire before he could engage it and his aircraft was wasted. After circling the convoy he bailed out and was quickly recovered from the sea. The first successful 'Hurricat' interception took place on August 3, 1941. Lieutenant Robert W H Everett of 804 Naval Air Squadron (NAS) was launched against a low flying Condor, which he found difficult to keep up with as the differential between the sea level speed of the two aircraft was only minimal.

The Fw 200 was well protected with defensive gun positions but after a brief fight, Everett set it alight and saw it crash into the sea. He was now faced with a dilemma, after attempting to bail out he elected to ditch the aircraft. As it struck the water the huge radiator forced the nose down but he managed to escape while the aircraft swiftly sank. He was

rescued and was no doubt warmly welcomed by the sailors, who had come to hate the Condors circling the convoys like birds of prey, spotting the weak and vulnerable.

Everett was awarded the DSO and his experience altered the orders for ditching a Hurricane. Pilots were advised to approach the water with the wheels and flaps retracted, the canopy was to be locked open and the starboard emergency access panel jettisoned. The deceleration when alighting on water was highly dangerous. To avoid being pitched into the gunsight, pilots took up all of the slack as they tightened the harness as far as was humanly possible. Piloting a catapult fighter took a special kind of bravery.

The launch itself was not without danger, then there was the prospect of being shot at by a determined and skilled enemy. But it must have been the landing that caused the most anxiety, either of the two options meant surviving in cold water waiting to be collected. Everyone knew that if an enemy submarine was in the area, then a convoy would not turn back to save a lone man bobbing up and down in the water.

They simply could not risk the loss of another vital ship. By the end of the year, a further five enemy aircraft were shot down in a similar fashion and an unknown quantity were driven away from the convoys. The system, limited as it was, worked. ➤

A Hawker Sea Hurricane MkIB in the markings of 880 NAS. **Keith Draycott**

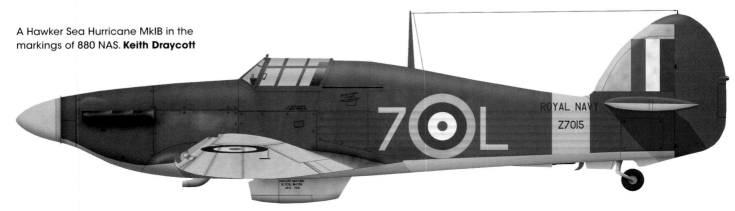

Hawker Sea Hurricane MkIA, LU-L P3620, being lowered on to the launch trolley of a CAM ship catapult at Gibraltar in March 1942. **Editor's collection**

CATAPULT EQUIPPED SHIPS THAT OPERATED SEA HURRICANES

Eight CAM ships were requisitioned from private owners, two of which were sunk. They were:

- Daghestan, Daltonhall, Eastern City, Helencrest, Kafiristan, Michael E (sunk), Novelist, Primrose Hill (sunk).

27 CAM ships were Ministry of War Transport owned Empire ships, 10 of which were sunk:

- Empire Burton (sunk), Empire Clive, Empire Darwin, Empire Day, Empire Dell (sunk), Empire Eve (sunk), Empire Faith, Empire Flame, Empire Foam, Empire Franklin, Empire Gale, Empire Heath, Empire Hudson (sunk), Empire Lawrence (sunk), Empire Moon, Empire Morn, Empire Ocean, Empire Rainbow (sunk), Empire Ray, Empire Rowan (sunk), Empire Shackleton (sunk), Empire Spray, Empire Spring (sunk), Empire Stanley, Empire Sun, Empire Tide, Empire Wave (sunk).

In addition to these there were five fighter catapult ships, collectively known as the Pegasus class:

- HMS Ariguani, HMS Maplin, HMS Patia (sunk), HMS Pegasus, HMS Springbank (sunk).

A CAM ship Sea Hurricane MkIA mounted on the bow catapult, showing the heavy struts that stabilized the aircraft at sea. These were removed for launch. **Editor's collection**

Two Sea Hurricane MkIAs, LU-L P3620 and LU-Y Z4867, being taken out to a waiting CAM ship by barge. From the barge, the Hurricanes would be raised by crane and mounted aboard the catapult. **Editor's collection**

The Fighter Catapult Ships were less successful, several operated the new two-seat Fairey Fulmar, but this was a large and ponderous aircraft and was unsuited to interception duties. HMS Patia and HMS Springbank were lost to enemy action, as were 12 of the CAM ships, indicating the severe attrition of this campaign.

HMS Maplin remained in service but had her launch rails removed in June 1942 when she reverted to her previous role. For some time the CAM ships provided the convoys with their only fighter cover in mid Atlantic. To service them, three UK based sites were established on the west coast along with one at Belfast.

Convoys departing from British waters were met by a CAM ship that had been re-equipped at Liverpool, Bristol or the Clyde. CAM ships protecting the American end of the Atlantic convoys could also be replenished at the Royal Canadian Air Force (RCAF) base at Dartmouth, Nova Scotia. For the Mediterranean convoys, catapult Sea Hurricanes were based at Gibraltar.

Convoys to the remote Russian ports began in 1942 as the British and Americans struggled to supply their new ally in the war against Nazi Germany. Empire Morn was the first CAM ship to accompany a convoy on this new and highly hazardous route on April 26, 1942, but did not launch her aircraft until

the return trip from Murmansk. Flying Officer Kendall shot down a Junkers Ju 88 and chased away a Blohm und Voss BV 138 flying boat, but was killed on impact with the water, having bailed out at too low an altitude.

The Empire Lawrence, on an outbound Russian convoy, also successfully deployed her 'Hurricat' on this day, destroying a Heinkel He 111 and damaging a second. Pilot Officer Hay was plucked from the icy waters by HMS Volunteer after bailing out, which was considered a safer option in the freezing conditions.

Several improvements were incorporated into the Sea Hurricane based on Canadian experience of operating the type in low temperatures. Heated clothing could now be plugged into the aircraft's 12 volt electrical system and a cockpit heater was installed. Long range tanks added a further 90 gallons (400 litres) of fuel, but their additional weight required greater catapult power to maintain an acceptable margin of safety.

The last CAM ship victory occurred on July 28, 1943, when a pair of 'Hurricats' from Empire Tide and Empire Darwin shot down two Fw 200s 800 nautical miles (1500km) west of Bordeaux. Flying Officer Flynn from the Empire Tide was picked up by HMS Enchantress and Flying Officer Stewart from the Empire Darwin was picked up by HMS Leith.

The CAM ships were an operational necessity and were not considered as anything more than an emergency measure. Despite the wastage in aircraft and the dangers faced by the pilots, it forced enemy aircraft to be more cautious and it is impossible to say how many hundreds of lives and thousands of tons of shipping were saved. Only a handful of the 50 'Hurricats' survived. They were officially referred to as Sea Hurricane MkIAs and some were stranded in Canada where they were handed over to the RCAF. In total there were nine combat launches, eight Sea Hurricanes and

The aircraft that prompted the development of the Sea Hurricane, the Focke-Wulf Fw 200 Condor, the long ranged maritime patrol bomber that was so effective at shadowing transatlantic and Russian convoys, reporting their position to U-Boat packs.
Editor's collection

one pilot lost in return for eight German aircraft destroyed and one damaged.

The Royal Navy's fleet carriers were in constant demand and they simply could not escort every convoy. Therefore several merchant ships were converted, simultaneously with the ongoing CAM ship operations into makeshift escort aircraft carriers. Some of these vessels lacked hangars so the Sea Hurricanes shared the exposed deck with biplane Fairey Swordfish torpedo bombers.

Sea Hurricanes destined for use on carriers were designated as MkIBs. They were fitted with full arrester gear, including a system of warning lights in the cockpit and a release mechanism to free the aircraft from the wires that had just hauled it to an abrupt

Hawker Sea Hurricane MkIB on the lift of HMS Argus in the Firth of Clyde with three Seafires and another Sea Hurricane toward the stern.
Editor's collection

A close-up of the underside of the Shuttleworth Collection's Sea Hurricane MkIB showing the arrangement of the arrestor hook and catapult strops.
Julian Humphries

A close up of the arrestor hook on Shuttleworth's Sea Hurricane MkIB.
Julian Humphries

The catapult strop attachment point on Shuttleworth's Sea Hurricane MkIB.
Julian Humphries

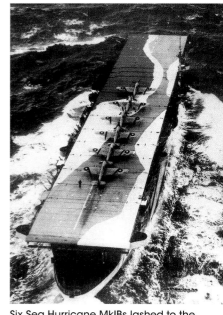

Six Sea Hurricane MkIBs lashed to the flight deck of escort carrier HMS Avenger.
Editor's collection

The Shuttleworth Collection flies the world's only surviving Sea Hurricane MkIB, seen at air shows in the UK every summer. **Constance Redgrave.**

stop. Three hundred Hurricane MkIs were converted into Sea Hurricane MkIBs and again, most of the work was subcontracted out and undertaken by General Aircraft Ltd.

The new variant retained the land fighter's Merlin III engine and machine gun armament. With the additional weight of the naval equipment it was some 40mph (64kmh) slower than its land based cousin and its rate of climb was also badly affected. It reached 10,000ft (3050m) in 6.2 minutes compared to the standard RAF Hurricane's 4.1 minutes. The MkIB was replaced by the cannon armed MkIC, which substituted the early outer wing panels for those of a Hurricane MkIIC.

In all other respects the aircraft was essentially the same. The modification posed no problems, although the greater weight of the four 20mm Hispano cannon inevitably had a detrimental effect on the aircraft's performance. The MkIC entered service with 811 NAS in January 1942. The Sea Hurricane

MkIC was an interim design and was the only Merlin III powered variant to carry the full complement of cannon.

Twelve Sea Hurricane MkICs of 802 and 883 NASs were embarked aboard the escort carrier HMS Avenger to accompany the Russia bound convoy PQ 18 in October 1942. The previous convoy, PQ 17, had been a disaster, losing 24 of its 35 merchant ships. Losses at such a rate, had they continued, would have ended the Russian supply operation.

During this trip alone, HMS Avenger's aircraft destroyed five enemy aircraft and damaged a further 17, of which three were so badly damaged that they were claimed as probably destroyed. One British pilot was lost during this action, but three others were rescued from the sea.

The final version of the Sea Hurricane was the MkIIC. This was introduced into service from December 1942 and was converted from the MkII land plane. The more powerful

Merlin XX engine of this type restored much of its performance. Folding wings were never installed on Sea Hurricanes, although they were considered at an early stage. This was a limitation that had to be accepted in order to prevent interruption of the production lines.

Despite now possessing a top speed of 318mph (510kmh), the Sea Hurricane was already being superseded by navalised versions of the Spitfire and the excellent new naval fighters from America, such as the Grumman Hellcat and Chance Vought Corsair. Hurricanes continued to be used in the Mediterranean and equipped the fighter component of several fleet carriers, 801 NAS aboard HMS Eagle, 800 NAS aboard HMS Indomitable and 885 NAS aboard HMS Victorious.

Disaster befell HMS Eagle when she was torpedoed and sunk on August 11, 1942, taking almost all of her aircraft with her. On the following day, HMS Indomitable was heavily damaged by dive bombers but remained afloat with many of her Hurricanes destroyed.

The last Sea Hurricane MkIIC, NF717, was delivered from the Austin Motors factory in August 1943. The type continued in service until September 1944, by which time only 825 NAS aboard HMS Vindex and 835 NAS aboard HMS Nairana were operational. A total of 443 Sea Hurricanes were converted from landplanes or built from new.

Fifty MkIAs, 290 MkIBs and 42 MkICs were converted from Hurricane MkIs, along with 60 new build MkIICs supplied to the Fleet Air Arm. Additionally, a small number of Sea Hurricane MkXIIs were converted from Canadian built Hurricane MkXIIs fitted with the Packard Merlin 29 and 12.303 Browning machine guns. These were followed by a few Sea Hurricane MkXIIAs which had eight .303 machine guns. ∎
Words: Tim Callaway and Julian Humphries

Sea Hurricane MkIBs aboard HMS Victorious. **Editor's collection**

Hurricane Mk.IIDs fitted with the Vickers 40mm 'S' guns in pods under the wings. **Editor's collection**

Refining
the breed
The Mk.II, IV and V

Service experience with the Hurricane Mk.I highlighted two operational requirements which would need to be addressed if the fighter was to continue in front line service. The first was for more firepower, the second for greater speed. Hawker began addressing these requirements as early as 1939, developing re-engined and re-armed variants that began entering service towards the end of the Battle of Britain. The increased firepower helped the Hurricane to fill new roles, and was to keep the aircraft on the front line until the end of the Second World War.

It was quickly realised that the need to improve the Hurricane's performance could not be met with the existing Merlin III engine. Two aircraft, L1856 and L2026, were therefore used for trials with two different versions of the Merlin during 1939, but it was not until mid-1940 that the fully developed Merlin XX was available.

The new engine initially produced 1185hp and very few changes were required to fit this to the Hurricane I airframe, designed as it was for maximum compatibility with earlier variants. The basic structure of the early Mk.II was virtually identical to the Mk.I; however, the opportunity was taken for detail design changes to solve issues revealed by service use. The machines that appeared from October 1940 onwards, known at this stage as Series 2, introduced a slightly longer, re-profiled nose and a semi circular oil splash guard behind the propeller.

On June 11, 1940, Hawker test pilot Philip Lucas took Hurricane P3269 on its first flight from the company's Langley airfield with the new engine installed. A Rotol constant speed propeller was fitted and the aircraft was fully armed with eight machine guns. The overall weight was just less than 6700lb (3040kg) and this machine was the fastest armed Hurricane ever built, capable of 348mph (560kmh) in level flight.

Hurricanes with the new engine were designated as Mk.IIs from December 1940, but production had begun in August 1940. A few were issued to front line squadrons, including 111, during the Battle of Britain. The increase in available power raised the Hurricane's top speed to a more respectable 342mph (550kmh); however, this was still some 15 to 20mph (24 to 32kmh) slower than the contemporary Spitfire I and Bf 109E.

A strange phenomenon was encountered with the Mk.II at this stage. It became uncontrollable at altitudes previously unobtainable by earlier versions of the Hurricane. The cause was found to be the lubricating grease used in the controls. This was unsuitable for high altitudes and froze, locking the flying surfaces. Early Mk.IIs were armed with eight .303 Browning machine guns and designated Mk.IIAs. The Mk.I remained in squadron service well into 1941, but was gradually replaced as the new aircraft rolled off the production lines. Many Mk.Is found their way into training units, where even a few very early machines with fabric covered wings continued to give good service.

The engine installation in a Hurricane Mk.II, note the semi-circular oil collector ring on top of the forward cowling, where it would be just behind the propeller. **Julian Humphries**

The Merlin XX was fitted to the Hurricane Mk.II, Halifax and Lancaster, and was one of the most produced variants of the famous Rolls-Royce engine. **Editor's collection**

INCREASING THE FIREPOWER

As early as 1939, consideration had been given to improving the firepower of British fighters. The eight Browning machine guns had a high rate and density of fire, but it was apparent that the rifle calibre bullets were becoming increasingly ineffective. As an interim measure, the number of machine guns was increased to 12 by fitting two additional pairs of .303 Brownings towards the wing tips, outboard of the wing leading edge landing lights.

To accommodate these guns it was necessary to mount them further forward than the main battery, so the muzzles projected beyond the wing's leading edge. The inner gun of each extra pair was mounted slightly higher than the other guns and was fed from a magazine inboard of it. The outboard guns were fed from the opposite side. The Hurricane's wing was so thick and spacious, even at this distance from the root, no blisters or other contour changes were necessary. Hurricanes so armed were referred to as Mk.IIBs.

Aircraft cannons had been investigated as early as the mid 1930s. Despite having a lower rate of fire than a machine gun, cannons were able to fire a wider variety of explosive and armour piercing ammunition. Several old airframes were tested on ranges and the effects of cannon fire were impressive, as it took only a few hits to cause lethal damage. The Air Ministry was in the process of negotiating manufacturing licenses from Hispano and Oerlikon for their 20mm cannons, but at this stage it was thought they would be too heavy for use in single engined fighters.

As a trial of the Swiss Oerlikons, two were fitted to Hurricane L1750 in 1939, carried below the wings. This installation was less than satisfactory and the aircraft was not used operationally. The French Hispano cannon was considered most suitable for the next generation of British fighters so arrangements were made for the parent company to establish a factory in Grantham, under the convoluted title the British Manufacturing and Research Company.

P2963, an early eight gun Hurricane Mk.IIA. **Editor's collection**

A close-up of Peter Tiechman's recently restored Hurricane IIB, showing the outer pair of .303 machine guns. This is the only flying 'Hurribomber' in the world. **Julian Humphries**

A close-up of the underwing pylon on Peter Tiechman's Hurricane IIB. This could carry a 44 gallon external fuel tank or 250lb bombs. The machine gun immediately above the pylon was often removed for ease of access to the mount. **Julian Humphries**

Several pairs of unserviceable wings were returned to Hawker to experiment with the installation of four Oerlikon cannon into the existing gun bays. The breeches could be accommodated in the vast bays, but the barrels projected well ahead of the wing. Small aerodynamic blisters on the gun access panels were necessary to clear the breech of each gun. Hurricane Mk.I V7360 was fitted with cannon wings and flew the full installation, but with drum fed guns, for the first time on June 7, 1940.

The first production version of the Mk.IIC, V2461, had belt fed guns. The additional weight of the guns and ammunition reduced the aircraft's speed considerably and it was unable to achieve even 300mph (482.8kmh). The potential to create a heavily armed fighter was recognised, but the limiting factor at the time was the relatively low power of the Merlin III engine.

During the Battle of Britain, V7360 was delivered to 46 Squadron at North Weald, still fitted with four cannons and used during the intense fighting in September. The gun feeds often failed to function correctly or jammed but at least one German bomber was claimed by Flight Lieutenant Alexander Rabagliati. The problems with the feed mechanism were overcome by the new Chatellerault feed, and with the introduction of more powerful versions of the Merlin, paved the way for full scale production of the cannon armed Hurricane Mk.IIC, which first flew on February 6, 1941. This mark would become the most widely used version of the Hurricane, with over 4700 built, mostly by Hawker at Langley. The wing was largely unchanged, except for the gun bays, which now had additional access panels on the undersurface to allow access to the cannon cocking levers and spent ammunition chutes. The cannons exerted a much greater recoil force than the machine guns which were dampened by prominent recoil springs around each barrel. Hurricane Mk.IICs entered RAF service in May 1941 and were among the world's most powerfully armed fighters at the time. ➤

A Hurricane Mk.IIC with 44 gallon underwing tanks in North Africa. This aircraft was one of several presented to the RAF by Lady MacRobert. **Editor's collection**

HURRIBOMBERS

The wing of the Hurricane Mk.II could also accept external stores. Either two 44 gallon (200 litre) external fuel tanks or a pair of 250lb (113.4kg) bombs could be carried, one under each wing. When bombs were carried it was usual practice to reduce the number of machine guns by two, the Brownings directly above the pylon attachment point being removed for better access.

The range of the 'Hurribomber', as they were unofficially known, was not greatly affected by the extra weight, but the aircraft's speed was considerably reduced. The first attack took place on October 30, 1941, when a pair of Mk.IIBs attacked an electrical distribution installation near Tingery. At about this time other modifications to the Hurricane were considered, a new Spitfire sliding canopy devoid of the heavy metal framework was tested on at least one aircraft and a four bladed Rotol propeller was flow as early as December 1940. Neither modification was adopted as the Hurricane was seen as belonging to a previous generation and Hawker was preparing to produce the Typhoon.

When operations over northern France began, it was quickly found that the Hurricanes could not operate without fighter escort. Even with the greater power of the Merlin XX, Hurricanes were outclassed by new versions of the Luftwaffe's Bf 109. Even more dramatic was the advantage enjoyed by the superb Focke-Wulf 190A, which outclassed even the latest incarnation of the Spitfire until the introduction of the Mk.IX. In a reversal of the previous year's fighting, 1941 saw the RAF go on to the offensive, using fighter sweeps often mixed with a few Blenheims or 'Hurribombers' to force the Luftwaffe to engage in combat. Spitfires were the obvious choice for the escorts, on occasion outnumbering their charges by as many as three to one in an attempt to draw enemy fighters into combat.

The 20mm cannon barrels of the Hurricane Mk.IIC extended well forward of the wing leading edge and featured large springs to absorb the recoil. **Julian Humphries**

Targets included forward Luftwaffe bases and the railway network, where the destructive power of the four cannon was proved beyond doubt. These operations confirmed the fighter-bomber concept; Hurricanes, once free of their bombs, were restored to being moderately useful fighters, whereas the slower Blenheim was a liability for the escorting fighters both to and from the target. By the latter half of 1941, it was apparent that the Hurricane was drawing to the end of its operational usefulness over Europe by day, despite the fact that more than 50 squadrons were equipped with the type.

German night raids on Britain continued throughout 1941. As a stop gap measure, Hurricanes were used to patrol high value target areas, often working in conjunction with Boulton Paul Defiants. Night fighter and night intruder operations will be covered later in this magazine. Hurricane IICs of 43 Squadron were among the first aircraft involved in the abortive raid on Dieppe on August 19, 1942, known as Operation Jubilee, which ultimately failed to achieve any of its objectives.

The RAF lost 106 aircraft in the action and nearly two thirds of the landing force of 6000 troops were either killed or taken prisoner. Despite this, crucial lessons were learned that would pay great dividends when the Allies returned to mainland Europe in 1944. This was the last occasion that Hurricanes were used in great numbers in an offensive capacity over Europe. The Hurricane Mk.IID was a ground attack aircraft fitted with a pair of podded Vickers 40mm 'S' guns for anti-tank missions. These are described later in this magazine.

ROCKET PROJECTILES

The next and perhaps the most important development in British aircraft armament was the rocket projectile (RP). Hurricane Mk.IIA Z2415 was selected as the test bed for the new weapon, as it had already been strengthened for previous aerodynamic trials. The aircraft was first flown on February 23, 1943, with six rockets under each wing. It was later passed to the Aeroplane and Armament Experimental Establishment (A&AEE) at Boscombe Down for further trials and development. The production RP had a 60lb (27.2kg) warhead and four stabilising fins at the rear of the tube containing the propellant.

As the weapon was being developed the number of rockets carried by an individual aircraft was increased to eight. The rocket had many advantages over bombs and cannon. With practice, ground attack pilots could deliver them with great accuracy and they were effective against almost every type of battlefield or surface target. There was no recoil as the rockets left the rails, although

The Hurricane Mk.IV had the universal wing and could carry eight 60lb rocket projectiles as shown here. **Editor's collection**

A side view of Hurricane Mk.V KZ193 shows just how big the armoured radiator installation was, extending even beneath the Vickers cannon pods. **Editor's collection**

The universal wing on the Hurricane Mk.IV could also carry the Vickers 40mm 'S' gun as shown here. These weapons were used extensively in the Far East and Western Desert in the anti-tank role. **Editor's collection**

KZ193, one of three Hurricane Mk.Vs built, showing the much larger under fuselage radiator required by the Merlin 32. This was armoured to increase the survivability of the aircraft in low level missions. **Editor's collection**

pilots experienced a brief period of turbulence as the launch aircraft passed through their wake.

The launch rails were mounted on a thin steel plate to protect the wings from the blast effects as the rockets were launched, in either pairs or in a salvo of all eight. Once the Hurricane had launched its rockets, it reverted to its fighter role and therefore did not require escort in the traditional manner. Rockets were used over mainland Europe for the first time by 137 and 164 Squadrons on September 2, 1943, against the lock gates at the Hansweert Canal in Holland.

This was among the last offensive actions undertaken by Hurricanes in Western Europe, but in the Middle and Far East the RP was to keep the Hurricane at the forefront of the fighting. A single Mk.IV was employed to test the massive Long Tom rocket during 1945. The warhead weighed 500lb (226.8kg) and only two could be carried, but the weapon was never used operationally by RAF Hurricanes.

HURRICANE MK.IV AND V

During 1942 the Hurricane was evolving into a specialist ground attack aircraft and as such would need an adaptable wing that could be reconfigured in the field for the varied missions the aircraft was expected to undertake. The universal wing was designed to accept bombs of 250 or 500lb (113.4 or 226.8kg), long range fuel tanks of 45 or 90 gallon (200 or 400 litre) capacity, or the Vickers 40mm cannon in pods. It was also wired to carry rockets and smoke generators to lay smoke screens. Just two Browning machine guns were retained for sighting purposes. This version was initially referred to as the Mk.IIE, but after production commenced a new designation was created.

Externally, the Mk.IV was identical to the standard Hurricane Mk.II, with the exception of the heavily armoured radiator, which now had an angular, flat sided appearance. Many liquid cooled aircraft were lost at low level through damage to the coolant system, so additional armour was fitted around this, the engine and cockpit. The Mk.IV weighed 6150lb (2790kg) empty, in comparison to the Mk.IIA's 5150lb (2336kg), and was powered by a Merlin 24 or 27 engine producing 1620hp. Hawker test pilot Philip Lucas flew the first Hurricane Mk.IV KX405 on March 14, 1943.

More than 500 Mk.IVs entered service with 20 RAF Squadrons, all of which were built in the UK by Hawker Aircraft and Austin Motors. In service the type upheld the Hurricane's reputation as a robust and reliable machine. The Mk.IV Hurricanes had serial numbers preceded by the following letters: HL, HM, HV, HW, KW, KX, KZ, LB, LD, LF, PG and PG. In Burma, Mk.IVs were frequently operated with an asymmetric payload of a single fuel tank and four rockets.

In early 1943, two Hurricane Mk.IVs were taken from the production line and converted to accept the Merlin 32 engine which was tailored to low level performance and produced 1700hp. To absorb this power, a Rotol four bladed propeller was installed. The intention was to produce an even more powerful low level attack aircraft coupled to the universal wing of the Mk.IV for use in the Far East. The new version was to be known as the Mark V.

The first, KZ193, was flown by Lucas shortly after he had tested the first MkIV, on April 3, 1943, and was fitted with Vickers 'S'

guns. The second conversion, KX405, was completed with a bulged engine cowling to fully accommodate the Merlin 32. A single prototype Mk.V, NL255, was built, but no further aircraft were ordered as production of a new version so similar in performance was considered unnecessary. The Mk.V was predictably the heaviest of all the Hurricanes at 6405lb (2905kg) empty. It was almost a third heavier than the Mk.I. Fully laden it had a maximum takeoff weight of 9300lb (4218kg).

As one would expect for such a widely used aircraft, the Hurricane was subject to numerous tests and trials. Alternative power plants were considered such as the Napier Dagger and the Bristol Hercules. At one stage the 2000hp Griffon was considered, but the engineers at Rolls-Royce were able to extract ever more power from the Merlin, making such measures unnecessary.

Other Hurricanes were employed to gather high altitude weather data by the meteorological flights. This lonely and unglamorous role was diligently undertaken by single flights in the UK, Egypt and Iraq. Hurricanes modified for this role had sensors and rudimentary recording equipment mounted on the starboard wing. As a stopgap measure, several Hurricanes were converted to carry out photo reconnaissance (PR) missions.

To meet the urgent need for a suitable high level reconnaissance platform on Malta, Hurricane V7101 was stripped of all non essential items to save weight and improve performance. At some time the empty gun bays were used to house additional fuel tanks probably salvaged from other aircraft on the island so the aircraft could reach Sicily. In the hands of Flight Lieutenant George Burgess it provided valuable intelligence about enemy activity.

Burgess stated that the aircraft displayed some undesirable flying characteristics at very high altitude, probably as a result of the rearward shift of the centre of gravity when two F.24 cameras were installed behind the pilot's seat.

The Hurricane was replaced by dedicated PR versions of the Spitfire as they became available. At least one Mk.II was also adapted for the role and was fitted with as many as four vertical cameras to give as wide a field of coverage as possible.■

Words: Tim Callaway and Julian Humphries

A side view of the second Hurricane Mk.V KX405 shows the bulged engine cowlings to fully accommodate the Merlin 32. **Editor's collection**

FLYING CAN OPENERS

Three Hurricane MkIIDs of 6 Squadron take off from Sidi Haneish in Egypt on June 20 1942. The twin 40mm Vickers cannon made the Hurricane MkIID a powerful anti-tank aircraft and its success in this role in the Western Desert campaign earned 6 Squadron its nickname.

Night Hawks

Clive Rowley tells the story of the Hawker Hurricane as a night fighter and night intruder, and of the remarkable pilots who achieved success against the odds.

The exploits of the RAF fighter pilots who fought the Luftwaffe by day during the Second World War have been widely publicised, as has the history of the Hawker Hurricane as a day fighter. However, the stories of the single seat fighter pilots who operated the Hurricane by night are less well known, partly because secrecy cloaked night operations at the time (especially when airborne radar was introduced) and also because the service record of the Hurricane in the night interceptor role was largely indifferent and 'nothing much to write home about'.

The odds against any tangible success for Hurricane night fighter pilots were extremely high and many were left with a feeling of utter impotence and frustration, arising from an abject failure to see anything of the enemy except perhaps a fleeting shadow. However, despite the odds stacked against them, a number of Hurricane night fighter pilots achieved considerable success against the enemy in the dark hours. They did this without the aid of airborne radar, relying simply on skill, courage, a sixth-sense for finding the enemy, and an individual streak of sheer daring that was an essential ingredient for success in the very singular nature of their particular task. This is the story of the Hurricane as a night fighter, the tactics used and of the remarkable night fighter aces who achieved success despite being faced with a seemingly impossible task.

FIRST HURRICANE NIGHT KILL – MAX AITKEN (601 SQUADRON)

Even before the Battle of Britain began in July 1940, it was apparent that the air war would have to be fought at night as well as by day, and RAF Hurricane and Spitfire pilots were called upon to engage enemy raiders operating under cover of darkness. The first major Luftwaffe night raid against England took place on the night of June 18-19, 1940 (the day that Prime Minister Winston Churchill gave his 'finest hour' speech in the Commons). In conditions of bright moonlight some 70 Heinkel He 111s attacked oil storage facilities at Canvey Island, the airfields at Leconfield and Mildenhall, and other targets. This bombing raid resulted in the first British civilian casualties of the Second World War.

No claims were made by Hurricane pilots that night, but Blenheim night fighters (then operating without the benefit of airborne radar) claimed five bombers destroyed, and the clear and bright conditions also allowed Spitfires of 19 and 74 Squadrons to operate almost as if in daylight. The Spitfire pilots shot down four of the bombers (two of them falling to the guns of the brilliant fighter ace, 'Sailor' Malan).

Extensive enemy bombing raids followed on four further nights in June 1940. On the night of June 26-27, 1940, Squadron Leader Max Aitken, the commanding officer (CO) of 601 (County of London) Squadron (popularly known as the 'Millionaires' Squadron') earned a DFC for what was probably the first successful kill by a Hurricane pilot at night.

A Hurricane night fighter taxies out. **Editor's collection**

Having waited for three nights in the readiness hut at Tangmere, sitting in a chair in his 'Mae West' life jacket without being called upon, he was scrambled at midnight on June 26. After about an hour on his designated patrol line, he was informed by the fighter controller that enemy aircraft were approaching his position. The searchlights, which had been weaving about beneath the light cloud below him, suddenly all converged on one spot. They illuminated the cloud brilliantly and silhouetted three German He 111s just above it. Aitken lost sight of two of the bombers immediately, but fastened on to the last of the three.

Closing in on it, he opened fire from point blank range. The enemy aircraft slowed so much that he nearly overshot it. He fired four more bursts from his eight .303 machine guns and noticed a dull glow developing inside the German aircraft as it began to burn. The Heinkel went into a shallow dive over the sea. Aitken continued to fire the rest of his ammunition into it and only broke away when

he was down to 500ft. He did not see the bomber crash, but he climbed up to 1000ft and fired off a parachute flare which illuminated the Heinkel lying on the water with a column of smoke rising from its rear section.

By the end of the war, Aitken had risen to the rank of group captain, been awarded the Distinguished Service Order and the Distinguished Flying Cross, and achieved a total of 14½ of which five were at night (four of these while flying radar equipped Beaufighters. He survived the war and became Sir Max Aitken, 2nd Baronet, chairman of Beaverbrook Newspapers and Member of Parliament. He died in 1985).

"A BLOODY DANGEROUS THING TO DO" – NIGHT FLYING HAZARDS

These early Hurricane night fighting sorties were occasional missions launched at times when aircraft could be spared from more urgent daytime tasks. They were usually flown only by experienced pilots who possessed the necessary night flying

expertise and who were more normally employed in the day fighter role. The difficulties and risks associated with operating a single seat fighter at night were considerable and the aircraft were not, initially, modified for night flying.

The accuracy of the ground control organisation – which proved adequate for daylight interceptions in conditions of reasonable visibility – was not of a sufficiently high order in darkness or poor visibility to ensure that the single seat fighter pilot, with no airborne radar, would be brought into visual contact with his quarry in a viable position to launch an attack.

At this time the Hurricane pilots generally operated at night in a more-or-less freelance role, on standing area or line patrols, under a very loose form of control from the ground, receiving only snippets of information from time to time about hostile movements in the area. They were left very much to their own devices, initiative, instinct and the whims of pure chance. ➤

The Rt Hon J W "Max" Aitken, pictured when he was a group captain and leader of the Banff Strike Wing. **Editor's collection**

Their best hope was that they might, by chance, spot an enemy bomber illuminated by searchlights or anti-aircraft (AA) fire. The anti-aircraft guns constantly failed to distinguish between friend and foe, but they could be of assistance in leading a night fighter pilot towards the enemy. There were few successful interceptions and night kills were even rarer, but in these circumstances the Hurricane night fighters' lack of success was entirely understandable.

Towards the end of 1940 and into 1941 some Hurricane squadrons – including Nos 73, 85, 87, 96 and 151 Squadrons – were dedicated to night fighting (later operating both Hurricanes and Boulton Paul Defiants). All these units suffered losses in accidents, as night flying proved to be difficult and dangerous even without the intervention of the enemy.

As one night fighter pilot of the time put it: "It was a bloody dangerous thing to do." Even taxiing the aircraft at night proved more problematic than by day and the swing on take off, caused by the enormous torque from the Hurricane's Rolls-Royce Merlin engine, was much more difficult to pick up and to control on dimly-lit airfields at night.

As a result, there were frequent ground collisions and accidents. Sometimes pilots crashed shortly after taking off at night, typically climbing to about 400 or 500ft and then, while trying to adjust their eyes from the visual take off to instrument flying, simply becoming disorientated, losing control

and sliding into the ground within a couple of miles of the airfield. Pilots also had to get used to night navigation over blacked-out countryside and perhaps above cloud, relying on flying accurate headings, using the stopwatch and adjusting for the effects of the wind. On clearer nights, patrol lines were marked by bright flares on the ground at 10 mile intervals, but if the night was not clear and the flares were not visible through cloud, the pilots had to rely totally on their basic stopwatch and compass navigation skills.

The Hurricane's TR9 radio proved unreliable and it was not always possible for pilots to obtain a navigation fix by using triangulation from voice transmission. It was no wonder that Hurricane pilots sometimes became uncertain of their positions and simply flew into hillsides trying to get back down in the dark. It was a sad fact that the single seat night fighter pilots had a greater chance of losing their lives to an accident than they did of finding and shooting down an enemy bomber; it was indeed one of the most dangerous of occupations.

The Hurricane did at least enjoy several advantages over the Spitfire as a night fighter. It had a fine forward view and was renowned as a steady and effective gun platform (especially effective once the Hurricane MkIIC arrived with its armament of four 20mm cannons), it was viceless if flown sensibly and its landing characteristics and sturdy undercarriage were better suited to less-than-perfect night landings.

AS ONE NIGHT FIGHTER PILOT OF THE TIME PUT IT:"IT WAS A BLOODY DANGEROUS THING TO DO." EVEN TAXIING THE AIRCRAFT AT NIGHT PROVED MORE PROBLEMATIC THAN BY DAY

The blitz destroyed vast areas of London and other British cities. Fighter Command was ill-equipped to stop the night raids, being predominantly a day fighter force. **Editor's collection**

The other RAF single engined night fighter at the time of the Battle of Britain, the Boulton Paul Defiant, seen here equipped with AI radar. **Editor's collection**

Night fighter Hurricanes of 30 Squadron warming up at their base in Egypt. They flew night partols defending the Suez Canal. **Editor's collection**

Dedicated night fighter Hurricanes were suitably modified for the task and were painted black; the rear-view mirrors, which were useless at night, were usually removed to reduce drag and increase speed, the cockpit lights were replaced with dim red lights to preserve night vision and engine exhaust anti-glare panels were fitted on the nose of the aircraft to hide the bright exhaust flames from the pilot. The gunsight aiming graticule, though, was always too bright for aiming the guns at night and shooting was done with a large pinch of TLAR ('that looks about right').

THE BLITZ

During the Blitz, between September 1940 and May 1941, the Luftwaffe made 127 large-scale night raids against Britain, 71 of which were targeted against London and the rest against cities and towns outside the capital. The Hurricane was Fighter Command's principal single seat night fighter during this period, although increasing numbers of airborne intercept (AI) radar equipped twin engined night fighters were gradually becoming available.

As the Hurricane night fighter pilots and the ground controllers gained experience and improved their tactics, the Hurricanes began to have some success against the raiders. In May 1941, the Luftwaffe launched its final series of full-scale night attacks of the Blitz. After this the weight and number of night assaults gradually decreased as the Luftwaffe turned its attention east towards Russia. During this month the Germans lost 138 aircraft to a combination of the British AA, radar equipped twin engined night fighters and the single engined non-radar night fighters.

In just one night, on May 10-11, 1941, with a full moon giving good night-time visibility, 1 Squadron, flying Hurricane MkIIAs and MkIIBs in the defence of London, was credited with the destruction of seven He 111s and one Junkers Ju 88, for the cost of one of the squadron's pilots, who was apparently killed by AA fire. In the course of three sorties that night, Czech pilot Sergeant Josef Dygryn personally downed two He 111s and the Ju 88. He was later promoted to warrant officer and achieved ace status with five kills, but was shot down and killed by flak on a Hurricane night intruder operation with 1 Squadron on June 4, 1942.)

RICHARD PLAYNE STEVENS (151 SQUADRON) – HURRICANE NIGHT FIGHTER ACE

The greatest Hurricane night fighter pilot of this period was the legendary Pilot Officer Richard Playne Stevens (later promoted to squadron leader) of 151 Squadron. Stevens was quite a different character in many respects from most RAF Hurricane pilots of the time. To start with he was older, having joined the RAF after the outbreak of war at the age of 30 – the maximum age for pilot training. Having been a commercial airline pilot before the war, flying the cross Channel route between Croydon and Paris with mail and passengers, Stevens already had some 400 hours of flying, much of it at night and in poor weather.

He seemed to possess a personal hatred of the Germans, although this was not, as commonly stated in contemporary accounts, because his wife and children had been killed in a German air raid. More recent research shows that his wife and son outlived him, although his daughter had tragically been killed in a house fire in October 1940. Although this was nothing to do with enemy

Squadron Leader Richard Playne Stevens, DSO DFC and Bar of 151 Squadron. **via Author**

action, Stevens may have, in some way, blamed the war for it and certainly pursued the German airmen with total ferocity and with no regard for his own safety, even into the thickest anti-aircraft fire.

Stevens joined 151 Squadron in October 1940 and he achieved his first night kill on January 15-16, 1941, by which time the squadron was operating a mix of Hurricanes and Defiants in the night fighter role. He took off in his Hurricane that night at 12.56am from 151 Squadron's forward base at Manston. Half an hour later he received reports of enemy raiders heading towards London. Attracted by shell bursts from AA batteries below, he spotted the slim shape of a Dornier Do 17. Positioning behind the bomber at extremely close range, he fired at it. As it dived away, Stevens followed it down, giving it another burst and seeing it burst into flames and crash into a wood near Hornchurch. ➤

A Hurricane MkIIb in the markings of Squadron Leader Ian "Widge" Gleed of 87 Squadron. Julian Humphries

This was not the only action Stevens saw that night, as just before dawn he was scrambled again and found an He 111 silhouetted over the burning fires of London. The Heinkel's rear gunner saw him and opened up, but Stevens raked the bomber with machine gun fire, it began to descend, trailing smoke, and two of its crew baled out. Subsequently, a Royal Observer Corps post confirmed that the Heinkel had crashed into the sea near Southend. Stevens was only the third RAF pilot to score a brace of kills in a single night. He was awarded an immediate DFC, but this was only the beginning of his killing spree.

After being grounded for a while due to ear trouble, Stevens returned to the battle with a vengeance, shooting down two Heinkels on the night of April 8, 1941. Two nights later he destroyed an He 111 and a Ju 88, which was enough to add a bar to his DFC, and on May 7 he shot down two more bombers in one night. By November 1941, Stevens had gained 14 night victories – far more than any other RAF pilot, including those flying radar equipped night fighters. Promoted to flight lieutenant, he was transferred to 253 Squadron and on December 12, 1941, the award of his DSO was announced. Three nights later (December 15-16, 1941) he took off in Hurricane Z3465, alone as always, on a night intruder mission over the Continent from which he did not return, having crashed to his death at Hulten, near Gilze, in the Netherlands.

A "Turbinlite" Hurricane of 486 Squadron seen at RAF Wittering in 1940. **Editor's collection**

Part of the reason for Stevens' success was his complete disregard for his own safety. He would move in to extremely close range against his targets before firing and his Hurricane would often return bearing scars of flying wreckage from his victims. According to his colleagues, Stevens could be a solitary and melancholy man; if he was unable to fly he would stalk around the officers' mess, avoiding talking to anyone, before tucking himself into a corner with a favourite book. At other times, though, he was good company and enjoyed squadron parties. Years later, the great RAF fighter ace Air Vice Marshal 'Johnnie' Johnson said of Richard Stevens: "To those who flew with him it seemed as if life was of little account to him, for the risks he took could only have one ending".

TOM DALTON-MORGAN (43 SQUADRON) – HURRICANE NIGHT FIGHTER ACE

While Stevens was by far the most effective Hurricane night fighter pilot of the period, there were other pilots who met with some success and even achieved ace status in the difficult and dangerous world of night fighting in single seat aircraft. Among these was the CO of 43 Squadron, Squadron Leader Tom Dalton-Morgan (later promoted to group captain). By 1941 Dalton-Morgan was an experienced Hurricane pilot and, with his squadron based at Drem in Scotland, his primary task was to train new pilots for service with the squadrons in the

south. The squadron was also called upon to conduct night patrols and, as a lone hunter on these missions, Dalton-Morgan destroyed six enemy aircraft at night. Three of his victims went down in successive nights on May 5-6 and 6-7, 1941, when the Luftwaffe embarked on a major offensive against the Clydesdale ports and Glasgow.

On the first night he was credited with two enemy bombers destroyed. Attacking the first, a Ju 88 he spotted over Anstruther at midnight, he opened fire from 400ft dead astern; observing no effect, he then closed to 100ft to give it another burst. There was a violent explosion, which flung his Hurricane upwards and off to one side and he saw pieces of the enemy aircraft flying through the air. On June 8, Dalton-Morgan achieved a remarkable kill when he shot down a Ju 88 having made initial contact by spotting its shadow on the moonlit sea. After two more successes at night, he was carrying out a practice interception on July 24 with a fellow pilot when he spotted another Ju 88.

Dalton-Morgan gave chase and intercepted it off May Island. Despite his engine failing and with fumes filling the cockpit, he attacked the bomber three times. He had just seen it hit the sea when the engine of his Hurricane stopped. Too low to bail out, he made a masterly ditching on the water, but lost two front teeth when his face hit the gun sight. He clambered into his dinghy before being rescued by the Navy.

Squadron Leader Tom Dalton-Morgan DFC of 43 Squadron. **via Author**

An RAF Douglas A-20 Havoc with a 2700-million candlepower 'Turbinlite' searchlight in its nose. **Editor's collection**

Squadron Leader Richard Stevens official Air Ministry portrait by Eric Kennington in 1940, seated in his Hurricane night fighter. **Editor's collection**

Hurricane night fighters of 486 Squadron. **via Author**

Dalton-Morgan was awarded a Bar to his DFC for his "exceptional skill". He scored another night victory on October 2, 1941, off Berwick-on-Tweed, bringing his total number of night kills to six. In February 1942, after 18 months in command, the longest spell by any of 43 Squadron's wartime commanding officers, Dalton-Morgan was rested. He went on to achieve a total of 17 kills, survived the war and died in 2004.

TURBINLITE –
NOT SUCH A BRIGHT IDEA

Between September 1942 and January 1943, demonstrating typical wartime ingenuity with what must have seemed like a good idea at the time, night fighter Hurricanes were employed as the 'gunner' element in the relatively short-lived and generally unsuccessful 'Turbinlite' operations. The concept was that a radar-equipped but unarmed Douglas A-20/DB-7 Havoc, with a giant 2700-million candlepower 'Turbinlite' searchlight in its nose, would find and illuminate targets for two Hurricanes flying in formation on its wingtips to shoot at.

Flying in formation at night and possibly through thick cloud is a particularly difficult and dangerous procedure (as a pilot who has tried it, I can attest to that). Added to this was the problem that even if an intercept and illumination of an enemy aircraft was

successfully achieved by the Havoc, the Hurricane pilots' night vision would immediately be destroyed by the brilliant light. Not surprisingly, the gunners in the German bombers tended to shoot back at the light and the temporarily blinded Hurricane pilots would find themselves dumped back into darkness with no visual on anybody.

One Hurricane pilot described the experience thus: "In practice the first thing the Hurricane pilot found was the slipstream of the target, then he was blinded by the brilliant light from behind obscuring the windscreen. There then followed a series of involuntary aerobatics terminating several thousand feet below, each Hurricane looking for the black Havoc in a very black sky."

Initial experiments with separate Havoc and Hurricane units proved difficult to coordinate so, in September 1942, mixed squadrons of Hurricanes and 'Turbinlite' Havocs were created. Eventually there were 10 such squadrons. The first 'Turbinlite' action occurred on the night of April 28-29, 1942, during the so-called 'Baedeker Raids'.

The target was illuminated by the Havoc, but escaped from the beam before the 'gunner' aircraft could get into position, although the Hurricane pilot had actually seen the target before the light was switched on. The first success came on the night of

April 30-May 1, when the target was located by the Havoc's radar and the Hurricane pilot got a 'visual' and shot down the enemy aircraft before the light was turned on.

'Turbinlite' formations only managed to destroy one He 111, one probable and two damaged. All these actions were by Havocs of 1459 Flight and Hurricanes of 253 Squadron – no other units made any claims. During the period from September 1941 to January 1943, the 'Turbinlite' units lost 31 aircraft and some crews, demonstrating the natural risks attached to night flying, especially in winter weather. In addition one of the RAF's own Stirling bombers was shot down in error by a 'Turbinlite' formation; fortunately the crew bailed out safely. This was hardly a 'finest hour' and all the 'Turbinlite' squadrons were disbanded in January 1943.

ATTACK IS THE BEST
FORM OF DEFENCE –
HURRICANE NIGHT INTRUDERS

In vindication of this failure in the 'Turbinlite' role, RAF Hurricanes flown by a small and elite band of extremely skilled and adventurous night fighter pilots demonstrated that attack is the best form of defence by setting out to fly night intruder operations into Europe, to attack and destroy the enemy bombers within their own airfield circuits, as they took off or landed on bombing raids against Britain. ➤

Two presentation Hurricane MkIICs "Nightingale" and "Night Duty", donated to 87 Squadron for night intruder operation, note the long range tanks. **Editor's collection**

Squadron Leader Ian "Widge" Gleed of 87 Squadron points out his cat motif on the cockpit door of his Battle of Britain Hurricane, a marking he kept when his aircraft was painted all black as a night fighter with 87 Squadron. **Editor's collection**

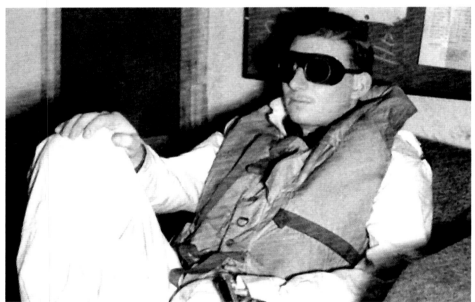

Squadron Leader 'Jay' or 'Mac' MacLachlan was sometimes known as 'One-Armed Mac' as he had lost an arm to a cannon shell over Malta. Here he can be seen wearing his "Hurricane arm" that enabled him to control the throttle, as well as red tinted glasses to preserve his night vision indoors. **via Author**

Squadron Leader MacLachlan DSO DFC and 2 Bars in the cockpit of his 1 Squadron Hurricane. **via Author**

An official portrait photograph of Flight Lieutenant Karel Kuttelwascher DFC, the Czech fighter pilot and greatest night Hurricane ace. **via Author**

The concept had already been proven with a number of individual night intruder missions, but the first unit to be given the role exclusively, for a period of three months, was 1 Squadron, from April 1942. Operating from its base at Tangmere, the squadron was to become the most successful single seat night intruder unit of any. The unit's Hurricane MkIICs, with their formidable armament of four 20mm cannons, carried a 45 gallon drop tank under each wing. They were initially painted with black undersides beneath their daytime grey/green camouflage, and given red code letters and propeller spinners, but eventually were painted all-over black. Night intruder missions often lasted three to three and a half hours and were generally flown around the period of the full moon, when the visibility offered some chance of success.

In addition to all the difficulties which confronted the Hurricane night fighter pilots over home territory, the intruder pilots also had to face long transits over the sea in their single engined mounts (with no chance of rescue until daylight, if they ended up in the water), they had to operate and navigate over hostile territory, locate the enemy with no assistance at all from ground-based radar, and were likely to come under fire from enemy anti-aircraft guns, especially near the well-defended airfields that were their hunting grounds. It was not surprising that some pilots met with no success at all, nor that some went out and were never seen again. Remarkably, some pilots met with considerable success.

'ONE-ARMED MAC' MACLACHLAN (1 SQUADRON) – HURRICANE NIGHT INTRUDER ACE

The commander of 1 Squadron was the remarkable, youthful but experienced fighter pilot, 23-year-old, Squadron Leader 'Jay' or 'Mac' MacLachlan. He was sometimes known as 'One-Armed Mac', due to having had his left arm shot off above the elbow by an enemy cannon shell while flying Hurricanes from Malta. Not one to let such a minor physical disability stand in his way, he persuaded the RAF doctors to let him return to operational flying, with a special mechanical arm specifically adapted for the Hurricane cockpit.

MacLachlan was a fine leader, much loved by his pilots and men, and he led from the front. He had an emblem painted on to the nose of his personal Hurricane MkIIC, BD983 coded 'JX-Q' – a severed forearm with a cannon shell passing through it, defiantly holding up two fingers in a 'V' sign!

MacLachlan's first night victory came on April 26, 1942, when he attacked a Dornier Do 217 which had just taken off from Evreux airfield in France, and which he saw silhouetted against the moon. He fired three short bursts at it from 600 yards dead astern and then his two port cannons jammed. Closing in to 200 yards, he fired several more short bursts. Showers of sparks erupted from the bomber's starboard engine, its nose dropped; it went into a shallow dive and crashed in a field about two miles from the aerodrome.

During the period that his squadron was involved in the night intruder operations, MacLachlan claimed a total of five night kills (three Do 217s and two Ju 88s destroyed, plus a further three Do 217s damaged) all over their own airfields in France. In addition, when he could not find any enemy aircraft to attack, he shot up numerous trains as targets of opportunity. MacLachlan died in captivity in July 1943, 13 days after being shot down by ground fire and mortally wounded while on a daylight intruder mission over France in a P-51 Mustang Mk IA. He had 16½ confirmed kills.

'KUT' KUTTELWASCHER (1 SQUADRON) – HURRICANE NIGHT ACE OF ACES

From April 1 to July 1, 1942, 1 Squadron flew 140 night intruder missions. These sorties were flown by a total of 19 pilots (the highest number of missions – 20 – being flown by 'Mac' MacLachlan). They accounted for 22 enemy aircraft destroyed at night and 13 damaged, plus 67 trains and five boats disabled or destroyed – an incredible achievement.

Only seven of the 19 pilots involved scored kills against enemy aircraft and of those, one – Czech fighter pilot Flight Lieutenant Karel Kuttelwascher – achieved no fewer than 15 kills and five damaged in only 15 intruder sorties. 'Kut' as he was known to his colleagues and friends became the paramount Hurricane night intruder ace. He ranks sixth in the list of the RAF's top-scoring night fighter pilots and those with more kills achieved most or all of them with the benefit of AI radar. Kuttelwascher is the highest scoring single seat night fighter ace.

Like Richard Stevens, he was different from most RAF fighter pilots of the time and was slightly older than many of his compatriots (he was 26 in April 1942). When he joined the RAF, he brought with him considerable flying and combat experience, having been a fighter pilot with the Czech Air Force from 1937 and having fought with the French Air Force during the Battle of France in 1940.

'Kut' was a complex, private character with more than a hint of contradiction. He managed to combine great coolness in the air with some irascibility on the ground, and his modesty in public was balanced by a strong personal ambition and a hatred of the Nazis who had invaded his country.

He was an uncompromising character, totally dedicated to his craft. He took his flying extremely seriously and his austere lifestyle excluded drinking, smoking and gambling. He was more of a loner than a leader and excelled when allowed to operate away from the pack. All these were attributes which lent themselves to being a lone night intruder. ➤

"Night Duty" one of a pair of presentation Hurricane MkIICs given to 87 Squadron for night intruder operations. **Editor's collection**

When 1 Squadron's night intruder phase began, 'Kut' had become a flight commander on the squadron and he had already destroyed three Messerschmitt Bf 109s and claimed a 'probable' against another in daylight. During this period his personal aircraft was Hurricane MkIIC BE581, coded 'JX-E', which bore his emblem – a scythe and banner with the inscription 'Night Reaper' – on the starboard side of the nose.

Kuttelwascher's first night victories came on April 1-2, 1942, when he found the flarepath lit at Melun-Villaroche airfield, on the far side of Paris, with a Ju 88 in the process of taking off. He slotted in behind it as it climbed to 1500ft, raked it with cannon fire from 100 yards and watched it dive into the ground. He then saw another Ju 88 on the runway and strafed it before the aerodrome defences woke up to his presence with searchlights and flak. He claimed one Ju 88 destroyed and one damaged. Further successes followed on almost every night that 'Kut' went out; he seemed to have an uncanny knack for finding the enemy and

then an unerring ability to make the kill.

On the night of April 30-May 1, 'Kut' destroyed two bombers in one night for the first time (a Do 217 at Rennes and an He 111 near Dinard) a feat he was to repeat twice more. By the night of May 4-5, 1942, he had destroyed five enemy bombers and damaged two more over their own airfields. On this night he found a gaggle of He 111s returning to the airfield at St Andre-de-l'Eure after a destructive bombing raid against Cowes on the Isle of Wight. The six He 111s were all showing white tail-lights and were circling in the landing pattern at 1500 to 2000ft. After stalking them carefully for two minutes Kuttelwascher positioned himself for a kill.

A two-second burst of cannon fire from 100 yards caused the first Heinkel to catch fire and dive into the ground north-east of the airfield. Immediately, 'Kut' positioned behind another of the bombers and a one-second burst of great accuracy sent that He 111 down on fire, into a wooded area to the east. Astonishingly, the Germans still did not seem aware of his presence, so 'Kut' lined up

behind a third Heinkel and a two-second burst of fire sent that one down too. Three bombers destroyed in four minutes and he had used only 200 of his 364 rounds of 20mm ammunition.

At this point the airfield lighting went out and the flak guns opened up at him. In a later BBC radio interview about the incident 'Kut' said: "They opened up all their anti-aircraft fire on me and I had to fly through it. It was like going through hell." Karel Kuttelwascher's eventual total score was 18 enemy aircraft destroyed (15 at night) plus one 'probable' and five damaged (all at night). Karel Kuttelwascher survived the war but died of a heart attack in 1959, still aged only 42.

In July 1942, 1 Squadron was replaced in the night intruder role by 43 Squadron, another famous Hurricane night fighter unit, but they were far less successful in achieving aerial kills, focussing more on attacking ground targets. After 43 Squadron's stint the night intruder role became the domain of radar equipped twin engined aircraft.

HURRICANE MKIIC (NF) – FIRST EVER AI EQUIPPED SINGLE SEAT FIGHTER

By the end of 1941 it was obvious that the future of night fighting lay with AI radar equipped fighters. The twin engined Bristol Beaufighter had entered service in limited numbers in the autumn of 1940. The first AI-assisted kill was made by a Beaufighter of 604 Squadron, flown by Flight Lieutenant John Cunningham (later promoted to group captain) on the night of November 19-20, 1940, the first of his 19 night kills. Improvements in the AI radar allowed the Beaufighter night fighters to really come into their own in 1941; on May 19-20, for example, Beaufighter crews claimed 24 victories in one night.

The need for AI radar led to a final, but sadly unsuccessful, chapter in the story of the Hurricane as a night fighter when, in 1942, 12 Hurricane MkIICs were modified to carry the AI Mark VI radar. The Hurricane IIC (NF) is a truly rare and little-known aircraft which, while singularly unsuccessful, entered the record books as the first radar

A rare colour shot of a Hurricane IIC of 87 Squadron being flown by Squadron Leader Dennis Smallwood in 1942. **via Author**

equipped single seat night fighter in the world. The AI MkVI radar had some automatic functions which, in theory at least, meant that it was possible for a single seat pilot to operate it. An 'automatic range strobe' was supposed to 'lock on' to the target radar echo, allowing the pilot to see the altitude, azimuth and range on the 'pilot's indicator' tube in the cockpit without having to continually adjust the set.

In the Hurricane the 4in diameter radar screen was placed in the position normally occupied by the undercarriage indicator, which in turn went to the position occupied by the clock, which was removed from the instrument panel. By June 1942, the prototype Hurricane MkIIC (NF), BN288, had completed its test flying with the Telecommunications Flying Unit at RAF Defford and the Fighter Interception Unit at Ford. The TRU/FIU report on the aircraft, dated June 7, 1942, was cautiously positive, but hinted at a problem by stating: "...inexperienced pilots are not recommended to fly an AI equipped Hurricane in bad weather at night".

The production of the 12 Hurricane MkIIC (NF) aircraft was completed by December 1942, and six aircraft each were deployed operationally with 245 and 247 Squadrons at RAF Charmy Down and RAF High Ercall respectively. In service the complex AI sets proved hard to maintain. It was found that moisture build-up could cause the radar aerials to 'squint' and often the automatic strobe found it difficult to 'stick' to a weak or rapidly evading target.

The maximum range of the AI MkVI in service was, disappointingly, only about one mile rather than the two to three miles that had been 'advertised'. Using the pilot's indicator effectively required "considerable skill and practice". The major shortcoming, though, was that the bright radar screen effectively destroyed the pilots' night vision, so that when they looked up for the target at minimum radar range they were unable to see anything in the darkness. ➤

The Battle of Britain Memorial Flight's Hurricane MkIIC PZ865 is painted in the markings of Flight Lieutenant Karel Kuttelwascher DFC. **Keith Brenchley**

Flight Lieutenant Karel Kuttelwascher DFC photographed in 1942. **via Author**

In addition, there was a significant performance penalty for the Hurricane with the extra weight and drag of the radar equipment. Pilots found the aircraft unpleasant to fly, saying that it felt "top-heavy" and was difficult to handle, especially when carrying long-range fuel drop tanks.

Pilot Officer Ken Gear of 247 Squadron said the Hurricane IIC (NF), overloaded with radar and long-range tanks, felt as if it was, "flying through mud". The Hurricane (NF)s were not quick enough to catch the fast aircraft that the Luftwaffe was now sending on raids so, in early 1943, the Air Ministry had the aircraft shipped out to India. They served from June 1943 onwards with 176 (NF) Squadron based at Baigachi, about 25 miles/40km north-east of Calcutta. The Hurricane IIC (NF) failed to score any victories, being too slow to catch the Luftwaffe bombers, and being denied the chance to test its mettle against the Japanese night raiders. The surviving Hurricane (NF)s were withdrawn from service by Christmas 1943, and struck off charge in 1944 – an ignominious end to a brief and disappointing career.

THE ACE FACTOR

In common with other single seat non-radar equipped aircraft, the Hurricane was, not surprisingly, generally rather ineffective as a night fighter. The difficulties, almost impossibilities, of the task that faced these pilots were extreme, but a small band of individualists showed that they could be overcome. The Hurricane night aces shared several things in common with each other. By and large they were older and more mature than most fighter pilots of the time, and they were experienced pilots with the ability to fly on instruments and at night without it sapping their capacity. They were quite happy operating alone, their gunnery skills were of a high order and they got in close to shoot.

This latter point was a common factor with most fighter aces of the period, but these men did it in the dark. The Hurricane night aces also shared a steely determination, in some cases almost a hatred and sense of vengeance against the enemy, and this translated into the patient stalking of their prey in the air and then heroic pressing for the kill. Without the benefit of AI radar to assist them, these pilots seemed to possess almost a sixth sense of where to find the enemy.

They seemed to be able to get inside the enemy airmen's heads and to know where they would appear. The most successful pilots of RAF single seat non AI equipped night fighters flew the Hurricane; some of them became night aces, and these men made the story of the Hurricane as a night fighter a success when it had every right to be a dismal failure. ■ *Words: Clive Rowley*

The ace factor. Aitken, MacClachlan & Kuttelwascher phtographed together in July 1942. **via Author**

One of the 12 Hurricane MkIICs modified to carry the AI Mark VI radar to become the Hurricane IIC (NF). **via Author**

THE HURRICANE WAS, NOT SURPRISINGLY, GENERALLY RATHER INEFFECTIVE AS A NIGHT FIGHTER. THE DIFFICULTIES, ALMOST IMPOSSIBILITIES, OF THE TASK THAT FACED THESE PILOTS WERE EXTREME, BUT A SMALL BAND OF INDIVIDUALISTS SHOWED THAT THEY COULD BE OVERCOME.

Rear view of a night fighter Hurricane MkIIb in the markings of Squadron Leader Ian "Widge" Gleed of 87 Squadron, photographed at the Sandown air show in 2006. **Julian Humphries**

A Greek in the RAF Eagle Squadron

As one of the foreign pilots who flew with the RAF before the American squadrons arrived in England, Spiros 'Steve' Pisanos of Greece became a double ace and the first American citizen to be naturalised in an overseas ceremony.

Spiros Pisanos was born in Athens, Greece, in 1919 and it wasn't long before he became completely infatuated with aviation. But his ambition to become a pilot was frustrated at first. He said: "I first fell in love with aeroplanes when I was young, and when I was 12 years old I was planning to attend the Greek Air Force Academy. Unfortunately, I was so bad in school that I did not have the qualifications to take the exams."

It was time for plan B.

"Near the end of high school, I began to dream about going to America to become an aviator," he said. "My first attempt was to stow away on the Italian liner Rex when it had arrived in Athens to pick up passengers bound for New York, but they found me."

Steve with his portrait in the International Aerospace Hall of Fame in 2012. **Norm deWitt**

Time to commence plan C. Steve said: "Later on I was playing football with my friends and a fellow wanted to join. He was an American from Buffalo, New York, visiting his uncle, who was a friend of my father. I told him about what I had attempted to do on the Italian liner.

"He told me that I would have probably died in the middle of the Atlantic Ocean, but that there was another way. 'Get a job on a Greek merchant ship and eventually when that ship arrives in an American port, just jump off, walk away and get yourself to New York. There you will find many Greeks'. So that is exactly what I did. The only places I knew about in America were New York City, Chicago with the gangsters, and the West with the cowboys."

Pisanos left Greece on March 25, 1938, and jumped ship while docked in Baltimore, Maryland, in the middle of April. He got on to a train bound for New York City.

"I arrived at Pennsylvania Station and when I walked out, honest to God I was crying like a baby that lost its mother at the shopping centre," he said. "There were Greek and American flags on a small theatre where they were playing the first movie made in Greece, a movie I had seen. Behind me I overheard two gentlemen talking about the movie in Greek."

Those two brothers he met in front of the theatre brought Pisanos to where they lived in Brooklyn.

"The older brother was a chef, and his friend worked for an employment agency for restaurants and bakeries," said Steve. "He got me a job at a bakery at 147th St and Broadway that was owned by a Greek family. I went to a recruiting office to join the Army, but they noticed my accent and discovered I wasn't an American, so they wouldn't take me." Trying a different angle now, all of Steve's spare money went towards taking flying lessons. "There was a flying school at the airfield in Brooklyn, like a flying club. You had to pay 25 dollars… and I started to fly," he said.

"Unbelievable! Well, I had a friend who told me about how in New Jersey I could pay eight dollars for instruction, and six dollars for solo (Brooklyn was 12 dollars and eight for solo). So, I quit my job and told the employment agency fellow that I needed to move to New Jersey.

"I got a job at the Park Hotel by the Westfield airport, where the cheap flying was. The owner of the hotel was a German guy who had come to America the same way. He had been a waiter on the SS Bremen and when they stopped in New York he said, 'to hell with this life'."

Steve impressed the owner to the point that he soon offered to send him to Cornell to learn the hotel business, but Steve wasn't interested. "I told him the centre of my heart was in the airplanes," he said. "In late April 1941, the newspaper

Late in 1944, Steve was posted to Wright Field, where he began a new career of evaluating and testing aircraft.
Steve Pisanos

Inside the ready room of 71 (Eagle) Squadron. **Editor's collection**

reported how the Germans were shelling the Greeks in Athens and stealing all the food they could and sending it to Germany. I was really upset and when I got to the airport my instructor spotted me and asked why I looked so angry. I told him what I had seen in the paper and if I could only get my hands on a plane to fight those damned Germans.

"He asked me 'do you really want to fight the Germans? How would you like to join the RAF? In New York they have a recruiting office at the Waldorf Astoria on the 13th floor, they are looking for aviators. Look for the sign on the door that says The Clayton Knight Committee'."

It was the HQ for the American Eagle Squadron which had been formed 18 months earlier, with Squadron 71 becoming operational early in 1941, equipped with the Hawker Hurricane. Eventually there were three RAF Eagle Squadrons, the 71, 121 and 133, and by this time some of the earlier issues, such as asking Americans to swear allegiance to the Crown, had been resolved.

Steve said: "My instructor told me to take my licence and logbook, as I had a private licence by that time with 170 hours. I got there and said that I was there to enquire about joining the Royal Air Force, so they introduced me to Squadron Leader George Graves, the man who was in charge of recruiting civilian aviators.

"He informed me that the minimum was 200 hours, and I told him if he would ➤

Pilots of 71 (Eagle) Squadron in 1941. **Editor's collection**

A Hurricane of 71 (Eagle) Squadron is rearmed. **Editor's collection**

allow me, I'd go back to fly some more and come back later on. Graves said 'that won't be necessary' and he turned to his secretary and asked her to help Mr Pisanos to fill out his application. Then he told me that he would call and let me know.

"I was so happy you have no idea… when I got back to the hotel, I didn't say anything to anyone. A month later the public phone rang in the dining area and a waiter said 'Steve, somebody wants you on the phone'. A voice said 'Mr Pisanos, this is Squadron Leader Graves from New York… you have been accepted to join the Royal Air Force. You need to take a flight check at Flushing Airport and take a physical'. I did the physical and then did my flight check with a Stearman biplane that I had never flown. The old pilot that gave me the check was a First World War fighter pilot. We did some acrobatics, this and that and he didn't say anything yay or nay.

"After the flight, we sat down for coffee. I was so damn anxious to hear from the guy… and then he said 'for never having flown that aircraft before, you did very well my boy. You are going to the Polaris flight academy where you'll get some more training'. I asked the

guy behind the counter to give us some apple pie with ice cream, I was so happy! This was in October of 1941.

"Now I was faced with… how do I tell my good German boss Albert Stender, who had helped me so much? I went to his office and told him that I had joined the Royal Air Force and that I was going to England to probably fight the German air force. He got up and came around to where I was sitting and said 'Steve, I have never approved of what Hitler and all his gang have done to Germany, my country. Germany is in my heart like Greece is in your heart. I want you to go there and give Hitler and his pals hell'.

"He had a big shindig for me with the newspapers about the boy from the Park Hotel who has joined the RAF… it was unbelievable. When I was over in England, you wouldn't believe all the packages of cookies and things I received from his wife. In November, I reported to the Polaris flight academy."

Soon it was off to England and flying with the RAF. Steve said: "I was with the 268 Squadron, flying the Hurricane, P-40s, and P-51s with the Allison engine, not the later model with the Rolls-Royce engine. Well, one day I got a phone call from a wing

commander of the Greek Air Force and he told me that he wanted me to come to London and that he needed to talk to me.

"I told my flight commander, who said 'you'd better go then'. This Wing Commander Kinatos was the aide to King George, who was also staying at this hotel since he escaped from Greece when the Germans invaded. The wing commander told me how many of the Greek Air Force pilots had escaped to Egypt, Malta, and Cyprus.

"To find his pilots he had sent his people to the Air Ministry for a list of every pilot in the RAF, to pick out the Greek names. I told him that I belonged to an RAF squadron here and that if I survived the war, I wanted to go back to America. He was getting kind of angry, telling me that I was a Greek soldier and that I had to go to Egypt… when I had nothing to do with the Greek Air Force.

"I walked out and figured I'd better go to the Eagle Club where the manager was Mrs Dexter, an American lady who had gone to England. I told her that I needed to talk to Squadron Leader Chesley Peterson, the commander of the 71st Eagle Squadron, who I'd met before. She got him on the phone, and I told him that I needed to speak with him about something important.

"So, I met him at the Regent Palace Hotel by Picadilly Square. He asked me 'do you want to go to Egypt?' and I said 'no sir, I want to stay here in the RAF'. So he told me that he was going to Fighter Command tomorrow, and to let him handle this. The following day, Wing Commander Anderson of 268 Squadron said 'what is this? I just got a phone call from Fighter Command telling me to release you immediately to report to 71 Eagle Squadron'.

"I got into the 71st Eagle Squadron of the RAF, flying Spitfires V's in the very beginning of September 1942. Don Gentile was my room mate during the rest of the war, and he ended up with 28 aircraft destroyed – 22 in the air and six on the ground.

"But it was mostly a 'rhubarb mission', what in RAF terminology meant strafing locomotives. That and convoy patrol. I destroyed a couple of locomotives in France. When the American Eighth Air Force came over to England, they didn't have any experienced fighter pilots then. Guys like Doolittle were looking with binoculars for

Two Hurricanes of 71 (Eagle) Squadron low over their home base of RAF Kirton in Lindsey. **Editor's collection**

The badge of 71 (Eagle) Squadron. **Editor**

The badge of 121 (Eagle) Squadron. **Editor**

The badge of 133 (Eagle) Squadron. **Editor**

pilots from the Eagle Squadrons – we had combat experience, and with dogfighting.

"The decision was made that the three Eagle Squadrons would transfer over to the Eighth Air Force. I figured that they were not going to take me, as I was not an American. Well, Peterson was the liason officer between the RAF and the Eighth Air Force and he said that they needed every one of us, including me. Well, I went to London to be interviewed, facing three Army Air Force colonels.

"They asked if I lived in America and I said 'yes sir' and explained how the RAF had trained me in California. They asked if I intended to go back to America and I answered 'yes sir'. They asked if I would accept a commission in the United States Army Air Force and that they needed every one of us. I just couldn't believe it.

"So, I was practising dogfighting with my room mate Gentile in our P-47s. We had to get 30 hours in the aircraft to be considered combat-ready. Over the radio, I was ordered

to return to base immediately. There was a staff car waiting for me with Chesley Peterson at the wheel, I was afraid that an order had come from the Greek wing commander that they had to have me in the Greek Air Force.

"Well, the Group Commander Colonel Anderson told me to sit down and called the ambassador at the American Embassy. Now I was afraid they were going to tell me that I could not stay in the air force. Well, the ambassador asked me 'lieutenant, how would you like to become an American citizen? There is a special envoy from Washington who is here to naturalize about half a dozen of you boys, and we want you to be the first one'.

"I looked at Peterson and he was smiling like nobody's business. He asked if I was surprised. 'Surprised? You almost gave me a heart attack, the Greeks wanted me to go to Egypt, I said'.

"On March 3, 1943, because of a recent Act of Congress, Steve Pisanos became the

first individual ever in American history to be naturalized as a US citizen outside the borders of the United States.

"Walter Cronkite was there, Ed Murrow was there, Andy Rooney was there… oh my God, Ed Murrow came up to me with that cigarette in his mouth and said 'lieutenant, what took place this afternoon in this room, I'm going to relate to the American people tonight'."

America had a new fighter pilot, forever to be known as 'the flying Greek'. Now flying the P-47 for the Americans in Squadron 334, Pisanos was to become an ace with six confirmed victories.

He said: "My first victory was on May 21, 1943, over Belgium. I got on this Fw 190's tail and I blasted him. Once, over Belgium, I came down on this damn 109. We found ourselves on the deck and I was still on his tail trying to get into position when out of the corner of my eye I saw these high tension wire towers. Knowing the area, this gentleman was trying to get me to fly into these wires, so I raced ➤

Canadian built Hurricane MkXII Z7381 in the markings of XR-T of 71 (Eagle) Squadron as it was operated by the Fighter Collection until 2002. Note the Eagle Squadron badge on the nose. **Keith Draycott**

Hurricane Mk XII Z7381, XR-T, comes in to land at Duxford. This aircraft is now owned by the Historic Aircraft Collection and appears as HA-C. **Keith Draycott**

Steve Pisanos and Major General Charles E 'Chuck' Yeager with the under construction replica of the Bell X-1 in which General Yeager became the first man to fly faster than sound. **Norm deWitt**

my P-47 and barely missed the top wire and got him on the other side.

"I made my report and they went to my aircraft and got the film. The film was completely blank. As far as I'm concerned, I killed that son of a bucket; he blew up right in front of me."

Steve got no official credit, although he still ended the war with 10 confirmed victories, six with the P-47 and four with the Mustang – a double ace. By 1944, he was to receive a P-51B.

He said: "It was the first one with the Rolls-Royce engine, but it did not have the bubble canopy. It was a good aircraft and I went on the first Berlin mission on March 3, 1944. After the war, I sat next to Adolf Galland at the Paris Air Show. He asked me 'what kind of airplanes did you fly?' I told him 'I don't fly any more general, but in the war I flew Spitfires with the 71 Eagle Squadron'.

"When I said 'Spitfire' I think he went about four inches up in the air. He said 'my friend... that was Colonel Blakeslee's organisation, the Fourth Fighter Group, 1016 victories. We knew him well in the Luftwaffe; he was one of the greatest aerial commanders. You know, when we learned that (Hubert) Zemke was shot down, I was in Berlin that day and told the marshal that if we could get this fellow (Don) Blakeslee, our problems with the Americans would be over'. Truthfully, looking back, they were

the two greatest commanders we had, Zemke and Blakeslee."

Blakeslee was grounded in September 1944, and it has been said that he flew more missions than any other American pilot of the war. By then, Steve Pisanos was similarly out of action, through entirely different circumstances. On May 5, 1944, while on a return flight after logging additional victories against Bf 109s while flying bomber escort, Pisanos was forced down behind enemy lines with mechanical problems.

Ironically it had been the same day that future aviation legend Chuck Yeager was shot down further south in France. Steve joined up with the French Resistance and participated in missions against the occupying German forces until that summer when the Allied armies reached his position in Paris. In 2010, he received the French Legion of Honor in a ceremony held in San Diego to honour his service as both a fighter pilot in the skies over France and his later efforts with the French Resistance.

Steve said: "I've been asked 'of the aircraft that you flew, which one did you prefer?' Well, the Hurricane was a good aircraft and if you recall your history, during the Battle of Britain it got more victories than the Spitfire. After I flew the Hurricane my instructor in the operational training unit (before Pisanos joined the 268 Squadron), who had 13 victories in the Battle of Britain, asked me,

'how did you like it?' I said that it was the best fighter I had ever flown. His response was 'wait until you fly the Spitfire'.

"If you wanted me to defend San Diego against enemy bombers or what-have-you I'll take the Spitfire. For aerial combat, the Spitfire was number one. Now if you wanted me to intercept a train full of enemy soldiers, east of San Diego, I'll take the P-47. If you wanted me to escort bombers up to San Francisco, I'll take the Mustang."

After the liberation of Paris, Pisanos was transferred back to the United States for his new role as test pilot.

He said: "In October 1944, after I had returned from France, I went to the Park Hotel in New Jersey to see my friends there. You have no idea – the entire hotel staff had come out to see Lt Pisanos who had come back from the war with 10 victories. They had a big dinner, the mayor, the chief of police, even the mayors from the surrounding cities were there – unbelievable.

"They wouldn't let me fly again in France, so they sent me to Wright field to test enemy aircraft – the Me 262, the radial Fw 190s, the Bf 109 and the Zero. I was a test pilot along with my good friend Don Gentile. Then, after the war, it was Chuck Yeager, Bob Hoover and me. When Colonel Bill Councill set the records in the Shooting Star going from West to East, actually I was supposed to fly the thing. I had like 100

Hurricane MkXII Z7381 in the markings of XR-T of 71 (Eagle) Squadron showing the nose art of a fighting rooster. **Editor**

Chesley 'Pete' Peterson, the Officer Commanding 71 Squadron when Steve Pisanos first arrived there. **Norm deWitt**

March 3, 1943, and Steve Pisanos becomes the first individual ever in American history to be naturalized as a US Citizen outside the borders of the United States. **Steve Pisanos**

Steve in the cockpit of a P-47D in the summer of 1943. **Steve Pisanos**

something hours in the YP-80 program."

He was later to be involved in the testing of other planes, such as the Delta Dagger and after further service flying in Vietnam, Colonel Pisanos retired in 1974.

Steve said: "The Eagle Squadron Association made up of those of us who served in the Eagle Squadrons 71, 121, and 133 – we made this museum, the San Diego Air & Space Museum, our home. Back in 1980-something, the president said 'you know, we don't have a Spitfire'. So, we prepared a letter and sent it to the Air Ministry. An Air Marshal came right back and said that 'we have a Spitfire for you boys, but we need a favour, we don't have a Mustang for our museum'.

"Where on earth were we going to get a Mustang? So, what we decided to do was to collect parts of a Mustang. We got the propeller from Australia, the engine from San Francisco, a wing from a Mustang that had crashed... well, we got this fellow with a big garage in El Cajon, and he knew about putting airplanes together."

There were huge challenges ahead for the Eagles. Steve said: "The biggest guy who helped us was the President of Federal Express, Fred Smith. He gave us $50,000. So, we put the Mustang together and went to the air force and asked them, but some guy came back and said 'we can't do it, if Congress finds out we've done this, they'll raise the dickens'. So, it was back to our friend Fred Smith.

"He sent a 747 to Miramar where we loaded the Mustang into boxes after we took it back apart and flew it to England. They got the Spitfire and brought it back."

That Spitfire now sits next to the Eagle Squadron display at the San Diego Air & Space Museum. Steve Pisanos has had a long life and an incredible adventure.

"Of course, this is a wonderful country," he said. "It is a country that believes in freedom, opportunity, equality and promise, and that's exactly what Uncle Sam did for me." One might add 'with a little help from the Royal Air Force'. ■

Words: Norm deWitt

Steve Pisanos in mess dress with full medals in 2004. **Steve Pisanos**

The BBMF's Dakota leads the Lancaster, four Spitfires and a Hurricane in a special flypast at their home base at Coningsby. **Constance Redgrave**

Battle of Britain Memorial Flight

An irreplaceable national treasure

The Hurricanes of the Battle of Britain Memorial Flight of the Royal Air Force are unique in many ways, not least due to the organisation they belong to. Constance Redgrave, with help from the Flight's public relations officer Yvonne Masters, takes a look at the Flight from her uniquely American perspective and finds that it is going from strength to strength and is now more available for people to visit than ever.

There are many things to inspire the heart and soul of an expat Californian living in London, England, but none come close to the joy of seeing and hearing the Battle of Britain Memorial Flight (BBMF) flying over the Mall at Buckingham Palace. The Brits do 'old' so very well and in my opinion the BBMF may be one of the UK's best kept secrets.

The BBMF is a flying memorial commemorating the Second World War; it consists of an Avro Lancaster flanked by a Supermarine Spitfire and a Hawker Hurricane. The symphony of Merlin engines, harmonised by age and loving care, as they fly over your head is guaranteed to bring a tear to the eye, even if you have no idea what you are seeing, such is the emotive power of that sound.

The Flight comprises 11 aircraft in total, including the impressive Lancaster, two Hurricanes, five Spitfires (soon to be six thanks to the tireless efforts of Dave Marshall, Paul Blackah and the rest of the engineering team), a Douglas Dakota and two de Havilland Chipmunks. The last two are used to train pilots in operating tail draggers, as we call tail wheel aircraft. The Flight's Hurricanes are very special aircraft. Why you ask? Well, LF363 is the last Hurricane to have entered service with the RAF and can be seen in a number of films including The Battle of Britain and Angels One Five. PZ865 was the last of 14,533 Hurricanes to be built and for many years the aircraft bore the legend 'The last of the Many!' on either side of the cockpit. These original cockpit doors have since been replaced, but can still be seen on display in the office corridor of BBMF headquarters building.

The charming and irrepressible Officer Commanding the BBMF, Squadron Leader Ian Smith, has every reason to smile from the cockpit of Hurricane LF363. **Constance Redgrave**

The BBMF often displays two fighters with either the Lancaster or the Dakota, all of which regularly change their colour schemes. Here is the Flight in 2005, none of these schemes are carried by the aircraft any more. **Constance Redgrave**

A typical scene in the BBMF hangar as a group of visitors are enthralled by their guide as they get a close-up view of the legends. **Yvonne Masters**

The record-breaking East Coast locomotive to be named 'Battle of Britain Memorial Flight' on June 2, 2012. **Jack Boskett**

As the Lancaster is one of the last two remaining airworthy examples left in the world, it is a real treat to witness it in the air. The Lanc also flies for official occasions of state and often leads a pair of the fighters in a display. This role is also taken at flybys and air shows by the Douglas Dakota. 2012 uniquely offers several opportunities to experience the Lancaster over London if you are coming to Britain, including the Queen's 60th Jubilee and the 2012 Olympics. Check the website for the current diary and event listings.

The Flight's home base at RAF Coningsby in Lincolnshire is a working RAF station, with the latest Typhoon fighters and the occasional glimpse of a Tornado seen just next door to the BBMF visitor centre. So as well as getting up close and personal with the classic vintage planes of the Flight, you can get some great photo ops of modern day jets as well. It's a great day out for the family, with guided tours available for a small charge for groups and school parties as well. Nothing beats being in the spotless hangar with these legends.

There are many ways to experience the magic of the BBMF, even if you can't get to the UK anytime soon. YouTube has some wonderful clips of displays and flypasts. My personal favourite is www.youtube.com/watch?v=ntmVPl3BlQw a clip just called bbmf flypast, 28 perfect seconds of smooth Merlin rumble to make you smile. Yvonne has been working very hard to fully establish the Flight on all of the electronic networks and tells me that those who wish to see more can subscribe to the Flight's own YouTube channel, keep up-to-

date with the Flight through Twitter and follow it on Facebook. The addresses of all these wonderful resources are on these pages. For those of you interested in supporting the Flight, there is now even an eBay shop where a variety of memorabilia can be purchased.

In 2012 there are two special events already planned. The RAF BBMF and Tattershall Castle, a property of the National Trust, will be joining together to bring you an exclusive view of the Flight and the aircraft that has never been seen before. Visitors will be able to view the aircraft on a usual hangar tour for the usual admittance price and then on production of their receipt they will be offered a special rate to enter Tattershall Castle to view the aircraft carrying out their practice displays from the high turret walls. This event is due to take place on Tuesday, April 24, 2012, and further details will follow on the RAF BBMF website soon.

There is also a spectacular ceremony and flypast to launch a nine-day festival, 'Railfest', at the National Railway Museum in York on June 2. The opening of the festival will be marked by the unveiling of a record-breaking East Coast locomotive to be named 'Battle of Britain Memorial Flight'. The locomotive will carry a special colour scheme featuring the aircraft and insignia of the Flight, and as it is unveiled, the Lancaster, a Hurricane and Spitfire will fly overhead. The Dakota will also be making an appearance over the special display of famous and record-breaking locomotives gathered for the festival.

How wonderful is that. Trains and planes… ■ *Words: Constance Redgrave and Yvonne Masters*

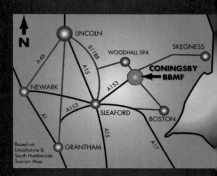

Comrades
in arms
Russian Hurricanes

The biggest Hurricane customer, other than the RAF, was the Soviet Air Force. The Russians received 2952 aircraft and used them in every possible role. It was almost a fifth of all Hurricanes built. The first aircraft to arrive were two RAF Squadrons, sent in August 1941. These two units trained Russian air and ground crews in operating and maintaining the Hurricane, before returning to Britain. A number of the aircraft were adapted to carry Russian guns, as supplies of British ammunition were often difficult to maintain.

Operation Barbarossa, the Axis invasion of the Soviet Union, began on June 22, 1941. The Soviets were caught in a state of unpreparedness, despite Stalin and other Soviet leaders and generals having publicly stated that war with Germany was inevitable.

Warnings were received from Allied intelligence that the Axis armies were massing on the borders, but little of practical use was done to ready the Soviet forces to defend their country. Instead, Stalin placed much faith in the prewar Molotov-Ribbentrop Pact and the German-Soviet trade agreements that followed it, and chose not to provoke Hitler in any way.

On June 22, nearly four million troops invaded the Soviet Union along a 1800 mile (2897km) front, the largest invasion ever staged in history. Supporting these troops were armoured and mechanised units, and of course the combined might of the Axis air forces.

The Luftwaffe's task was to destroy the Soviet Air Force as quickly as possible on the ground and in the air. Luftwaffe attacks on Soviet airfields found lines of aircraft laid out as if for an inspection, and claimed more than 1400 machines destroyed on the first day. By the third day, according to Russian sources, the Soviet Air Force had lost 3922 aircraft. The Germans had achieved air superiority over the entire front, and would maintain it for over a year.

Obviously, something had to be done to help the Soviets, and quickly before they were overrun by the rapidly advancing Axis forces. While it is true that the attack on the Soviet Union relieved the pressure on Allied forces in several theatres, the capture of the oil fields of the Caucasus and the industrial might of Russia by the Axis would be an unmitigated disaster for the Allies. Vehicles, tanks, aircraft and ships were all earmarked for supply to Russia.

Unfortunately, there was only one way to get them there, by convoy to the Arctic ports around the North Cape. These convoys had to run the gamut of German surface and subsurface forces, as well as the bombers and torpedo aircraft based at captured airfields in Norway. The cold weather was a factor that made many of these convoys face a battle for survival as much as anything else, friend and foe finding themselves at the mercy of the freezing seas and icy storms.

Some of the convoys suffered terrible losses, the fact that they made it at all is testament to the courage and determination of the often unsung heroes of the Merchant fleet, men in the front line as much as their uniformed colleagues.

Conditions on the Russian front were primitive, bloody, muddy and harsh, but there was one fighter in the British arsenal that was ideally suited to the challenges of operations in such a place, the Hawker Hurricane. Fortuitously, Canadian production of the aircraft was now supplementing the factories in the UK, so there was a small surplus of aircraft that could be spared to supply to Russia.

The first consideration was to protect the ports where the convoy ships were being unloaded. To this end, it was decided to establish 151 Wing RAF at Vaenga airfield, near Murmansk. Under the command of New Zealander Wing Commander Ramsbottom-Isherwood, 151 Wing comprised 81 Squadron under the command of Squadron Leader Rook, and 134 Squadron under Squadron Leader Miller, with a full support

151 Wing Hurricanes at Vaenga airfield near Murmansk shortly after arriving in Russia. **Editor's collection**

Russian troops cheerfully digging out parking revetments at Vaenga airfield. **Editor's collection**

Russian crews running up a Hurricane MkIIB.
Editor's collection

THE LUFTWAFFE'S TASK WAS TO DESTROY THE SOVIET AIR FORCE AS QUICKLY AS POSSIBLE ON THE GROUND AND IN THE AIR.

RAF pilots of 151 Wing with one of the Russian guards. **Editor's collection**

staff of engineers, communications officers and interpreters.

The entire wing was transported to Russia by convoy. Some of the Hurricane MkIIBs were aboard the carrier HMS Argus which left Scapa Flow on August 30, 1941, with a further 16 in crates aboard the merchant ship Llanstephan Castle. On September 7, 24 of the Hurricanes flew off HMS Argus to a warm and rather vodka fuelled reception by their enthusiastic hosts. The Llanstephan Castle had docked at Archangel, some 400 miles away, on September 1.

The crated Hurricanes were taken to Keg Ostrov airfield then rebuilt by RAF ground crew led by Flight Lieutenant Gittens, under the keen eyes of their hosts who wanted to learn as much as possible about the new aircraft. The 16 Hurricanes were flown to rejoin the wing in two waves on September 12 and 15. Early operations encountered a number of snags, not least of which was the unavailability of 100 Octane fuel, which caused reduced power and other problems.

The severe cold of the region affected both the weapons and the lubricants of the Hurricanes, but steadily fixes were found by the inventive crews. The first operations began on September 11 with familiarization patrols. The following day combat began in earnest, with the wing claiming four German aircraft, including three Bf 109Es destroyed.

Patrols over the harbours and intercepting incoming raids were interspersed with escort missions for Soviet bombers. The reputation of the wing steadily grew with the Russians and a number of prominent pilots, including the Commanding Officer of the Soviet Northern Fleet Air Force, Major General A A Kuznetsov, coming to fly and assess the Hurricane. The intended secondary role of 151 Wing was always for it to act as an operational training unit, teaching Russian crews to operate and maintain their aircraft prior to handing them over.

Increasing numbers of Russian pilots were trained on the Hurricanes, with A Flight of 81 Squadron being handed over on October 13,

Russian pilots wait at Vaenga while RAF ground crew refuel a Hurricane MkIIB. **Editor's collection**

followed by B Flight on October 22, together forming the nucleus of 1 Russian Hurricane Squadron commanded by Lieutenant Yakovenko. Although this was intended to act as an operational training unit, the squadron continued combat patrols, shooting down its first enemy aircraft, a Bf 110, on October 26.

With the foundation of the squadron, the rest of the Hurricanes were soon in Russian hands, the first operational unit being the 78th Regiment of the Red Naval Air Fleet, the first Soviet regiment to be equipped with a foreign aircraft. By October 30 three more regiments, the 72nd, 152nd and 760th, were fully formed and operational, repainted with red stars and white aircraft numbers.

The commander of the 78th Regiment was one of the first Russian pilots to fly the Hurricane, the popular and charismatic Captain Boris Safanov. By the time he began to convert on to the new fighter, Safanov was already a Hero of the Soviet Union and an ace with 14 victories to his credit. By October 31 more than 100 Hurricanes had been delivered and were now being assembled solely by the Russian engineers.

The RAF personnel of 151 Wing returned to the UK by sea, arriving on December 7, 1941, in Rosyth, Scotland. In their short career they had accounted for 16 enemy aircraft destroyed, but more importantly had

introduced the Soviet Air Force to a potent new weapon, replacing as it did the outclassed and open cockpit Polikarpov I-16.

The 78th Regiment was soon in action but it was not to be until November 16 that it claimed its first confirmed victory, when a Junkers Ju 52 three engined transport was shot down near the Finnish border. Safanov was at the head of two Flights of Hurricanes on December 17 when they fought an engagement with the Bf 109s of JG77, damaging one, but losing one Hurricane.

Safanov's own aircraft was so badly damaged he was forced to land on a frozen lake, a process he survived intact, but he had to leave his aircraft when it was attacked and destroyed by more German fighters. Sadly, the personable Safanov was to be killed in action flying a P-40E on May 30, 1942.

Nine Hurricanes were to be lost by the end of the year, mostly to enemy action, but some due to the extreme weather and freezing temperatures of the region which continued to cause problems with the Hurricane's coolant and lubricant systems. At the same time, however, the regiment claimed 10 enemy aircraft destroyed, even in the harsh conditions, so on January 18, 1942, the 78th Regiment was granted a much prized honour, that of the status of Guards Regiment. ➤

A Hurricane cocooned in protective wraps against the extreme cold of Northern Russia in an attempt to protect the coolant and lubricant systems. **Editor's collection**

A Tupolev SB-2 bomber over the 151 Wing base at Vaenga. **Editor's collection**

Deliveries from Britain and Canada more than offset the losses of Hurricanes, and the regiments grew in strength through the months of extreme winter weather. The deliveries were to continue throughout the war in increasing numbers, even after the Hurricane production line had closed in 1944. Stocks of stored airframes were supplied, mostly through the northern convoy system, but also via an overland route through Africa and the Middle East which began in 1943. Of the original batch of 151 Wing Hurricanes, only one survived the war, BD823, the rest were either lost to enemy action, in accidents, or scrapped.

Even though convoy support and protection measures developed through the war, large numbers of crated Hurricanes were lost when the ships they were on were sunk, especially when the Germans stepped up their attacks on the ports and convoys in April and May of 1942. Along with these aircraft, much of the ammunition intended for them was also lost and these shortages caused the Russians to try fitting their own guns to the Hurricane.

A pair of ShVAK 20mm cannon and two Berezin UBT 12.7mm heavy machine guns were fitted as a trial installation. Flight trials with the new armament began on February 24, 1942, and proved extremely successful, both in increasing the firepower of the Hurricane and in reducing Russian dependence on vulnerable overseas ammunition supplies. The underwing long range tank and bomb racks were modified to carry a variety of Russian weapons, including pairs of the RS-82 air to surface unguided rocket.

These were electrically fired and the necessary modifications were all carried out by Russian personnel, often in the field, to the majority of Hurricanes supplied to Russia. A number of Hurricanes were also converted into two seat trainers in Russia, with either a second seat ahead of the existing cockpit or behind it. Since the former required removing the fuselage fuel tank, few of the conversions were built this way. Neither arrangement included an enclosed cockpit, so the instructor must have been well attired for training flights in the Russian winter.

It is unclear as to how many were converted, or the level of equipment in the instructor's cockpit, but addressing their need in such a direct way was typical of the Russian approach to the war. They were in a desperate and murderous fight for survival, so anything that was seen as a requirement was built or modified in as practical and expedient a method as possible.

This practical approach often horrified western observers, but Russian made equipment was built to cope with open air storage and rough and ready engineering practices. Supposedly inferior Russian aircraft could function well with even the most frugal of support, in conditions that would quickly wreck the superior products of the west. It may be that this 'expediency first' attitude to engineering is why the Russians considered the normally

tough Hurricane a somewhat fragile machine by comparison to some of their own.

There are many gaps in the historical records regarding the use and history of the thousands of Hurricanes supplied to the Soviet Union, but it is known they were widely employed as fighters, ground attack aircraft, reconnaissance platforms and trainers. They served well, and were regarded as more reliable and easier to maintain than some of the other machines Russia was supplied with.

With the fall of the Soviet Union, more details are emerging, as are a number of surviving airframes from some very remote areas. One of these is Hurricane IIB Z5252, an aircraft recovered from the bottom of a lake near Murmansk, having force landed on the frozen surface on June 2, 1942. In 2004, the aircraft was successfully raised almost completely intact, having been preserved in the low temperature water. It is planned to restore this airframe to flying condition as a tribute to the pilots of the Great Patriotic War.

It may be that more questions about Hurricane operations in Russia are answered as time goes on and more records and aircraft are found. I hope so. It would be fitting to celebrate the courage of the many Russian pilots who operated the type, and to tell the whole story of their achievements. ∎
Words: Tim Callaway

Hurricane MkIIB Z5252 at Vaenga, this aircraft has recently been recovered from a lake near Murmansk. **Editor's collection**

Hurricane MkIIB Z5252 was presented to the Commanding Officer of the Soviet Northern Fleet Air Force, Major General A A Kuznetsov, in November 1941. It was flown by 78th Regiment until it force landed on a frozen lake after being damaged in battle on June 2, 1942, but has since been recovered for restoration. **Keith Draycott**

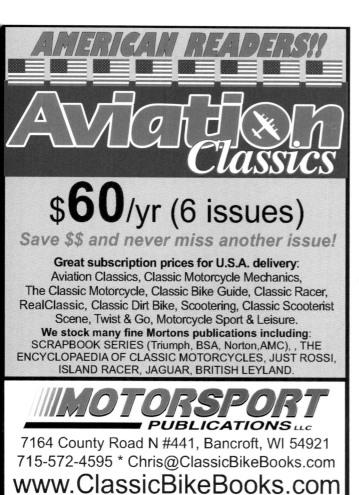

Inside the
Hurricane
Exploring the secrets of a legend

Every year, as part of their rigorous and detailed maintenance, the aircraft of the Battle of Britain Memorial Flight are taken apart and thoroughly inspected in preparation for the forthcoming display season. *Aviation Classics* was allowed to photograph one of the flight's two Hurricanes during this process and the resulting images show views of the airframe that usually would be concealed by the aircraft's skin. We would like to thank the Officer Commanding BBMF, Squadron Leader Ian Smith, and everyone at the flight who made us so welcome.

THE UPPER PORTION OF THE COCKPIT SECTION WAS MADE OF WOOD AND WAS SOMETIMES REFERRED TO AS THE 'DOG KENNEL', WHICH IT RESEMBLED BEFORE BEING MOUNTED TO THE MAIN FUSELAGE.

The Hurricane was one of the larger single seat prewar fighters, its wide stance on the ground giving it a pugnacious appearance. It was both slightly longer and of greater span than the Spitfire, but it was the much thicker wing and greater height that really made it look the larger of the two. Compared to the Bf 109, it was a veritable giant, but it was quickly surpassed in size by the next generation of fighters such as the Republic P-47 Thunderbolt and the Hawker Tempest.

As already discussed, the construction of the Hurricane posed no problems for the Hawker workforce. They were well versed in the techniques of Warren truss airframe manufacture, and indeed, so similar was the new fighter to the company's previous products that under the skin it was difficult to differentiate it from the earlier Fury on the production line. Designer Sydney Camm's influence on the aircraft was a constant and ensured that the end product was as simple and as light as possible.

FUSELAGE

In modern terms the Hurricane's internal structure is a lightweight space frame around which the remaining assemblies were attached. Four steel tubular longerons ran from the forward bay behind the engine to the rudder post. These were connected by cross members using bolts or large tubular rivets through pressed steel flange plates. In this fashion a series of bays were created along the fuselage length and no welding was required. This eliminated the need for highly skilled labour in the factories and at the Ministry of Aircraft Production (MAP) repair units. The end of each tube was milled into a rectangular shape to present a flat surface area for the plates which held it in place. ➤

The fuselage reserve self sealing fuel tank. Note it is immediately above the rudder pedals and behind the electrics of the instrument panel. **Julian Humphries**

Hurricane MkIIC LF363 of the Battle of Britain Memorial Flight stripped for winter maintenance in its Coningsby hangar. **Julian Humphries**

The large metal panels on the sides of the fuselage are easily removed, allowing open access to all the aircraft's major systems. **Julian Humphries**

The thick wing and height of the Hurricane add to its impression of solid bulk. **Julian Humphries**

Sydney Camm and Fred Sigrist, another Hawker engineer, had jointly developed the steel tube method and first used it in the Hawker Heron and Harrier. To further strengthen the structure, tensioned bracing wires were used to reduce any flexing of the bays under torsion. The fuselage sat across the large and immensely strong centre section bringing additional rigidity to the whole structure. This skeleton structure was then fitted with plywood frames which were clipped to the longerons at intervals.

These were raised to form the rounded shape of the rear fuselage and tapered towards the tail. The whole structure was then covered in high quality aviation grade fabric which was treated to make it taut over the wood and metal frame. A large access panel to the tail wheel area was provided on the port side under the tail and the whole lower fuselage covering could be easily removed.

No aircraft built with a monocoque skin could ever offer such unlimited access, as the whole strength of the structure would be totally compromised by large access panels. The multi-faceted skin bestowed by this construction technique is obvious when viewing the Hurricane's rear fuselage, a feature in sharp contrast to later Hawker products.

The front of the forward fuselage bay formed the engine firewall. This served two purposes. Its construction gave some protection from an engine fire but when properly sealed also acted as a barrier to dangerous engine fumes. The firewall sat on the upper beam of the centre section's front spar and the top half was canted forward towards the rear of the engine. It was constructed from a sandwich of asbestos

A rare view of the reduction gearbox and propeller shaft. **Julian Humphries**

The firewall showing the seals around all the items that pass through it, and the edge seal, all aimed at keeping engine fumes out of the cockpit and sealing it against fire. **Julian Humphries**

Inside the rear fuselage showing the four longerons, bolted and riveted spacers and the plywood formers that gave the aircraft its external shape. **Julian Humphries**

The cockpit showing the inside of the windscreen. **Julian Humphries**

The outside of the windscreen with the rear view mirror mounted on top. **Julian Humphries**

The left hand wall of the cockpit featured the throttle and fuel mixture controls, these were mounted on top of the upper longeron tubing. An undercarriage warning buzzer was fitted to alert the pilot that the wheels had not been deployed at low throttle settings. This feature saved many a novice pilot from the humiliation of explaining to his commanding officer why he had damaged one of the King's valuable aeroplanes.

The pilot was provided with a small internal lamp at the top left hand side with a dimmer switch. The gun sight illumination was controlled by a dimmer on the right. Adjustment to both elevator and rudder trim was achieved with two wheels lower down by the front left edge of the seat. On the right hand side of the seat was the undercarriage and flap selector box which had the appearance of a modern car's manual gear lever and gate.

The joystick controlled the elevators and ailerons in the usual fashion, it also carried the gun firing switch known most frequently to the pilots as the 'tit'. This was fitted with a safety catch to prevent inadvertent firing. Unlike early German fighters, the British articulated the upper section of the joystick allowing it to swing from side to side further than the lower section allowed, giving much greater freedom of movement and reduced stick forces. To the rear of the circular grip at the top of the control stick was a lever operated by the right hand which controlled the main wheel brakes. ➤

The left side of the cockpit showing the ease of access to the electrical cables and systems like the elevator trimmer, the wooden wheel in the centre. **Julian Humphries**

Looking down into the cockpit showing the trays for the pilot's feet to operate the rudder. Note the complete lack of a floor. **Julian Humphries**

The cockpit canopy in its fully open position. **Julian Humphries**

Two views of the uncovered tailplane structure showing the twin dumbbell spars that mounted on to the rear fuselage longerons to support the fin and tailplane. **Julian Humphries**

The engine radiator also contains the cylindrical oil cooler in the centre. **Julian Humphries**

THE CENTRE SECTION, WINGS AND TAIL

As previously described, the wing centre section formed part of the fuselage and provided most of the aircraft's strength. The two main spars protruded several feet on either side of the fuselage and were mounted parallel to each other and perpendicular to the fuselage. To carry the higher loading at the wing root the centre section was skinned in metal which also protected the aerofoil shape from wear as pilots and crew clambered into the cockpit.

This section accommodated the two main fuel tanks, undercarriage and radiator. The spars were made from high-tensile steel rolled into flat sided tubes with 10 faces. A slightly smaller tube of the same shape was inserted to double the strength of the spar and each tube had a lengthwise slot with a large flange on either side.

A metal web was slid into this slot to connect the upper and lower spars. When viewed end on, this arrangement had the appearance of a dumbbell and was developed by another Hawker engineer, Roy Chaplin. The front and rear spars were made up in the same way and connected together by girder work at the two ends and towards the centre bracing tubes were attached to the top of this box only.

The lower area was completely open to avoid fouling the undercarriage. No interconnecting ribs were used in this section of the wing and the aerofoil section was achieved by riveted light metal fairings.

The two main fuel tanks of 34.5 gallon (159 litre) capacity were carried on either side in the upper part of the centre section between the two spars and the engine oil tank was mounted on the left forward spar only. The capacity of this tank was later increased and was shaped to form part of the wing leading

The rear access panel on the fuselage is open showing easy access to the control runs and elevator and rudder actuators and trimmers. **Julian Humphries**

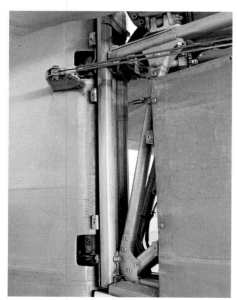

The rear spar of the fin also acts as the sternpost on which the rudder is mounted. **Julian Humphries**

The carburettor air intake under the rear of the engine bay and a view of the large wheel well under the wing. **Julian Humphries**

A rear view of the radiator cover showing the adjustable flap to help control engine and oil temperatures. **Julian Humphries**

The trim tab and navigation light on the rear of the rudder. **Julian Humphries**

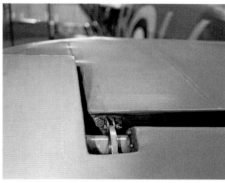

Close up of the outer elevator hinge. **Julian Humphries**

edge, a filler cap flush with its upper surface was provided for replenishment.

The Hurricane's characteristically wide stance was created by placing the main undercarriage legs at the extreme ends of the centre section. The aircraft's weight was carried mainly by the front spar to which each main leg or strut with oleo-pneumatic shock absorbers was attached. The wheels were supplied by the Dunlop Company and were of 10¼in (27.3cm) diameter, the tyres were from the same source.

Pneumatically operated brakes were fitted and undercarriage retraction was achieved via jacks driven by the high pressure hydraulic system. In normal operation an engine driven pump generated hydraulic pressure but was complemented by a hand operated lever in the cockpit. A large letter 'B' shaped cut out in the lower centre section allowed the wheels to lay flush with the underside of the wing when retracted.

An oxygen tank for the pilot was installed within the wheel bay and was mounted on the forward spar. Directly ahead of the wheel bay was the carburettor air intake and to the rear was the large centrally positioned radiator. An oil cooler was installed in the centre of the radiator matrix and a movable flap was provided at the rear of the radiator fairing. In flight the flap normally lay flush with the undersurface of the radiator faring, on the ground or in hot conditions it was opened to increase the cooling airflow.

The outer wings were attached to the centre section by bolts at the four tube ends of each spar structure and carried the aircraft's armament. Any under wing stores that were introduced with later variants of the Hurricane were attached to these panels, as no centre-line pylons could be attached because of the geometry of the undercarriage and the position of the radiator. ➤

The entire undercarriage leg with the door attached and brake cable running down it. **Julian Humphries**

A close up of the rear of the oleo, hub and brake assembly. **Julian Humphries**

Looking up into the wheel well with the cockpit blanking plates removed. The right hand rudder pedal tray is visible, as is the pilot's oxygen bottle mounted against the back of the front wing spar. **Julian Humphries**

The hub, axle and brake assembly with its wheel removed. **Julian Humphries**

Looking down the leading edge box of the outer wing, showing the ribs and tube built spacers that gave it its shape and rigidity. **Julian Humphries**

The main wing flap in the open position, showing the structure. **Julian Humphries**

The wingtip navigation light in its plexiglass fairing. **Julian Humphries**

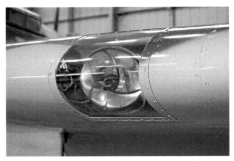

A landing light is mounted in the leading edge of the outer wings. **Julian Humphries**

The various armament configurations will be considered later and the fabric covered wings of early production MkI aircraft were completely interchangeable with the later, more resilient metal wings. For a brief period, while the remaining stocks of the old fabric covered wings were used up, aircraft left the factory with either type of wings, so great was the need to get the type into service. The outer panels of the wing were made up from two spars built in the same tube and web system as the centre section.

The spars carried most of the wing loads which decrease towards the tips. Correspondingly, the spar thickness was reduced by using shorter outer tubing, the inner tube extending out to the wing tip. Nine diagonal trusses connected the two spars in each wing, the pair closest to the wing joint passed through the gun bays. Lightweight metal ribs were fixed to the spars at right angles, which carried the skin covering be it fabric or metal.

A single spar and metal ribs formed the backbone of the ailerons which were fabric covered. Below the wing's trailing edge were the expansive hydraulically operated flaps, which were completely built up from metal components. A clever design feature prevented flap deployment above an airspeed of 100mph. Although mechanically connected, the inner sections of the flaps were separate and were installed in the wing centre section.

A landing lamp was built into the leading edge of each wing outboard of the gun bays. If fitted, the gun camera was installed in the leading edge of the starboard wing inboard of the gun bay. The lens projected through a small square shaped fairing which was hinged and formed the access panel to service the camera.

The Rotol variable pitch propeller off the aircraft. **Julian Humphries**

The left main fuel tank bay in the centre section seen from below, showing how the retracting undercarriage fitted around it. **Julian Humphries**

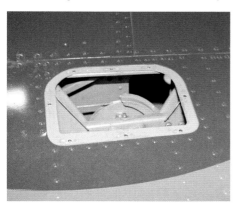

The aileron control run inspection panel is removed. **Julian Humphries**

The retractable stirrup under the fuselage to the rear of the left wing. **Julian Humphries**

The 11ft (3.35m) span fixed portion of the tail plane and fin were of metal construction. The elevators and rudder were made up from metal tubes and ribs covered with fabric. A lead weight in the top portion of the rudder provided its balance and it had a movement of 28 degrees either side of the centre line. A navigation lamp was fitted above the movable trim tab on the rudder's trailing edge. The elevators had a range of 29 degrees' movement above and below the horizontal plane. Once the decision to fix the tail wheel and install the ventral strake was made, the Hurricane's tail unit remained unaltered throughout all versions, with the exception of the arrestor hook for naval variants. Some later production MkI aircraft and all subsequent Hurricanes had an improved Dowty oleo-pneumatic tail wheel leg.

The construction techniques described, although entirely conventional at the time, presented modern restorers with huge engineering difficulties for some time. The machines that produced the longeron and spar tubes have long been scrapped, as this technique was abandoned in favour of monocoque construction methods. As a result, up until quite recently there were very few airworthy Hurricanes as the cost of reproducing unserviceable or missing parts was prohibitive.

These issues have now been completely overcome by specialist aircraft restoration companies in the last decade or two and Hurricanes, and even their older Hawker stablemates, are returning to the air in unprecedented numbers. ■ *Words: Tim Callaway and Julian Humphries*

The hand hold on the side of the fuselage. When this was closed, it retracted the stirrup. **Julian Humphries**

The tailwheel off the aircraft. **Julian Humphries**

A close-up of the propeller hub. **Julian Humphries**

Looking at the centre section to wing joint from the rear, note the rear bolts are vertical, the front horizontal. **Julian Humphries**

Through a glass darkly... well, lightly in this case

The Hurricane by Maurice McElroy of Flyinglass

Maurice McElroy discussed his images of classic aircraft created using the traditional techniques of stained glass in Issue 11 of Aviation Classics. This is an unusual medium for portraying aircraft, unique to this artist as far as we are aware.

At the time, he had constructed a Harrier in glass which we featured as he had kindly offered the piece as a prize to our readers. Maurice has now created a Battle of Britain period Hurricane depicted flying over the fields of south east England, and again offers it to Aviation Classics readers as a unique prize. We caught up with Maurice at his home in north London and asked him about how he came to create these stunning and colourful artworks.

"I first got into working with glass about four years ago," he said.

"I was looking for something to do and spotted an advert for a weekend course in Somerset working with hot glass – fusing and slumping. This was great fun and I really got into it. Once back home however, I realised that without a kiln I wasn't going to be able to do much and started looking for something in London where I live.

"Fortunately there's a place called Lead & Light in Camden Town that sells glass and also runs workshops. I did several of these run by Lynette Wrigley who, aside from being a wonderful glass artist and writer, is a great teacher. She taught me the basics of copper foil and lead work which meant that I could do projects at home. All my work is done on the kitchen table so I tend to eat off my knees these days.

"As most of my time is spent being a musician I haven't done a huge number of pieces. I'm still learning and fitting it in with the rest of my life means a fair amount of juggling. Mostly they've been small panels that I've given away to family and friends. I'm not going to be able to do the big stuff until I get a bigger kitchen table. The aviation pieces started with a panel I did as a birthday present for the editor of Aviation Classics, he has since mounted it in a window and it fills the room with patterns of light. The Hurricane is my third one following the Harrier I did for a previous issue of this magazine.

"What I like about glass is the glass itself, the colours and textures, and the way light comes through it. Most stained glass is exactly that: glass that has been 'stained' by putting paint on to it. Aside from that fact that my painting ability is nonexistent, I prefer to work just with the colours and textures of the glass. Therefore the Hurricane, as with the Harrier before it, is

WIN
A BEAUTIFUL PIECE OF AVIATION ART
ENTER ONLINE

Maurice hard at work on the Harrier. **Constance Redgrave**

The Flyinglass Hurricane by Maurice on the lightbox. Imagine the light streaming through this into your room. **Maurice McElroy**

not a specific aircraft complete with squadron markings but more of an evocation or illustration of general 'Hurricaneness'.

The inspiration came from a photograph I saw of a Hurricane flying over Southern England. All the lead work on this piece follows exactly the field boundaries in the photo. Somehow that aircraft over those fields is a very powerful image for me.

"Like most small boys I read a great many war comics when I was at school and spent a large proportion of my pocket money on Airfix model plane kits. While I loved the lines and romanticism of the Spitfire I always found myself drawn more to the Hurricane. There is something about it you can't quite put your finger on. When, in later life, I discovered that while the Spitfire got all the glory, it was the Hurricane that did most of the hard work, I wasn't in the least surprised.

"I hope that I've managed to capture the spirit of it. It's certainly what I was trying to do but others will have to be the judge of that."

You can learn more about Maurice's work at www.spikedrivers.co.uk/flyinglass.html ■
Words: Tim Callaway

ENTER ONLINE

If you would like to win this unique and beautiful piece of aviation art, simply go to the Aviation Classics website at www.aviationclassics.co.uk and enter the competition there.

THE INSPIRATION CAME FROM A PHOTOGRAPH I SAW OF A HURRICANE FLYING OVER SOUTHERN ENGLAND. ALL THE LEAD WORK ON THIS PIECE FOLLOWS EXACTLY THE FIELD BOUNDARIES IN THE PHOTO.

Maurice with the Hurricane. Even in the poor light the luminous quality of the glass colours is obvious. **Editor**

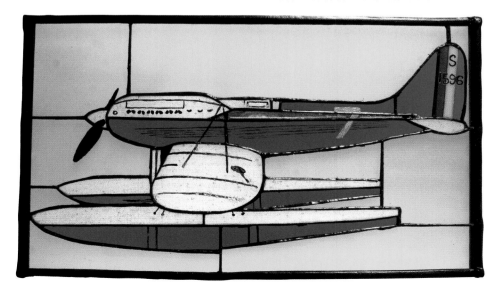

Maurice's first aviation piece, the Supermarine S6B. **Constance Redgrave**

Displaying a legend

Squadron Leader Clive Rowley was one of the fighter pilots with the RAF's world famous Battle of Britain Memorial Flight, eventually becoming the commanding officer of the unit in 2003. Here Clive recounts his experiences of flying and displaying the Hurricane.

PZ865 in company with the Battle of Britain Memorial Flight's Spitfire MkV. The Hurricane's most often on display in company with a Spitfire. **Luigino Caliaro**

I first flew a Hurricane on April 17, 1996. I was a new fighter pilot with the Royal Air Force Battle of Britain Memorial Flight (BBMF) and this was my first conversion to type. With no dual instruction available on the Hurricane it was, of course, a case of going solo on my first trip in the aircraft and hoping that I would cope. Fortunately I did, and I was then allowed to continue to fly the BBMF's precious Hurricanes (MkIIs, LF363 and PZ865) for a total of 11 display seasons. My logbook shows that I made 165 flights in Hurricanes, with my last one being on September 23, 2006.

For the last three years of that time, as the officer commanding the BBMF and the 'fighter leader', I also trained other pilots to fly the Hurricane, passing on my experience via dual instruction in the DH Chipmunks and with verbal briefings, before sending them off on their own solo 'voyage of discovery'.

As a 'modern' RAF fighter pilot, whose primary duties at that time involved flying the Tornado F3, I was extremely privileged to be allowed the rare opportunity to fly such a classic and iconic 'warbird' as the Hawker Hurricane. I also flew the BBMF Spitfires (actually many more times than the Hurricanes) and so had the chance to make comparisons between the types. So what is it like to fly a Hurricane? Let me try to put you in the pilot's seat.

Walking out to a Hurricane to take it flying, you cannot fail to be impressed by its sheer size; its hunched-backed stance and height off the ground make it seem more imposing than other similar-sized aircraft. I think it looks strong, purposeful and potent, especially with four 20mm cannons protruding from the wing. I wonder how the wartime pilots felt about it as they walked out for an operational mission in one. The pull-down step on the fuselage, just behind the trailing edge of the port wing, is very necessary to enable you to make the

big step up on to the wing; clever the way it automatically opens up the hand hold in the fuselage side as you pull the step down. The cockpit switches are safe, so I jump down to the ground again to carry out my 'walk-round' external checks. This is more of a tradition than a necessity as the ground crew have already completed the most thorough of inspections before releasing the aircraft to me.

External checks complete, I clamber back up on to the port wing and use the kick-in footstep to climb into the cockpit, pausing to give the canopy an upwards tug to confirm its security. Settling into the seat, that special smell of oil and petrol and I don't know what else, assails my nostrils; so different from the smell in a modern cockpit. I am assisted to strap in by the ground crew technician standing on the wing beside the cockpit, who then plugs in the lead of my flying helmet and, with a final pat on my shoulder in response to my thumbs up, leaves me alone in the cockpit.

Despite the relative simplicity of the controls in the Hurricane compared with modern jet fighters, I am reminded as I scan the cockpit of how complicated it seemed when I first flew the aircraft. They obviously had not invented ergonomics when this cockpit was designed. Controls, instruments and warning lights seem to be scattered about in an almost haphazard manner. One example is the fuel system controls. At the lower left is the fuel cock, marked 'off – main tanks on – reserve tanks on', with a spring-loaded catch to prevent inadvertent off selection (the 'main' fuel tanks are in the wings on both sides and hold 33 gallons of petrol each; the 'reserve' tank is in the nose, behind the instrument panel and above the pilot's feet, and contains 28 gallons, which will gravity-feed to the engine if necessary).

Over on the right side of the instrument panel is the fuel gauge and just above it a rotary control knob marked, 'port – centre –

stbd'. Making a selection with this knob and then pressing it in brings the fuel gauge to life to indicate the contents of the selected tank. What has to be remembered is that this knob controls only the fuel indications not the actual selection of the fuel tanks. Apparently, many years ago a senior-ranking BBMF pilot made the mistake of forgetting this golden rule and attempted to select the fuel tanks with the fuel gauge knob. When his wing tanks ran dry, it suddenly went very quiet as his engine stopped.

Fortunately, a rapid selection to the reserve tank with the correct cock restored normal power and noise levels, and no harm was done except to the pilot's heart rate and reputation. I was told this horror story to reinforce the lesson when I first converted to the Hurricane and have passed it on to others since. It is an example of how the cockpit of the Hurricane, with its lack of ergonomic design, contains 'gotchas' for the unwary.

The cockpit left-to-right checks are simple and logical and are completed in a minute or

two. I take a strange enjoyment in pumping the flaps down 20 degrees with the manual hydraulic pump handle (I have been grateful for this manual pump handle on several occasions, not least on my first ever flight in a Hurricane, when a weak engine-driven hydraulic pump led to my having to pump down the undercarriage by hand and then to make my first ever landing in a Hurricane). I leave the flap selector lever in the 'up' part of the 'H' gate so that when the engine starts and the hydraulic pump comes on-line it will raise the flaps, proving the serviceability of the system.

As usual I have left myself some spare time before I need to start the engine to make my planned take off time. I appreciate this time to myself in the cockpit, free from all outside distractions, able to focus on whatever it is I am going to do on the sortie. As I look around, I take the opportunity to refresh myself on the picture I will be seeing on landing, in terms of the height of my eye line from the ground and the nose-up angle of the aircraft. ➤

One of the Battle of Britain Memorial Flight's two de Havilland Chipmunks, used for training pilots in handling tail wheel aircraft. **Julian Humphries**

It's time to start up. I load the Kigas fuel priming pump by pumping it in and out until there is resistance and then, as the engine hasn't been run today and taking into account the air temperature, I give it seven pumps of fuel. I signal for start clearance to the ground crew and a confirmatory signal from him means I'm clear to start. Confirm wheel brakes on, throttle just off the idle stop, control column (stick) held fully back to prevent nose-over, magneto switches on, press the boost coil button for two seconds with my index finger then, keeping it pressed, also press the start button with my middle finger.

Meanwhile I'm holding the stick back with my legs and my right hand is ready either to use the priming pump or to move the throttle (a third arm and hand would be quite useful). The prop turns very slowly and jerkily for three or four blades then the engine kicks and the Rolls-Royce Merlin V12 bursts

sweetly into life, with puffs of smoke from the exhaust stacks and a cacophony of noise. What a wonderful sound – I always get a 'buzz' from that on start-up.

The engine instruments, particularly the oil pressure, show that all is well so I set the 'holding' RPM of 1000 with the throttle. The after start checks are completed in seconds. The flaps have travelled up so the flap selector lever is set to neutral and then the magnetos are checked individually. A quick radio call gets me clearance to taxi so I throttle back to idle and signal for the chocks to be removed. The ground crew man removes the chocks, carefully avoiding the lethal propeller arc and then flings them any old where, out of the way.

Taxiing the Hurricane is easy; the view over the nose is not bad at all, especially if the pilot's seat is raised, although it can be improved by weaving slightly from side to

Squadron Leader Clive Rowley photographed when he was the officer commanding the Battle of Britain Memorial Flight. **BBMF**

side. The brakes, controlled by a lever on the control column spade grip, are easy to use and give differential braking via the rudder pedals for steering. The brakes will fade if overused so it's worth keeping that in mind and keeping some braking in hand for when it is really needed. It is important to keep the stick fully back, especially when braking or opening the throttle, to prevent nose-over.

The Hurricane is not prone to overheating on the ground because the large radiator is

The cockpit of one of the Battle of Britain Memorial Flight's Hurricanes. **BBMF**

The Battle of Britain Memorial Flight's LF363 over Lincolnshire, home county of the Flight. **Luigino Caliaro**

sensibly located on the centreline under the fuselage behind the prop wash. Indeed, it is necessary to allow enough time for the engine to warm up for the engine run-up. Once the engine run-up checks are complete and air traffic control has given take off clearance, I line up on the centre of the runway, slightly canted off for a clear view down the strip. I won't put the aircraft straight until I'm about to roll. It wouldn't do to run into something unseen over the nose.

I set the throttle friction very tight so that the engine will not throttle itself back after take off when I take my hand off the throttle to raise the undercarriage. With the Hurricane, the final important check on the runway is to move the undercarriage safety catch to 'select' – this catch prevents the inadvertent 'up' selection of the landing gear while on the ground (nothing else does), but needs to be in the 'select' position to permit the gear to be raised after take off.

It's take off time and I'm cleared to go. I release the brakes and gently open the throttle to give +6in of boost (less power than might originally have been used but more than adequate for take off and the maximum I will use in the interests of engine conservation). On take off the aircraft tries to swing to the left as power is applied and again when I raise the tail at about 50 knots but the rudder control is powerful and it is easy to keep straight with right rudder.

Acceleration is moderate and at 70 knots I ease gently back on the stick to lift off, the aircraft feeling quite heavy on the controls. When safely airborne I squeeze the brakes to stop the wheels rotating and then comes the tricky part. I take my left hand off the throttle and place it on the spade grip of the stick – it's now that you'll regret it if you forgot to

The Hurricane cockpit is a long climb for a fighter. **Luigino Caliaro**

tighten the throttle friction because the throttle will gradually close and the aircraft will sink earthwards.

Now, flying the aircraft with my left hand, I find the undercarriage lever with my right hand without looking in and, pressing the thumb catch, I slam it hard into the 'up' gate, trying not to replicate the movement of my right hand with my left, but to continue to fly the aircraft smoothly. The air speed is increasing rapidly towards 100 knots as the gear slowly begins to retract. I have to pull the aircraft up into quite a steep climb or the undercarriage limiting speed of 104 knots will be exceeded and the gear will fail to lock up because of the aerodynamic load on the doors. After what seems like an age, two thumps and the red 'up' light on the undercarriage position indicator tell me that the gear is locked up.

These undercarriage indications do not conform with the modern convention of green for down, red for travelling up or down, lights out for locked up. With the undercarriage locked up, I can now lower the nose to a more normal climbing attitude, permitting the speed to increase to 140 knots, while selecting neutral with the undercarriage lever and then setting +4in boost with the throttle and 2400 RPM with the prop pitch control lever. This reduction in engine RPM slightly reduces the absolute cacophony of engine noise which has been present during the take off run at maximum RPM but the noise levels are still unbelievably high, even inside a modern flying helmet. As the speed reaches 140 knots, I start a climbing turn away from the airfield and then when I reach the cruising altitude I level off and set the power to maintain 150 knots. ➤

ONCE AIR TRAFFIC CONTROL HAS GIVEN TAKE OFF CLEARANCE, I LINE UP ON THE CENTRE OF THE RUNWAY, SLIGHTLY CANTED OFF FOR A CLEAR VIEW DOWN THE STRIP. I WON'T PUT THE AIRCRAFT STRAIGHT UNTIL I'M ABOUT TO ROLL. IT WOULDN'T DO TO RUN INTO SOMETHING UNSEEN OVER THE NOSE.

The rare sight of all seven fighters of the Battle of Britain Memorial Flight in the air together, seen at the 50th anniversary display at Duxford. **Julian Humphries**

Even with cruise power set the Hurricane cockpit is an extremely noisy place. The engine makes a tremendous racket and there is always a small gap between the windscreen and the canopy (which can be locked open but not shut) that creates considerable wind noise. I have the radio volume control turned up high in the air and I may still sometimes have difficulty hearing incoming radio calls, particularly if what is said is unexpected. I try to avoid flying through rain because of the potential for damage to the airframe, paintwork or the propeller but sometimes this is unavoidable and then, inevitably, I'll get wet inside the cockpit.

There is absolutely no heating or cooling system in the Hurricane and the cockpit can become either very hot or very cold depending on the ambient conditions outside. As I become accustomed to the cockpit environment again, I can't help wondering, as I have done on many occasions, how the wartime pilots coped with these problems on operational sorties. My discomfort at low altitudes and in temperate climes is a small price to pay for the pleasure of flying this wonderful machine; theirs would have been of a different order. While cruising, I do not relax for a moment, I am constantly monitoring the engine instruments for any

hint of an engine problem and I continually update my forced landing plans in the event that such a problem should occur.

Where is the nearest runway and which field is the best within gliding distance for a wheels-up forced landing? Every few minutes I check the fuel tank contents by turning the fuel gauge button to the tank I wish to interrogate and pressing it in. I am also keeping a check on the navigation. However, there are still some moments when I can snatch a few seconds just to look out through the Hurricane's latticed canopy at the wing tips, twist round to see the tail, imagine I am transported back in time and wonder how it might have been.

Prior to flying a display in the Hurricane I complete my pre-display checks including setting 2650 RPM with the prop pitch lever and +6in of boost with the throttle, setting the throttle friction tight. I also press in the cage button on the directional indicator (DI). I will have no heading reference during my display other than what I can see out of the 'window' and the DI would topple as soon as I exceeded 60 degrees of bank if it was not caged. The artificial horizon will also topple and become useless during my routine and the altimeter will be of limited value in indicating height because of pressure errors.

The only instruments I will be referring to during my display are the air speed indicator (ASI) and the engine performance gauges. I trim the aircraft – elevator and rudder – at display power settings and at a speed of 180 knots. From here on I'll be constantly moving the rudder pedals to maintain balanced flight against the changes in speed and the gyroscopic forces from the massive propeller disc.

LF363 under maintenance in the Battle of Britain Memorial Flight's immaculate hangar at RAF Coningsby. The incredible efforts of the engineers are why these vintage aircraft are such reliable performers at air shows throughout Europe. **Luigino Caliaro**

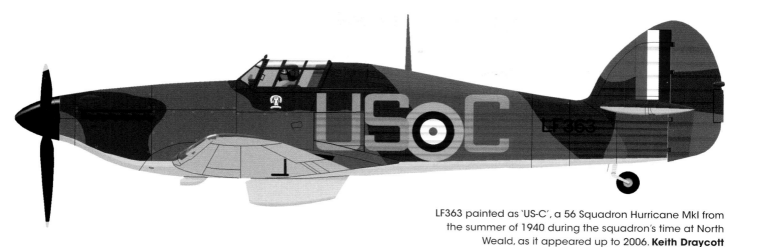

LF363 painted as 'US-C', a 56 Squadron Hurricane MkI from the summer of 1940 during the squadron's time at North Weald, as it appeared up to 2006. **Keith Draycott**

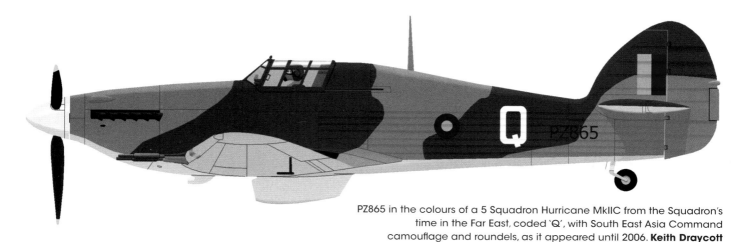

PZ865 in the colours of a 5 Squadron Hurricane MkIIC from the Squadron's time in the Far East, coded 'Q', with South East Asia Command camouflage and roundels, as it appeared until 2006. **Keith Draycott**

I run into the display in a shallow dive, building up speed. A final confirmation that I have display power set and I tighten the throttle friction fully and put both hands on the control column spade grip. As I dive down to level off at 100ft on my run in, the speed builds to 250 knots and the controls are becoming very heavy indeed. I will need both hands to roll and pull sharply into the initial break turn. I wonder again how on earth the wartime fighter pilots manoeuvred these aircraft at speeds considerably in excess of the 270 knots to which I am now limited.

Approaching the display datum, I roll the aircraft left with full stick and a large input of left rudder and pull into a level 3G break turn. This takes care, as in the interests of preserving airframe life the BBMF restricts the positive acceleration on the Hurricane to a maximum of 3G. The natural in-built longitudinal stability of the Hurricane, for which it is famed, means that an initial small movement of the control column to pitch the aircraft produces little, if any, effect – it doesn't want to move.

The pilot's natural reaction is to pull harder to increase the control column deflection from the neutral position; doing this will produce a rapid reaction from the aircraft so that it may pitch more than intended and the pilot then finds himself backing off the control inputs. I have only flown the two BBMF Hurricanes, but they both behave the same in this respect and I can only assume that all Hurricanes have similar reactions to control inputs for pitch.

Even with only 3G applied this aircraft can really turn; it is easy to see why its turn rate and small turn radius were strengths in combat. Rolling out of the turn, I pitch up to approximately 30 degrees nose up – judged by when my feet seem to be on the horizon – for a 'wingover'.

As I stop the roll at the top of the manoeuvre, I check the air speed, before pulling round the corner. If the speed reduces below 110 knots, the Hurricane can tend to 'tuck in' slightly, but if flown smoothly and gently with appropriate pitch-up angles the speed should not fall this low. On this 'wingover', started from high speed, I still have 140 knots over the top.

On the way 'down hill' I check the engine instruments – all is well – and then I concentrate on rolling out on the display line and levelling off at 100ft. I'm enjoying myself. As I roar down the line on the so called 'high speed' pass the aircraft is bumping in turbulence – it's really quite uncomfortable and it's a good job that I'm tightly strapped in. As the speed builds I have to feed on rudder to keep the nose straight. Sometimes, depending on the venue, I will fly this 'high speed' pass as a top-side pass, in a gentle, banked curve, using top rudder to hold the nose up. In a Spitfire this is really easy to do, but in a Hurricane, out-of-balance rudder input at higher speeds causes the aircraft's nose to dip markedly, which can be quite disconcerting at 100ft if you are not ready to catch it with some back stick. At these sort of heights, there is little margin for error. Pull up into another 'wingover' and on with the display sequence.

Karel Kuttelwascher's 'Night Reaper' markings on the nose of PZ865 at the 50th anniversary of the Battle of Britain Memorial Flight at Duxford. **Julian Humphries**

The final manoeuvre in the BBMF display routine is the so-called 'victory roll'. Such 'showboating' was, of course, strictly frowned upon during wartime, as there would be uncertainty over what battle damage aircraft might have suffered and whether a stray bullet may have partially severed a control cable, which might snap if subjected to unnecessary loads. No such worries for me though, as I position the aircraft on the display line at 100ft and ensure that I have at least 180 knots before pitching up, just before display centre, until it feels like my feet are on the horizon, wait until I'm passing 500ft and then roll left with full stick deflection and rudder to co-ordinate. ➤

The Battle of Britain Memorial Flight's unique display most often features a Spitfire, a Hurricane and the Lancaster bomber. **Julian Humphries**

LF 363 currently wears the colours of Hurricane MkI, P3878 'YB-W', the aircraft of Flying Officer Harold Bird-Wilson of 17 Squadron during the Battle of Britain. **Keith Draycott**

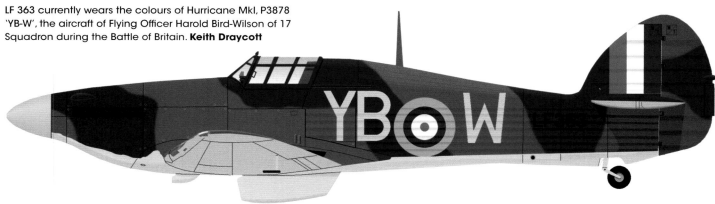

In 2006 PZ865 was painted to represent Hurricane MkIIC, BE581, 'Night Reaper', the aircraft flown by the Czech fighter ace Flight Lieutenant Karel Kuttelwascher during night intruder operations from Tangmere in 1942 with the RAF's legendary No 1(F) Squadron. **Keith Draycott**

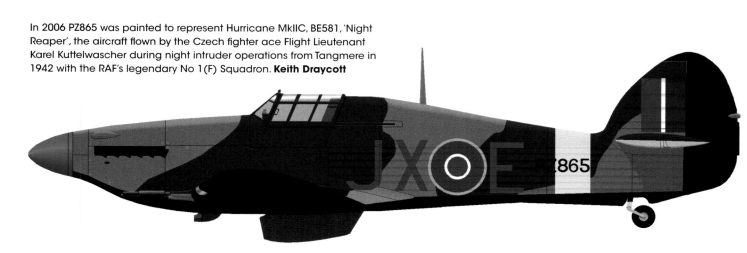

Four Spitfires of the Battle of Britain Memorial Flight are led by PZ865 over the top of the Flight's hangar at RAF Coningsby, Lincolnshire. **RAF Coningsby**

The roll rate in the Hurricane is quite slow, considerably slower than the Spitfire, and it takes several seconds to roll through 360 degrees. We don't use anything less than 1G on the aircraft, partly to conserve fatigue life and partly because negative G may cause the engine to cut. During a 1G roll, the nose will drop so it is important to have it high enough to start with. Rolling out, display complete and I'm suddenly aware that I'm breathing quite hard. That was actually quite physical. The engine oil and radiator temperatures have risen slightly and I reduce the RPM to let the engine cool down.

Now I have to concentrate on the circuit and landing. For a 'tail-dragger' the Hurricane is relatively forgiving of errors of judgement on landing because of its wide, strong undercarriage, although it will tend to bounce if the touchdown is misjudged. Any tail-wheel aircraft demands respect when landing, though, and today is complicated by a 10 knots crosswind on this runway.

These aircraft were really designed to land on grass airfields, more or less into wind, and are not ideally suited to modern airfields and hard runways. Mind you, I'd much rather be in a Hurricane having to land with a limited crosswind than in the far more skittish Spitfire. I level off downwind at 800ft, tight enough to the airfield to be able to glide to a suitable surface if the engine should quit, throttle back to just above idle to reduce speed and complete the pre-landing checks,

including putting the RPM lever fully forward and opening the canopy, which provides a welcome blast of fresh air.

When the speed is below 104 knots, I lower the undercarriage. I select the flap fully down as I tip into the final turn and correct the big nose-down pitch trim change with a large movement of back stick and lots of nose-up trim. I fly the final turn at 85 knots with about 30 degrees of bank, aiming to fly a continuous curved approach to roll wings level at about 200ft, enough time lined up straight-in on the approach to assess the effects of the crosswind. As the aircraft reaches the correct approach glide path, about four degrees, I apply a trickle of power to hold that runway aspect and then roll wings level for the final part of the approach. I gradually raise the nose, making sure that I am in trim, and let the speed reduce to 75 knots by about 20 to 30ft. On this straight part of the approach I am 'crabbing' in sideways with the nose pointing into the crosswind, if I pointed at my touchdown spot I would drift sideways.

One final check of the speed at 70 knots and I start the landing 'flare', gently raising the nose into the touchdown attitude and slowly closing the throttle. In the Hurricane, closing the throttle sharply causes the nose to drop and it takes more back stick than can normally be achieved in time to prevent the aircraft touching the ground early, with an inevitable bounce, so it is important to throttle back gently.

Just before I believe that I am going to touch down, I use the rudder to yaw the aircraft so that the wheels are lined up with the runway, keeping the wings level with aileron as I do it. Now I am looking directly ahead to ensure that I keep the aircraft pointing straight, but as the nose comes up in the flare it blocks my view and I have to use peripheral vision to monitor the runway edges either side of the nose. Hold it off, hold it off and with a squeak from the tyres and the gentlest of skips we are down. Stick right back now for maximum ground stability and concentrate on keeping straight with rudder, resisting the aircraft's tendency to swing into the crosswind. No time to relax yet; the ground roll after landing can be the most exciting part of the sortie in a strong crosswind. Now I'm down to taxiing speed, I can relax slightly and start weaving for a better view ahead.

When I have stopped in my designated parking place and carried out a final engine run-down at 1500 RPM, I check the magneto switches for 'live and dead', before throttling back to idle and pulling the slow running cut-out control to stop the engine. Suddenly it is very quiet, just the ticking of the hot exhausts as they cool down. Standing up on the seat, I discover that the back of my flying suit is wet with sweat; I hadn't noticed it while I was sharing another few precious moments of my life with an icon. ∎
Words: Clive Rowley

Hurricanes in the Mediterranean

Greece, East Africa, Malta and the Western Desert

Hurricanes began to be sent overseas as the war spread. Hurricane squadrons were sent to Greece, Malta and Iraq to defend against German and Italian attacks. The South African Air Force used the Hurricane in East Africa where they drove the Italian Air Force out of the area. These South African units then moved to Egypt to join the Western Desert Air Force, which boasted many Hurricane squadrons employed as fighters, fighter bombers and anti-tank aircraft. One of these, 6 Squadron, was to operate the Hurricane until 1946 and was the last RAF Hurricane squadron.

GREECE AND CRETE

The Italian invasion of Greece from Albania on October 28, 1940, prompted the deployment of several RAF units to assist the poorly equipped Greeks. The Blenheims and Gladiators sent to Greece were initially able to match the threat posed by the Regia Aeronautica, but the intervention of the Luftwaffe forced the redeployment of Hurricanes from the Western Desert.

At this time Hurricanes were desperately needed everywhere and only 33 and 208 Squadrons could be spared. 80 Squadron was gradually re-equipped with Hurricanes at Paramythia and claimed the first Hurricane victories over Greece on February 20, 1941. South African born Flight Lieutenant 'Pat' Pattle led an engagement against Italian Fiat

G.50 monoplane fighters claiming all four destroyed, 33 Squadron also claimed four enemy aircraft as destroyed on February 27.

Both squadrons were in action the next day when a large formation of Italian fighters and bombers were intercepted on the Albanian border and a huge running battle commenced. Pattle claimed six kills in two sorties, four of his victims were CR.42 fighters but it was an Australian, Flying Officer Cullen, who received an immediate DFC for his five victories. Pattle was promoted to the rank of squadron leader in March and was posted to 33 Squadron as its commanding officer.

When the Germans entered the arena, the balance was heavily tipped against the RAF. Instead of enjoying a marked superiority in fighter performance the Hurricanes were

outclassed as Messerschmitt Bf 109Es were encountered in increasing numbers. The German Army quickly swept aside the Greek defenders and the small British army contingent. As the ground forces yielded, the RAF was also obliged to withdraw and the surviving fighters were concentrated at Eleusis airfield to the south. April 20 was disastrous for the remaining Hurricane force. That afternoon the enemy launched a major attack on the harbour town of Piraeus. Only 15 Hurricanes were pitted against more than 100 bombers including Ju 88s and Do 17s with heavy fighter escort. Pattle shot down at least one Bf 110, but was himself attacked and killed by two others that sent his aircraft crashing into the sea. No parachute was observed and the RAF lost its highest scoring

Malta based Hawker Hurricane MkIs of 261 Squadron in late 1940. **Editor's collection**

261 Squadron Hurricanes scramble from Ta Kali to meet another raid on Malta. **Editor's collection**

IRAQ, SYRIA AND LEBANON

The large RAF base at Habbaniyah, Iraq, had been established several years before the war. In April 1941, the base found itself surrounded by the Iraqi army on the orders of a new regime sympathetic to the Axis powers. For a brief period the British were obliged to defend themselves, but after a few weeks the Iraqis withdrew having caused little damage.

Later, German aircraft began to appear over Northern Iraq operating from bases in Vichy France controlled Syria. To counter this, 94 Squadron, with four Hurricanes and two flights of Gladiators, was based at Habbaniyah from May 17, 1941. These were joined by additional Hurricanes including a Tac R reconnaissance machine. The threat to the eastern Mediterranean and Suez Canal from enemy aircraft based in Syria was a serious one, so an offensive was launched against the pro-Axis Vichy French Forces in Syria and Lebanon on June 8 by Arab, Australian, British, Czech, Free French and Indian Army units based in Iraq and Palestine. Hurricanes of 80 and 94 Squadrons fought alongside Curtiss Tomahawks and Fleet Air Arm Fairey Fulmars. Their opponents were Vichy French fighters, including the modern Dewoitine D.520. By July 12, the Vichy French Government in Syria requested a ceasefire, handing over the control to Free French forces. Vichy troops mostly returned to occupied France rather than join the Free French. ➤

ace to date, 33 Squadron losing a skillful and very popular leader.

The attrition caused by further enemy attacks whittled the RAF's strength down to just seven Hurricanes as 13 had been destroyed on the ground at Argos on April 23. As the pressure intensified, the Greek Government and those Allied forces that could make the journey decamped to neighbouring Crete. Resistance on mainland Greece came to an end shortly afterwards on April 30.

No one could have anticipated the rapid enemy progress and the defences on Crete were ill prepared to say the least. The remnant of 33 Squadron was based on the island while what little was left of 80 Squadron was retired to Egypt. The lack of spares and tools for the Hurricanes meant that by May 20 none were

left operational on the island. That day, the anticipated German invasion of Crete began with a massive but costly parachute assault on strategic points.

The fighting was intense and at times finely balanced as the locals and British troops held on, desperately inflicting many casualties on the invaders, but the Germans gradually expanded their hold on Maleme airfield and were able to fly in decisive numbers of fresh troops. Two attempts were made to re-establish a credible fighter defence on the island.

The first failed, and although the second saw the arrival of a depleted squadron of Hurricanes at Heraklion, these were destroyed on the ground within hours of landing. The few survivors of the campaign were withdrawn by sea under intense attack by the Luftwaffe to Egypt.

NO ONE COULD HAVE ANTICIPATED THE RAPID ENEMY PROGRESS AND THE DEFENCES ON CRETE WERE ILL PREPARED TO SAY THE LEAST.

MALTA

The beautiful island of Malta lies just 60 miles south of Sicily and sits astride shipping routes between Italy and North Africa. It formed a strategically important base of operations throughout the central Mediterranean for the Allies, so capturing the island was seen as vital by Italy.

When the Regia Aeronautica commenced air attacks on June 11, 1940, Malta was defended by a few Gloster Sea Gladiators and a handful of pilots. Despite their valiant efforts there was an urgent need for modern fighters to counter the Italian fighters and bombers appearing over the island.

Hurricanes had been staging through Malta en-route for Egypt since the beginning of the month and five were retained to bolster the venerable biplanes of the Hal Far Fighter Flight. On July 3, 1940, Pilot Officer Waters made the first Hurricane kill over Malta when he shot down an Italian tri-motor SM.79 bomber.

With the fall of France new supply routes had to be instigated to bring fresh aircraft

The Malta Night Fighter Unit was based at Ta Kali. **Editor's collection**

Squadron Leader Marmaduke Thomas St John 'Pat' Pattle DFC & Bar (July 3, 1914 – April 20, 1941) was born in South Africa. Pattle is arguably the highest scoring British and Commonwealth pilot of World War II. He has been unofficially credited with about 50 victories. **Editor's collection**

and pilots to Malta and the RAF in North Africa. Twelve Hurricanes were embarked on HMS Argus and successfully launched on August 2, 1940, some 360 miles west of the island. This was at the extreme range of the Hurricane but despite this all the aircraft reached Malta.

The mission was code named 'Operation Hurry'; whether that was in honour of the aircraft type or their urgent need, it seems a most appropriate title. RAF ground personnel to service the new arrivals could only be brought in by Sunderland flying boat or in converted submarines under the cover of darkness. The next resupply mission, Operation White, again aboard HMS Argus, took place in November but was an unmitigated disaster.

Fearing enemy surface units were in the vicinity, the aircraft were launched at the very edge of their endurance. Of the 14 aircraft despatched, only four of the 12 Hurricanes arrived. Only one of the pilots was rescued from the sea, which was a double blow as many of the missing were experienced fighter pilots whose skills would have been of incalculable value. By the end of the year there were 14 Hurricanes on the island but not all were airworthy through a chronic lack of spares.

The New Year brought grave news for the defenders when Luftwaffe units began to arrive in Sicily as Germany lost faith in its ally's ability to extinguish this troublesome pinprick of resistance. German aircraft made their first attack on January 10, 1941, when they dive bombed the carrier HMS Illustrious out at sea. The carrier was so seriously damaged that it had to slip into Malta's famous Grand Harbour to effect emergency repairs.

Six days later, Illustrious was still tethered to the dock when the whole port came under heavy attack from German Ju 87s and Ju 88s. The defenders put up a fierce resistance and five bombers were claimed as destroyed for no loss. Further costly raids were mounted over the following days, but Illustrious, now patched up, limped out of port and was eventually refitted in America.

In the face of such determined defence the German bombers switched to night operations. Even so, Hurricanes in close co-operation with the island's searchlight crews achieved several successes. Night activity was but a brief interlude though, and the fortunes of the defenders took a dramatic turn for the worse on February 12, 1941, when the Bf 109Es of JG 26 arrived over the island. In their first action they shot down three Hurricanes as they climbed to intercept a formation of Ju 88s.

Further reinforcements arrived from Egypt in the form of 274 Squadron, at a time when very few of the island's Hurricanes were serviceable, but another five aircraft and all of their pilots were lost on March 3. On April 3, 12 Hurricane MkIIs took off from HMS Ark Royal and all but one, which crash landed, arrived safely in the company of the customary Blackburn Skua lead aircraft.

Three Hurricanes were lost on April 11, including two of the new arrivals, all victims of JG 26. Under the code name 'Operation Dunlop' HMS Ark Royal returned on April 27 and delivered 24 Hurricanes. These new machines were a mix of MkIIA and 12 gun MkIIBs. After some confusion, 'Operation Splice' delivered three fresh Hurricane Squadrons, 213, 229 and 249, on May 21, from the decks of two fleet carriers.

An 80 Squadron Hurricane and crews at Eleusis airfield. **John Vane**

It was intended that they should merely use Malta as a staging post for their onward journey to Egypt, but 249 Squadron was ordered to remain in place of the hard pressed 261 Squadron. 249 Squadron claimed the 1000th enemy aircraft destroyed since the commencement of hostilities a few days after becoming operational.

Meanwhile German units were beginning to disengage from the Mediterranean theatre to participate in 'Operation Barbarossa', the ill fated invasion of Russia. JG 26 departed Sicily for North Africa and this shifted the balance once more. With the departure of the Luftwaffe the situation improved as more convoys arrived relatively unscathed and increasing numbers of offensive aircraft arrived.

Air strikes were made against enemy air bases in Sicily and against Axis convoys to Rommel's forces in North Africa. Combat over Malta by day was mainly between fighters as Italian bombers were relegated to night sorties. To counter the threat at night, several Hurricanes were painted all black and were formed into the Malta Night Fighter Unit (MNFU), which operated with some notable success and was later renamed 1435 Flight. On November 12, 1941, 'Operation Perpetual' delivered the Hurricanes of 242 and 605 Squadrons from the carriers HMS Ark Royal and HMS Argus. The first German aircraft of Fliegerkorps II appeared in mid December, bringing with them two new threats in the form of night fighter Ju 88Cs and the latest Messerschmitt Bf 109F, which was capable of 388mph (624kmh).

The Germans mounted increasingly effective raids, which caused severe damage to the three main airfields and destroyed or damaged many parked aircraft including most of the Wellington bombers at Luqa. In January 1942 there were about 80 Hurricanes defending the island facing over 600 Axis aircraft based on the much larger island of Sicily.

Despite the return of the Luftwaffe, offensive operations continued and heavy damage was inflicted on the enemy airfields by light and medium bombers from Luqa airfield. By this time Malta had endured over 1000 air raids. There was an urgent request for Spitfires to be based on Malta, but none were forthcoming for some time. On January 25, five Hurricanes were shot down intercepting yet another raid.

By the end of March fewer than 10 Hurricanes were serviceable, but relief came in the form of Spitfires flown from HMS Eagle during 'Operation Spotter'. Hurricanes continued to be delivered to the island but these were used mainly in the fighter bomber role or were issued to units conducting air-sea rescue patrols.

The Hurricane's part in the successful defence of the strategically vital island of Malta can never be overstated. In an action remarkably similar to, but on a smaller scale than the Battle of Britain, they bore the brunt of the fighting at a crucial time. Had Malta been captured, the Allies would not have been able to disrupt enemy shipping to Rommel's forces in the desert so effectively, nor would they have been able to use the island as a base for the successful invasion of the Italian mainland.

EAST AFRICA

Beginning on January 18, 1941, a twin pronged attack was launched by Allied forces in the Sudan and Kenya to eject the Italians from Eritrea and Somaliland to protect the Suez canal and prevent interference with shipping in the Red Sea by land based enemy forces. In early 1941, 1 Squadron SAAF under the command of Major L Wilot was based at Azzoza in Sudan, equipped with a mix of Hurricane MkIs and Gladiator MkIIs.

As the offensive advanced, 1 Squadron occupied the former Regia Aeronautica bases in Eritrea. In the south, 3 Squadron SAAF supported the advance into Somaliland from Kenya. On April 3, Captain J Frost shot down a Fiat CR.32 and three Caproni bombers. All this was witnessed by cheering ground troops who rounded up the Italian airmen as they landed by parachute.

The pace of the fighting quickened after the fall of Mogadishu and the Hurricanes were now operating at longer ranges. On March 13, Lieutenant Venter made a forced landing in the desert as a result of fuel starvation. He was rescued by his fellow squadron member Lieutenant Theron, who landed beside his forlorn Hurricane.

Between them they siphoned sufficient fuel into Venter's aircraft to return to their base, and as if they had not had enough adventure for the day, they arrived during an air raid and shot down a CR.42 each.

To keep up with the rapidly advancing ground troops, the SAAF occupied former enemy bases closer to Addis Ababa, which was captured on April 5, 1941. Enemy aircraft were encountered less frequently after this date but Captain Frost claimed his eighth victory when he shot down an SM.79 on April 30.

Later the SAAF units were moved to Egypt and played an important part in the desert campaign. South African pilots served with both their own air force and the RAF with distinction throughout the war, and as a memorial Hurricane MkIIC LD619 is displayed at the South African Museum of Military History in Johannesburg. ➤

Hawker Hurricanes of 185 Squadron at Hal Far, Malta, in September 1941. **Editor's collection**

Stone and sandbag revetments were built around Malta airfields to protect the aircraft from the many raids on the island. **Editor's collection**

WESTERN DESERT

Mussolini exploited Britain's perceived vulnerability in North Africa and declared war on Egypt on June 10, 1940. With Italy's entry into the war, the supply of British forces in Egypt required new routes to be established from bases in Western Africa.

From September 1940, Hurricanes were delivered in crates to Takoradi on the Gold Coast where they were reassembled and then flown via numerous refueling stages to Egypt. The long cross country flights took seven days and were accompanied by twin engined aircraft, most frequently Blenhiem MkIVs also destined for the Desert Air Force.

Now that Hurricanes were being flown over extreme distances with the aid of additional fuel in under wing tanks, it was necessary to increase the size of the engine oil tank, a modification introduced at the factories to all subsequent aircraft. The British fighter force in the Mediterranean was gradually built up as carrier deliveries of 104 Hurricanes and 12 Fulmars were made in three consignments between September and January 1941.

By December 1940 there were sufficient Hurricanes to convert 208 Squadron, whose aircraft were modified to carry a forward facing camera in the wing and used for low level tactical reconnaissance. Hurricanes so modified were referred to as Tac R MkIs. Later aircraft were more extensively modified and had a pair of F.24 cameras installed behind the pilot's seat. A fairing under the rear fuselage behind the radiator accommodated the lenses and an army radio was fitted.

In early 1941, the British Army had repulsed the Italians and was advancing west into Libya from Egypt forcing a rapid enemy withdrawal. The pilots of 33, 73 and 274 Squadrons were also demonstrating the superiority of their Hurricanes over the Regia Aeronautica CR.42s. The Germans then took a hand in the campaign and the leading echelons of General Erwin Rommel's Africa Korps began to arrive in Libya in February 1941.

The first German aircraft to be shot down over the Western Desert, a Ju 88, was claimed by Flying Officer J Saunders of 3 Squadron on

A formation of 94 Squadron Hurricane MkIIBs and MkIICs. **Editor's collection**

February 15, 1941. In April the land battle began to swing towards the Axis. As the fighting for the important coastal town of Tobruk turned into a siege, the first German single engined fighters began to appear and the British fighters had a tougher time.

In March, two further Hurricane Squadrons, 231 and 229, arrived from England and they were joined by 1 Squadron SAAF from its previous deployment in Sudan. Operation Battleaxe was drawn up to relieve Tobruk in June. While supporting the assault, 1 and 73 Squadron lost several pilots including some of their most experienced men. The air fighting was fiercely contested now that the Bf 109Es had bolstered the enemy's fighter strength, but the ground fighting had come to a standstill.

Further east, 30 Squadron commenced operations in the area of the Suez Canal. Their all black Hurricanes engaged several enemy aircraft and deterred night attacks on the strategically vital supply route between the Mediterranean and the Indian Ocean. As

the year progressed the nine Hurricane squadrons in the desert faced new and more deadly fighters in the form of JG 53's Bf 109F-4s, which arrived from Sicily in August. Among the German pilots was one of their most successful aces, Hans-Joachim Marseille, who would later claim 158 victories, 17 of which were in a single day.

The Allied forces were on the retreat by May 1942 and were obliged to retire east towards the previously inconspicuous village of El Alamein. The Hurricane MkII had now replaced the earlier versions but these were still no match for the Bf 109F and Spitfires were desperately needed to redress the balance. In June, Tobruk finally succumbed and Rommel continued his offensive eastwards.

The Axis forces eventually ran out of steam on the ground and the pause allowed Montgomery, who now commanded the 8th Army, to deliver the first decisive defeat to the German forces. The battle of El Alamein began with a tremendous artillery bombardment on October 23 and Hurricanes of 213 Squadron were in action early the next day against Ju 87s. 73 Squadron was employed on night intruder missions attacking enemy transport and deterring Luftwaffe activity.

Rommel was forced to withdraw, starved of supplies. From this time Hurricanes were increasingly employed as ground attack aircraft as tropicalised Spitfire Vs began to be delivered to handle the enemy fighters. A major contribution to the success of the Desert Air Force was the numbers of recovered aircraft put back into service by the repair and salvage units. They retrieved more than 1000 wrecked aircraft from the desert, of which over three quarters were returned to service while the remainder provided a useful source of spare parts.

Using a fleet of Queen Mary low loaders and vehicle mounted cranes, the recovery crews lived a semi-nomadic lifestyle driving hundreds of miles to recover Hurricanes and other types from the desolate sand dunes.

30 Squadron operated as night fighters in Egypt, protecting the Suez Canal. **Editor's collection**

The Hurricane again proved its worth as it was easily dismantled and repaired in makeshift conditions.

The difficulties in bringing aircraft to Egypt made these measures not only prudent but essential. By June 1942, there were 22 Hurricane squadrons in the Western Desert, making it the most significant Allied type in the region.

The Hurricane MkIIC's 20mm cannon were adequate for dealing with soft skinned transport targets but lacked the punch to destroy the latest German tanks. Experiments had commenced as early as 1939 and both Rolls-Royce and Vickers had been investigating the potential of a lightweight quick firing 40mm weapon.

The Air Ministry approached Hawker and suggested that the Hurricane MkII might be able to carry a pair of the Vickers 'S' guns. The detailed design work began in May and by September 18, 1941, Hurricane Z2326 was delivered to Boscombe Down for trials with a pair of the new guns. The cannon were suspended under the outer wing panels and the large 15 round magazine occupied the gun bay.

The outboard machine guns in each bay were retained solely for aiming purposes. The machine guns were loaded with tracer ammunition and were mounted to converge at 500 yards to save valuable main armament rounds as the pilot took a bead on the target. An aerodynamic fairing enclosed the guns and the barrels were mounted with a two degree angle of depression.

The heavy guns could not be jettisoned in flight and had a considerable detrimental effect on the aircraft's performance and handling. 6 Squadron was the first unit to convert to the MkIID, which was almost exclusively issued to squadrons in the Far and Middle East. The squadron's pilots spent several weeks adjusting to their role, shooting up abandoned tank hulks for practice.

Their operational debut came on June 6, 1942, supporting the Free French Brigade at Bir Hakim. The squadron quickly earned the nickname the 'Flying Can Openers' for its exploits against enemy tanks and adopted a cartoon of the winged kitchen utensil as its unofficial emblem.

The Allied invasion of Algeria, code named Operation Torch, spelt the beginning of the end of the Axis presence in North Africa. The landings commenced on November 8, 1942, and were covered by Canadian built Sea Hurricane MkXIIs from 800, 802, 804, 883 and 891 Naval Air Squadrons (NAS). They escorted the first raids by Fairey Albacores on the Vichy French airfields at Oran and shot down several Vichy French fighters, but could not prevent the loss of many of the Albacores.

The landings were successful and Allied aircraft were soon operating from the former French airfields. The German and Italian forces in North Africa initiated a major build up to counter the Allied forces over the winter of 1942, but to no avail. By May 13, 1943, after heavy fighting on two fronts, the

The Historic Aircraft Company's Hurricane MkXII is painted to represent a Malta based MkIIB of 126 Squadron. This aircraft returned to the island in September 2005 as part of the 'Merlins over Malta' project. **Julian Humphries**

Pilots of 30 Squadron brief for that night's sorties over Egypt. Aircrew clothing in the desert was a matter of practicality over everything. **Editor's collection**

South African aircrew from 1 Squadron SAAF. 1 and 7 Squadron SAAF operated Hurricanes in the Western Desert. **Editor's collection**

The Lone Star Flight Museum's Hurricane MkXII is painted to represent a 30 Squadron aircraft in desert markings. **Luigino Caliaro**

Axis forces surrendered and the war in Africa was effectively over.

By now, the Hurricane was being steadily withdrawn from service with the Desert Air Force, replaced by more capable types as it prepared for the invasion of Italy, but a number of units were to continue to operate it in the Mediterranean right up to the end of the war. 6 Squadron was active with a new weapon, rocket projectiles, after the invasion of Sicily in July 1943.

The squadron had become a highly specialised ground attack unit and established many of the principles and tactics for the operational use of the new weapon. 6 Squadron achieved exceptional results against enemy shipping around the Italian and Albanian coastline between May and June 1944 when they sank 22 enemy vessels of various types.

In October 1944 it was joined by a second Hurricane Squadron, 351, which was made up of Yugoslavians. This unit was later transferred with its aircraft to the Yugoslav Air Force after the war in Europe ended. The last operations by Hurricanes will be covered later in this magazine.■

Words: Tim Callaway and Julian Humphries

Versatility
in action

India, Burma and the Far East

The Hawker Hurricane was to serve with great distinction in the South East Asia Command or SEAC. Beginning with near disasters in Singapore, Sumatra and Java, defending Ceylon and then playing vital roles in the offensives and counter offensives that were to see-saw back and forth across Burma for over three years. All of these were to test the tough and reliable Hurricane to the limits and to see it used in roles Hawker never foresaw.

Following their audacious attack on the American fleet at Pearl Harbor on December 7, 1941, the Japanese commenced a series of strikes through Malaysia towards Singapore. The Japanese Army moved more rapidly than anyone could have anticipated, supported as they were by strong naval and air forces. Facing them were a few RAF squadrons equipped with several obsolete types, including the woeful Brewster Buffalo fighter and elderly Vickers biplane torpedo bombers.

Malaya and Singapore were already under attack when reinforcements arrived from the UK. The first 51 Hurricane Mk.IIBs were shipped in crates, reaching Singapore on January 3, 1942. The aircraft were accompanied by 24 pilots and were intended to bolster the Dutch, New Zealand, Australian and British fighter forces already in the region. The crated aircraft were hastily reassembled at Seletar airfield by engineers from 151 Maintenance Unit who, despite their unfamiliarity with the type, had 21 of the Hurricanes ready to fly in just three days, a heroic effort.

By January 17, sufficient aircraft were tested and armed to form a single squadron. Personnel from four different units, 17, 135, 136 and 232 Squadrons, were among the 24 pilots who had arrived with the convoy, so they were provisionally grouped together as 232 Squadron under Squadron Leader Landels. Nine more of the Hurricanes were issued to 488 (New Zealand) Squadron at Kallang airfield to partially replace its Brewster Buffalos, the two squadrons forming the basis of 226 Group on January 18. Two days later, 232 Squadron was in action against a heavy raid comprising more than 100 enemy aircraft.

Leading the Hurricanes into action, Landels was quickly shot down by the nimble Nakajima Ki-43 Hayabusa 'Oscar' escort fighters, who also shot down two more Hurricanes as the battle developed. Sergeant J Parker claimed the first Japanese aircraft to fall to the guns of a Hurricane when he dispatched an Oscar, the remainder of the squadron made attacks against the force of Mitsubishi Ki-21 'Sally' bombers, claiming a total of eight bombers and three fighters destroyed. The next senior pilot, Squadron Leader Richard 'Rickey' E P Brooker, took over command of the unit.

Vickers Vildebeests of 100 Squadron at Singapore in 1942. **Editor's collection**

Squadron Leader Richard Brooker force landed his Hurricane, BE208, on February 8, 1942, and is seen here surveying the damage on the East Coast Road in Singapore. **Arthur G Donahue DFC**

JAPANESE FIGHTERS

The quality and performance of the enemy aircraft came as a shock to the Allies who had previously been dismissive of both Japanese technology and pilots. The excellent Oscar was to shoot down more Allied aircraft than any other Japanese fighter type during the war. Its manoeuvrability was legendary and the type achieved air superiority for the Japanese over Malaya, Burma, Java and New Guinea in the early stages of the war in the Far East.

On January 21, the Hurricanes met a new and deadly foe, the superb Mitsubishi A6M Zero. The Japanese carrier Ryujo with her aircraft complement of 22 Mitsubishi

A6M Zero fighters and 16 Aichi D3A 'Val' dive bombers supported both the Malayan campaign and operations in Sumatra and Java later in February.

On January 26, having driven down the Malay peninsula, the Japanese began landings at Endau, only 250 miles (402km) from Singapore. Twelve Vickers Vildebeests from 36 and 100 Squadrons were escorted by Hurricanes and Buffalos, but five of the biplane bombers were shot down. 36 Squadron tried again later that day with eight more Vildebeests and three Fairey Albacores, again with fighter escort. This time six of the Vildebeests and two Albacores were lost. Reinforcements were en-route aboard HMS Indomitable in the

shape of the 242, 258 and 605 Squadrons, all three units equipped with Hurricane Mk.IIAs. By the time they arrived in the area Singapore was under intense air attacks day and night, so the convoy was diverted. The 48 Hurricanes were flown off the carrier to secret airfields at Pangkalan Benteng, code named 'P1' and Praboemoelih, 'P2', near Palembang in Sumatra on January 27.

258 Squadron deployed to RAF Tengah in the east of Singapore, but lost four aircraft in this brief excursion as airfields at Tengah, Seletar and Sembawang were in range of Japanese artillery at Johor Bahru. Thirty of the precious new Hurricanes were destroyed on the ground in Sumatra by Japanese air raids on February 7. After the Japanese landings on Singapore on the night of February 8, fierce fighting took place over the beachheads. Ten Hurricanes from Kallang airfield, the only operational strip left in Singapore, met a force of 84 Japanese aircraft over Sarimbun Beach, shooting down six of them for the loss of one Hurricane.

Intense air fighting continued throughout the day, Hurricanes landing at Kallang, refueling, rearming and taking off again to rejoin the battle they had just left. By the evening it was clear that operations could not continue, so the remaining eight Hurricanes were sent to Palembang. It was intended that Kallang was to be used as a forward operating base, but by February 10 it had become unusable, cratered by Japanese air attacks. No more Allied aircraft were to appear above the island, and on February 15, 1942, the ground forces in Singapore surrendered. ➤

Squadron Leader R F T Doe with personnel of 10 Squadron Indian Air Force and one of their Hurricane Mk.IICs. **Sqn Ldr R F T Doe**

SUMATRA AND JAVA

This was not the end for the Hurricane units in the area, rather it was the beginning of a nightmare. Palembang came under repeated air attack, with Japanese paratroops landing around P1 airfield and the vital oil refinery complex at Pladjoe on February 13. A Japanese landing force approached Sumatra on February 14 and was attacked by Lockheed Hudsons and Bristol Blenheim Mk.Is, sinking one of the transport ships.

Hurricanes strafed the Japanese landing craft on February 15 as they moved up the Musi, Salang and Telang rivers to link up with the paratroops, but that afternoon all Allied aircraft were ordered to move to Java, where another Japanese attack was expected. The last left Sumatra on February 16, by which time only 18 of the 99 Hurricanes sent to the area survived.

In the early hours of March 1, the Japanese landed at three points on the Javan coast, Bantam Bay and Eretan Wetan to the west and Kragan to the east. Both invasion forces had been involved in naval battles prior to the landings, the western force fighting the Battle of Sunda Strait, the eastern convoy the Battle of the Java Sea, both of which actions had inflicted heavy casualties on the Allied navies.

The surviving Hurricanes and personnel had been formed into 242 and 605 Squadrons and were based at Tjililitan and Tasikmalaya airfields in Java. On March 1, 12 of the Hurricanes were joined by nine Brewster Buffalos and three Glenn Martin 166 bombers of the Royal Netherlands East Indies Army Air Force (Militaire Luchtvaart van het Koninklijk Nederlands-Indisch Leger or ML-KNIL) in launching attacks against the western Japanese invasion forces at Eretan Wetan.

Despite this and other attacks by a wide variety of American, Australian, British, Dutch and New Zealand aircraft, the Japanese forces advanced under their umbrella of superior air support. On March 8, the Dutch commander surrendered his forces in Java. Some of the pilots and ground crews were evacuated to Australia, but the remaining Hurricanes were destroyed on the ground to prevent their capture. One Hurricane, V7476, did survive and was transferred to the Royal Australian Air Force, becoming the only Hurricane to be used in Australia.

Typical conditions outside the monsoon season as a Hurricane almost disappears in the dry dust of a Burma airfield. **Editor's collection**

BURMA AND CEYLON

As the Japanese extended their reach across southern Asia, fighter aircraft were desperately needed everywhere at once so it seemed. Hurricanes were needed in the Western Desert and on Malta, on night intruder missions over Europe, for supply to Russia and on board aircraft carriers as Sea Hurricanes, protecting the vital convoys. Again, a function of its simple construction, production of the aircraft always kept pace with demand, and so it was that the first Hurricanes arrived at Rangoon, now Yangon, in Burma on January 23, 1942. With the Japanese advances in China, Malaya, the East Indies and the Pacific, it was inevitable that their attention would turn westward towards the considerable resources of Burma and India. While the might of the Japanese forces was focused on its advances through Singapore and Java, it gave the newly arrived aircrews and engineers in Burma a chance to train and prepare.

Rangoon based 267 Wing comprised of the reformed 17, 135 and 136 Squadrons led by a number of veteran British pilots with an unusual mix of British, American and Australian personnel. Shortly after their arrival, the officer commanding 135 Squadron, Squadron Leader Frank Carey was promoted to lead the wing. Carey was to end the war the second highest scoring Hurricane ace with 28 confirmed victories.

Offensive patrols over Thailand and the Malay peninsula were undertaken in early February, the wing's Hurricanes meeting Oscars over Bangkok. After the fall of Singapore, the Japanese turned their attention north and west, beginning a concerted effort against the Allied forces in Burma on February 21. Again, Japanese ground forces moved with unexpected speed, reaching Rangoon and capturing the city on March 8. The wing was divided between Magwe and Akyab airfields, which were hit simultaneously by heavy air raids, eliminating any kind of organised air defence at a single stroke.

Only a few victories were claimed by the Hurricanes as the enemy eventually mopped up the last resistance in May, forcing the Allies to retreat back into India. The monsoon season came, and the few roads and tracks through the mountainous terrain of the Indian/Burmese frontier became impassable, halting the Japanese advance at the Chindwin River and giving the Allies a much needed pause.

A Tac R modified Hurricane Mk.IIC of 3 PRU is rearmed and has the underfuselage camera replaced in Burma, 1944. **Editor's collection**

A Hurricane PR.IIB, BM969, from 3 Photographic Reconnaissance Unit in March 1943. **Editor's collection**

The ease of access to the vital systems of the Hurricane made it popular with ground crews, particularly in the heat and discomfort of the Burmese theatre. Aside from the conditions, aircraft made excellent shelters for a variety of venomous snakes and insects, bringing yet another level of danger to operations in SEAC. **Editor's collection**

A Hurricane IIC of 42 Squadron attacks a bridge in Burma in mid 1944. The bombs can just be seen leaving the underwing pylons. **Editor's collection**

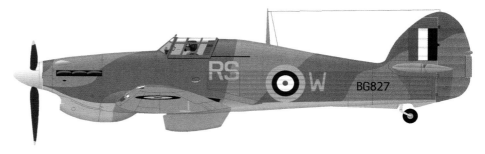

A Hawker Hurricane Mk.IIB in 30 Squadron markings at the time of the Battle of Ceylon. This aircraft was flown by Pilot Officer Jimmy Whalen. **Keith Draycott**

THE DARKEST HOUR

Radio intercepts during the Java campaign had suggested that Ceylon, the former name of Sri Lanka, may be the next subject of Japanese attack. A major sortie by the Imperial Japanese Navy into the Indian Ocean was expected in support of the Japanese advances in Burma and to drive the Royal Navy from the area, the hope being to catch and destroy the British carrier forces.

To bolster the island's defences, 30 Squadron was shipped to the island aboard HMS Indomitable from Port Tewfik on the Suez Canal. The squadron's first 20 Hurricanes flew off the carrier to Ratmalana airfield, near Colombo, on March 5, 1942, still in their desert camouflage. Four days earlier, 258 Squadron had been reformed around G Squadron and several surviving members of the Singapore disaster, and was based at Colombo racecourse. By the end of the month there were 36 Hurricanes with some very experienced pilots on strength, as well as 24 additional Hurricanes with 30 Squadron.

The Japanese navy launched its attack from a carrier task force in the early hours of April 5, which coincidentally was Easter Sunday, taking the defenders by surprise, because for no explicable reason, the radar stations protecting Colombo were unmanned, despite a warning of the Japanese fleet being received from a 413 Squadron Catalina the previous evening.

The Japanese commander Admiral Nagumo had hoped to catch the British Eastern Fleet at anchor but it had been withdrawn to the Maldives so there was no repeat of Pearl Harbor. When the Hurricanes were belatedly scrambled to intercept the dive bombers almost overhead they were immediately set upon by Zeros diving from higher altitude. The superiority of the Japanese fighter at low level

was brutally demonstrated as they shot down eight Hurricanes for the loss of four Vals and a Zero. The Japanese sank several ships in Colombo harbour as well as attacking the airfield at Ratmalana. A second attack was made against two cruisers they discovered out at sea, resulting in the sinking of HMS Cornwall and HMS Dorsetshire.

A second attack was made four days later on April 9 against the harbour at Trincomalee. Eight Hurricanes and a Fleet Air Arm Fairey Fulmar were lost, along with three warships, including the aircraft carrier HMS Hermes. Several Hurricane pilots were successful against the Japanese fighters, which were lightly built and lacked the self sealing fuel tanks and armour plate then standard in Western fighters.

In fact, it was not unusual for Japanese aircraft to literally break up under the weight of fire of the Hurricane's guns. When the enemy fleet withdrew it was claimed as a victory, however, the Japanese did not really have the resources to mount an invasion at that time, stretched as they were by other territorial gains.

The 'Doolittle Raid' of April 18 on the Japanese homeland caused the First Carrier Striking Force to be recalled to close the 'Pacific Frontier' and protect Japan from the US Navy. However, had Ceylon fallen it would have been a strategic disaster for the Allies as the enemy would have had almost total control of the Indian Ocean and been able to threaten mainland India and the routes to Australia. In his history of the war, Sir Winston Churchill noted: "The most dangerous moment of the war, and the one which caused me the greatest alarm, was when the Japanese fleet was heading for Ceylon and the naval base there.

"The capture of Ceylon, the consequent control of the Indian Ocean, and the possibility at the same time of a German conquest of Egypt would have closed the ring and the future would have been black."

By mid 1942 the situation had improved considerably with 50 new Hurricane Mk.IIs being delivered to the island. This made a force of 10 fully equipped squadrons operating a mix of eight and 12 gun Hurricane IIAs and Bs. Later that year the 44 gallon (200 litre) drop tanks became available and were widely used to extend the Hurricane's relatively short range in patrols from the island. ➤

INDIA AND BURMA – VERSATILITY WITH WINGS

The British and Indian Armies conducted the Arakan campaign between December 1942 and March 1943, advancing into Burma to capture the strategically important island of Akyab. This was repulsed by the Japanese, who drove the Allies back towards the Indian border until stopped again by the coming of the monsoons in May. North India was now under threat and again it was the Hurricane squadrons that provided the only effective fighter defences. By now most of the other obsolete types had been withdrawn or had been destroyed in action. This was to be the last use of the Hurricane exclusively as an air defence fighter.

The variety of roles for the versatile Hurricane in the Far East theatre grew along with their numbers. By June 1943 a total of 23 Hurricane squadrons were operational in the region, the majority of which were now cannon armed Mk.IICs. These frequently operated with long range fuel tanks or underwing pylons to carry ground attack munitions, a role the tough aircraft excelled in.

A number of aircraft were modified to carry cameras for low level reconnaissance and an extra radio to liaise with ground forces. Known as 'tactical reconnaissance' or 'Tac R' Hurricanes, these aircraft often had two machine guns or cannon removed to compensate for the extra weight of the equipment. Aside from reconnaissance, the Tac Rs would often act as forward air controllers for ground forces, directing other aircraft onto targets.

The 12 Hurricane IIC (NF)s modified to carry the AI Mk.VI radar, were allocated to 176 Squadron to counter Japanese night raids. Lastly, the latest version of the Hurricane Mk.II family made its debut in the region in June 1943, when the Mk.IID with its pair of 40mm cannon entered service with 11 Squadron at Baigachi, near Calcutta.

Conditions could be primitive in Burma. The ground crews and armourers did everything by hand, including loading bombs. **Editor's collection**

The demand for Hurricanes in this theatre now rivaled the needs of the Russians. Soon the first of eight squadrons of the Indian Air Force (IAF) were equipped with Hurricanes, commencing with 1 Squadron IAF in August, followed by 2 Squadron IAF in September and 6 Squadron IAF on December 1, 1942. By 1943 the war was beginning to turn against the all conquering Japanese as the US Navy quickly recovered from the early losses and began to inflict defeats in the Pacific.

By October 1943, Allied troops, mainly British, Chinese, Indian and Australian, had begun to return to Burma in strength and several Hurricane squadrons adopted the role of tactical reconnaissance in support of the advancing Armies. The ground attack sorties necessitated the introduction of new tactics, some already refined by the Desert Air Force in North Africa. The 'cab rank' system involved pairs of aircraft patrolling just behind friendly lines to be summoned by radio at the request of forward observers.

This cut down the amount of time between the call for assistance and the arrival of the fighter bombers to a matter of minutes and was greatly appreciated by the infantry. Another tactic was nicknamed 'Earthquake' and preceded a local ground offensive. The area would be thoroughly worked over with bombs and cannon fire prior to the advance, then, at 'H' hour, the Hurricanes returned to keep the enemy's heads down.

In this fashion the Hurricanes delivered the service traditionally supplied by the Royal Artillery, which was somewhat disadvantaged by the difficult terrain and long supply chain in the area. Several major advances were made into Burma, from China in the north and towards Arakan from the west in 1944, before the monsoons came again.

In March 1944, the Japanese attempted to restore their fortunes on the border between India and Burma and launched a huge ground offensive of their own, aimed at severing the Allied supply lines and the air transport route across the Himalayas. The

The 60lb rocket projectiles were an effective ground attack weapon, giving each Hurricane the firepower of a broadside from a light cruiser. They were also easier for the ground crews to handle than bombs. **Editor's collection**

14th Army's IV Corps, supported by five Indian Divisions, called on the close air support provided by the Hurricanes of 1 (IAF), 11, 28, 34, 42 and 113 Squadrons to stem the tide of the Japanese assault.

By April the Japanese had practically surrounded the important towns Imphal and Kohima and the skills of the fighter pilots was severely tested as they made repeated attacks at low level with cannon, bombs and rockets. On most of these missions, the Hurricanes carried either two 250lb (113.4kg) bombs or eight 60lb (27.2kg) rocket projectiles. Imphal was completely cut off and could only be resupplied by air until the enemy was forced to withdraw.

The Japanese troops were at the limit of their supply lines, suffering from malnutrition and disease as well as being almost continually harried by Hurricane ground attack aircraft. The Allied armies concentrated their reinforcements in counter attacks which broke the siege on June 22 and the Japanese were forced to withdraw. The Hurricane squadrons were hard pressed to meet the demands of the ground forces, but when the enemy attack finally ran out of steam it was they who cleared the way for the Allied troops to advance.

At times they attacked enemy positions only a few miles from their own bases and enemy infantry came close to reaching the airfields on several occasions. The Japanese made little use of armour and the few tanks they deployed were relatively small, lightly protected and poorly armed. Whenever they did emerge they were quickly dispatched with heavy cannon or rocket fire. 20 Squadron destroyed 13 tanks with cannon and rockets in a single day ahead of the Army's 20th Division, saving it from being outflanked.

After the withdrawal from Kohima and Imphal, the Japanese were pushed back to the Chindwin River by July. The monsoon season delayed the main push into Burma which commenced in August 1944. The fighting would last for almost another year until the last Japanese resistance was finally overcome. As the Allies pushed the weakened enemy south through Burma, encounters with Japanese aircraft became increasingly rare.

The Hurricanes were now solely employed in the ground attack and low level tactical reconnaissance roles as Spitfire Mk.Vs and VIIIs took over the pure fighter roles. Many reconnaissance Hurricanes were stripped of a pair of cannon and later of all armament in an effort to lighten them for the specialist tasks carried out, often below the jungle tree canopy, in support of the advancing Allied troops. Fighter bombers were also fitted with a single long range fuel tank under one wing and four rockets under the other to extend their endurance over the battlefield.

The versatile Hurricane undertook another more unusual task, one that prevented many casualties among Allied servicemen as they entered the marshlands of the Kabaw Valley. Aircraft were fitted with chemical dispensers which were used to spray DDT pesticide to kill mosquito larvae and prevent the spread of malaria.

An 11 Squadron Hurricane Mk.IIC is loaded manually at Sinthe in Burma. **Editor's collection**

Hurricanes remained the most numerous aircraft in front line service in the Far East, although some squadrons were beginning to receive the Republic P-47 Thunderbolt. The final version of the Hurricane, the Mk.IV, optimised for ground attack, was operated very successfully by 11, 20, 34, 42, 60 and 113 Squadrons. As the Burma campaign came to a close many Hurricane squadrons were gradually withdrawn to India, to be rested and re-equipped, but 28 Squadron retained its venerable machines until August 1945, when Japan surrendered after the two atomic attacks on Hiroshima and Nagasaki.

The Hurricane had distinguished itself in yet another theatre. Initially outnumbered and often outclassed, they performed every task asked of them and excelled in the fighter ground attack role. The pilots and ground crew worked in indescribably difficult conditions, the heat, monsoon rains, poisonous snakes, insects and tropical diseases made this one of the toughest campaigns of the war against a tenacious and brave enemy.

The remote battles in the Far East have often been overlooked and many servicemen felt, with some justification, that their suffering and achievements were neglected by the general public. However, their efforts in this theatre were as important as any other to the final defeat of the Axis powers. ∎

Words: Tim Callaway and Julian Humphries

If you don't have a bomb jack, call Jack. Astounding efforts were a daily routine for ground crews on the Far East theatre Hurricane Squadrons. **Editor's collection**

Warrant Officer Michael Dewing took this shot of Pilot Officer Muff in Hurricane 342 of 11 Squadron over Burma on January 23, 1944. This gives a clear idea of the terrain over which the armies fought. **via Julian Humphries**

The shape of things to come. The Republic P-47D Thunderbolt replaced many SEAC Hurricanes in the ground attack role from mid 1944 onwards. **Editor's collection**

Hurricanes abroad
Overseas service and production

Aside from the two biggest overseas customers as already discussed, India and Russia, the Hurricane was also supplied to Argentina, Australia, Belgium, Canada, Egypt, Finland, France, Iran, Ireland, Netherlands East Indies, New Zealand, Poland, Portugal, Rumania, South Africa, Turkey, and Yugoslavia. As well as these countries, RAF squadrons were formed with aircrew from Czechoslovakia, Free France, Greece, Norway and Poland, all of which were equipped with the Hurricane at some stage of their history.

CANADA

Twenty Hurricane Mk Is were received by the Royal Canadian Air Force (RCAF) prior to September 1939, and they were given the RCAF serial numbers 310 to 329. Two were lost in accidents, before an additional machine, L1848, was supplied as a pattern aircraft for the Canadian Car and Foundry Company in Montreal, which had commenced tooling up for Hurricane production in spring 1939.

The first order received was for 40 aircraft. To facilitate this, parts and engines were sent from England and by January 1940 the first aircraft, P5170, was completed. This was a standard MkI with a Merlin III engine which was shipped to England for comparison. It was later used for propeller trials at Brooklands.

With the success of this first batch, an order for 340 more Hurricanes followed. To distinguish the aircraft built in Canada the mark number X was used. This allowed for any future versions of the British built Hurricanes to have sequential numbering. Hurricane MkXs were broadly similar to the standard Hurricane MkIIB, but introduced Packard licence-built Merlin 28 engines, the first being delivered in 1941. Many Canadian built Hurricanes were allocated to the RCAF, but a large proportion were crated up after their test flights and sent to England by convoy.

Many were lost at sea, but significant numbers reached their destination where they were gratefully received by the RAF and the Soviet air force. Many Hurricanes built in Canada were fitted with Hamilton Standard Hydromatic three-bladed propellers which usually operated without spinners, making identification an easy matter. The Hurricane MkXI was a slightly modified variant which incorporated a different throttle layout and was generally retained for the RCAF, although a few were used to train American fighter pilots. The most widely produced and exported version was the MkXII, which initially carried 12 machine guns but was later equipped with four cannon.

The MkXIIA reverted to the traditional eight gun armament and some of these were converted for naval use. The MkXII version was powered by the Packard Merlin 29 with the majority of these aircraft being exported directly to the Soviet and Indian Air Forces by sea. Two of the RCAF Hurricanes retained in Canada were modified to operate on a fixed ski undercarriage which allowed the aircraft to be operated from packed snow or ice.

Altogether, 1451 Hurricanes of all marks were built in Canada, representing almost one 10th of the total production number. Canadian built Hurricanes can be identified by their serial number. Early MkIs carried the prefix P, T or Z, later versions of the MkX, XI and XII carried AE, AF, AG, AM, BW, BX, JS or PJ.

Another spinnerless Canadian built aircraft, this time in the special camouflage scheme used by 13 (Photo) Squadron RCAF. **Editor's collection**

YUGOSLAVIA

The Yugoslavian government had long been a customer of the British aircraft industry and a good relationship existed between their air force and Hawker Aircraft Ltd. Already operators of the Hawker Hind and Fury biplanes, it was natural for the Yugoslavs to show an early interest in the new monoplane fighter.

Yugoslavia became the Hurricane's first overseas customer when an order for 12 Hurricanes was placed in 1938. The first, Hurricane MkI L1750, was delivered from Brooklands on December 15, 1938, and was fitted with fabric covered wings and a Watts two bladed propeller. A second batch of 12 aircraft was ordered in early 1939 and plans to build 100 further Hurricanes under licence, minus their engines, were well advanced. It was anticipated that the two factories engaged in Hurricane production would be able to deliver eight completed aircraft per month provided the engines could be procured from Rolls-Royce in England.

As a contingency, and in an attempt to improve the performance of the Hurricane, a single aircraft was converted to accept the Daimler Benz DB601A engine at the Ikarus factory near Belgrade. This required a complete new set of engine bearers and as the German engine was designed to be installed inverted, it was also necessary to redesign the cooling system. This changed the nose profile considerably. Air tests of this hybrid revealed that the aircraft was faster than the Merlin powered version and had a better rate of climb.

Often the Canadian Hurricane MkXIIs with the Hamilton Standard Hydromatic three-bladed propellers operated without spinners, as here on RCAF5398. **Editor's collection**

A Hawker built Hurricane MkI for the Yugoslav Royal Air Force on a test flight from Brooklands. **Editor's collection**

YUGOSLAVIA BECAME THE HURRICANE'S FIRST OVERSEAS CUSTOMER WHEN AN ORDER FOR 12 HURRICANES WAS PLACED IN 1938. THE FIRST, HURRICANE MKI L1750, WAS DELIVERED FROM BROOKLANDS ON DECEMBER 15, 1938

Another view of the Hurricane MkI for the Yugoslav Royal Air Force with 'George' Bullman at the controls. **Editor's collection**

After the war, the Yugoslav Air Force, as it now was, operated 16 Hurricane Mk IICs and Mk IVs. These aircraft were brought back by 351 (Yugoslav) Squadron RAF when they returned home. This aircraft is now in the Museum of Aviation in Belgrade, Serbia. **Keith Draycott**

When the Germans invaded Yugoslavia on April 6, 1940, there were 44 Hurricanes, 20 Hawker built, the rest made locally by Zmaj. They were divided between three squadrons based in Sarajevo and Zagreb. Interestingly, the Yugoslavian Royal Air Force (JKRV) also operated a number of Bf 109Es. Despite having a total strength of over 800 aircraft, this was not enough to resist the combined German and Italian onslaught and the Yugoslavian government sued for peace 11 days later.

Many Hurricanes were destroyed on the ground by their crews or were wrecked on the production lines before the enemy could capture them. After the war, 16 Hurricane MkIICs and MkIVs, the equipment of 351 (Yugoslav) Squadron RAF, were used by the now Yugoslav Air Force (JRV), when 351 returned home, until the last were retired in 1951.

BELGIUM

The Belgian Air Force placed an order for 20 Hurricane MkIs in early 1939 and negotiated the rights to build a further 80 examples at the Avions Fairey factory at Gosselies. Only 15 of the Hawker built aircraft were delivered before the German invasion of Poland, the remainder being retained for the RAF. However, five RAF Hurricanes were impounded when they landed in Belgium after becoming disorientated or were short of fuel.

Squadron Leader Coope of 87 Squadron gifted Hurricane L1628 in this way when he force landed on a road. Only three of the Belgian-built aircraft were completed, one of which was awaiting an engine, when the capitulation put an end to any further production. The license built Hurricane's armament comprised four 12.7mm heavy machine guns.

SOUTH AFRICA

Seven Hurricanes were supplied to the South African government from 36 Maintenance Unit in early 1940 and were eventually issued to 1 Squadron SAAF at Pretoria. The early exploits of the SAAF in Eastern Africa have been related earlier and Hurricanes supplied to this nation were delivered in the standard RAF day camouflage.

As well as 1 Squadron, 2, 3, 7, 40, 41 and 43 Squadrons SAAF operated Hurricanes as part of the Desert Air Force, while 11 Operational Training Unit and the SAAF Central Flying School both trained pilots on Hurricanes in southern Africa. After the war several MkII machines remained on charge and were operated mainly by the operational training units as late as 1946, by which time the SAAF had received Spitfire Mk22s. ➤

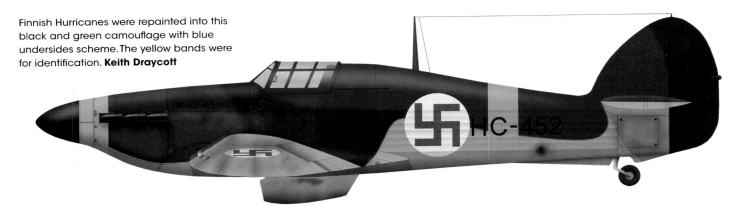

Finnish Hurricanes were repainted into this black and green camouflage with blue undersides scheme. The yellow bands were for identification. **Keith Draycott**

FINLAND

In order to avoid the political difficulties involved in directly supplying arms to the beleaguered Finns, the British government sold 12 Hurricanes to the Gloster Aircraft Company in late 1939. In turn, Gloster sold them to Finland, but two aircraft were damaged beyond repair during the delivery flight. The remaining 10 arrived just days before the signing of a peace treaty that ended the fighting in March 1940. They therefore took no part in what was called the Winter War.

When the Germans attacked Russia in June 1941, the Finnish government seized the opportunity to recover its losses from Russia. The resulting fighting is now referred to as the Continuation War. The Hurricanes had little impact and only five and a half enemy aircraft were claimed by Finnish Hurricane pilots. The supply of spare parts and replacement engines in Finland dried up, limiting the type's use. Since the Russians were now receiving large numbers of Hurricanes it is possible that Finnish and Soviet pilots met each other in similar machines. Several Russian Hurricane MkIIBs were recovered and at least one was used against its former owners.

On delivery, the Finnish Hurricane MkIs wore the standard RAF day fighter scheme with Finnish markings, the blue swastikas which were an ancient good luck symbol. **Editor's collection**

PORTUGAL, WHICH HAD REMAINED NEUTRAL THROUGHOUT THE WAR, RECEIVED 40 REFURBISHED HURRICANE IICS FROM RAF STOCKS HELD AT THE VARIOUS MAINTENANCE UNITS. THIS PROBABLY SAVED THEM FROM THE SCRAP HEAP. THE THREE HURRICANES USED IN THE 1951 FILM ANGELS ONE FIVE WERE SOURCED FROM THE SURVIVING PORTUGUESE EXAMPLES.

The single two seat trainer conversion for the Iranian Air Force, 2-31, began with two open cockpits, but a modified Tempest canopy was fitted later to protect the instructor. **Editor's collection**

CZECHOSLOVAK AIR FORCE IN EXILE IN GREAT BRITAIN
- No. 310 Czech Fighter Squadron
- No. 312 Czech Fighter Squadron

FREE FRENCH AIR FORCE
Free French Squadrons were formed in North Africa, their Hurricanes were marked with the Cross of Lorraine not the French roundel, to avoid confusion with the Vichy French units also in North Africa.
- Escadrille de Chasse No. 1
- Escadrille de Chasse No. 2
- Groupe de Chasse II/3 'Alsace' (341 Squadron RAF)

ROYAL HELLENIC AIR FORCE
The few hundred air force survivors of the disastrous Greek campaign formed a cadre around which the Royal Hellenic Air Force (RHAF) was rebuilt. Serving alongside the RAF in Egypt they became a valuable part of the Desert Air Force.
- 335th Fighter Squadron (335 Squadron RAF)
- 336th Fighter Squadron (336 Squadron RAF)

ROYAL NORWEGIAN AIR FORCE
- No. 331 Squadron Royal Norwegian Air Force
- No. 332 Squadron RAF

YUGOSLAV SQUADRONS IN THE RAF
- No. 351 Squadron RAF
- No. 352 Squadron RAF

POLISH AIR FORCES IN EXILE IN GREAT BRITAIN
- No. 302 Polish Fighter Squadron 'Poznanski'
- No. 303 Polish Fighter Squadron 'Warszawski Dywizjon im. Tadeusza Kosciuszki'
- No. 306 Polish Fighter Squadron 'Torunski'
- No. 308 Polish Fighter Squadron 'Krakowski'
- No. 309 Polish Army-Cooperation Squadron 'Ziemi Czerwienskiej'
- No. 315 Polish Fighter Squadron 'Deblinski'
- No. 316 Polish Fighter Squadron 'Warszawski'
- No. 317 Polish Fighter Squadron 'Wilenski'
- No. 318 Polish Fighter-Reconnaissance Squadron 'Gdanski'

IRAN

Iran, then referred to as Persia, ordered Hurricanes before the war, but only a single example, MkI P3270 (Iranian serial 2-52), was given Iranian markings and test flown by Hawker test pilot Richard Reynell on May 16, 1940. The aircraft was then disassembled and shipped to Iran where its fate is unknown. Ten more Hurricanes were left in Iran by 74 Squadron RAF when they were transferred to Egypt in May 1943 to convert on to Spitfires.

At the end of the war, 18 tropicalised MkIICs were delivered in the place of the original order, fitted with Merlin 22 engines. These were intended as single seat trainers and had their armament removed. One of these, 2-31 (formerly KZ232), was converted into a two seat trainer and was delivered to the Fighter School at Dosham Teppeh.

THE SUPPLY OF SPARE PARTS AND REPLACEMENT ENGINES IN FINLAND DRIED UP, LIMITING THE TYPE'S USE

Initially it had open cockpits with just a pair of windscreens for protection. A roll bar was mounted between the two cockpits and the full armament of four cannons was retained. Later, the aircraft was fitted with a modified Tempest sliding bubble canopy for the instructor's rear cockpit and the guns were deleted. The Iranian aircraft are often referred to as Persian Hurricanes and served as trainers for another Hawker piston engined fighter, the magnificent Fury monoplane, a radial engined development of the Tempest, which Iran received in 1946.

IRELAND AND PORTUGAL

During the war, the Irish had taken possession of the three MkI aircraft that had made forced landings in the neutral country. The Irish Air Corps received 12 surplus Hurricane MkIIB and Cs in 1944, just as the production of the type was being wound down in England. The Irish Hurricanes were based at Baldonnel and were retired in 1947 after a short career.

Portugal, which had remained neutral throughout the war, received 40 refurbished Hurricane IICs from RAF stocks held at the various maintenance units. This probably saved them from the scrap heap. They saw service with the Portuguese BA2 and BA3 Squadrons and ultimately the Lisbon Defence Squadron into the 1950s. The three Hurricanes used in the 1951 film Angels One Five were sourced from the surviving Portuguese examples. ➤

The Portuguese Air Force purchased 40 Hurricane MkIICs postwar and kept them in service until the 1950s. **José Jorge**

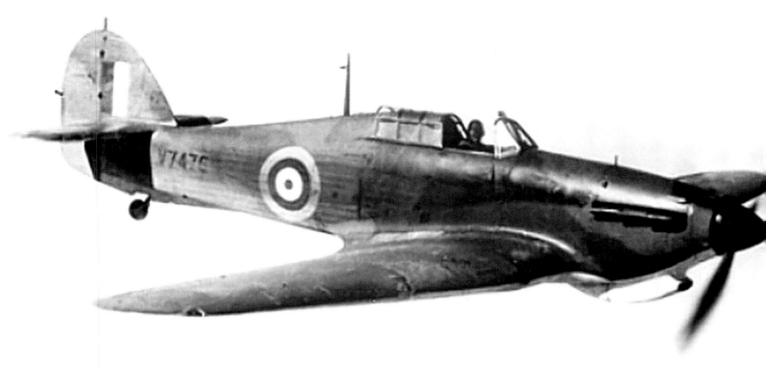

The only Royal Australian Air Force Hurricane to fly in Australia, V7476. **Editor's collection**

ROMANIA, EGYPT AND FRANCE

Fifty Hurricane MkIs were ordered by the Romanian government in 1939, of which 12 were earmarked for urgent delivery, but their history is somewhat obscure. The Rumanians, like the Yugoslavs, operated aircraft from a diverse number of nations including Poland, France, Germany and Britain, alongside several types of indigenous design.

It is known Hurricanes equipped the Grupul 7 vanatoare and Grupul 5 vanatoare of Fortele Aeriene Regale ale Romaniei (FARR or Royal Romanian Air Force), where they operated alongside Messerschmitt Bf 109s. Escadrila 53 vanatoare of Grupul 5 was detached from the attack on the Soviet Union to provide fighter cover for Constanta and the Black Sea Coast. On June 23, 1941,

Lieutenant Horia Agarici from that unit engaged a Soviet bombing raid on the Romanian Fleet. Despite his Hurricane being damaged, he shot down two or possibly three of the attackers, later in the war becoming an ace and eventually a group commander.

The Egyptian Air Force operated 20 Hurricane MkIIBs and Cs alongside the Desert Air Force in the role of local airfield defence. These were replaced by Spitfires during the war.

Aside from Hurricanes supplied to Free French units operating in the Mediterranean theatre, after the war a handful of Sea Hurricanes were also briefly used by the French Navy, prior to their acceptance of Seafires and several different types of American built naval aircraft.

AUSTRALIA, NETHERLANDS EAST INDIES AND NEW ZEALAND

Three Royal Australian Air Force Squadrons operated the Hurricane as part of the Desert Air Force, 3, 450 and 451. One other Hurricane actually saw service in Australia. V7476 been shipped from the UK as part of a consignment intended for service with the RAF's 226 Group in the Dutch East Indies. In the face of the Japanese advances, it was evacuated from Java and flown to Australia by Brian Eaton, RAF, in 1942. The only Hurricane in the region, it was designated A60-1 and used by communications and training units before being retired in 1946 and scrapped.

A number of Hurricane MkIs, possibly as many as 24, were supplied to the Militaire Luchtvaart van het Koninklijk Nederlandsch-Indisch Leger (ML-KNIL) or Royal Netherlands East Indies Army Air Force. These were all lost in fighting the Japanese during the invasions of Malaya, Singapore, Sumatra and Java.

468 and 488 Squadrons of the Royal New Zealand Air Force also operated Hurricanes. 486 formed at RAF Kirton in Lindsey in Lincolnshire in March 1942 and operated as a night fighter unit alongside 1453 Flight which was equipped with the "Turbinlite" Havoc. By July, the Squadron was re-equipped with the Hawker Typhoon. 488 Squadron was formed in New Zealand in September 1941. Equipped with Brewster Buffaloes, the Squadron received nine Hurricane IIBs at the end of January 1942, while based in Singapore. With the fall of Singapore, the Squadron returned home via Batavia and Freemantle in Australia, where the personnel formed the nucleus of 14 Squadron RNZAF.

POLAND ONLY RECEIVED A SINGLE HURRICANE, L2048. POLAND HAD ORDERED 10 HURRICANES, BUT ONLY THIS ONE HAD BEEN DELIVERED BY THE TIME OF THE GERMAN INVASION ON SEPTEMBER 1, 1939.

One of the second batch of Hurricane, MkIICs, supplied to Turkey in 1942. **Editor's collection**

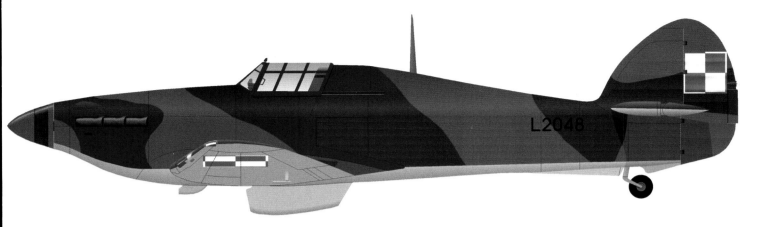

Hurricane MkI L2048, the only one of the Polish order to be delivered before the German invasion in September 1939. **Keith Draycott**

ARGENTINA, POLAND AND TURKEY

A single Hurricane MkIV, KW908, was presented to the Argentine Government in 1947. After some time on public display in Buenos Aires, it was sent to the Argentine Air force flying school at Cordoba, where it was used until the early 1960s.

Like Argentina, Poland only received a single Hurricane, L2048, but for very different reasons. Poland had ordered 10 Hurricanes, but only this one had been delivered by the time of the German invasion on September 1, 1939. The remainder of the Polish order was diverted to Turkey.

The Turkish Air Force, or Inspectorate of Air Forces, part of the Ministry of Defence, as it was properly known then, had expressed an interest in the Hurricane during early 1940. The remaining nine MkI aircraft from the Polish order were supplied later that year. With Axis powers on three sides of the country by 1941, Turkey purchased as many new aircraft as it could afford to ensure its defence.

While it was a neutral country, German ambitions in the region were obvious. Fourteen more tropicalised Hurricane MkIICs were supplied from stocks in the Western Desert in 1942. Eventually a wide variety of Allied types were in service, with Turkey joining the Allies in February 1945.

CAPTURED HURRICANES

Enemy fighters are always highly prized acquisitions and inevitably several Hurricanes fell into the hands of the Axis powers. The Germans came across many wrecked Hurricanes in France but captured an airworthy example in Libya. V7670 was repainted with large crosses over the RAF roundels and flown by several German pilots, remarkably it was recaptured intact in January 1943 when the Allies occupied Gambut airfield.

At least one other MkI Hurricane is known to have been tested in Germany but in truth the Luftwaffe was dismissive of the type and saw little value in carrying out extensive comparative tests. One of the strangest fates befell Hurricane MkI W9147 which flown to Holland by the traitor Augustin Preucil on September 18, 1941. He was a Czech national who had been recruited by the Gestapo in 1939 and made his way into the RAF following many of his countrymen through Poland and then France.

When he eventually reached England he was posted to 43 Squadron and then to 55 Operational Conversion Unit. While on a training flight over the North Sea he broke away and flew to Holland. His Hurricane was recovered intact, other than a smashed propeller and was displayed in the Berlin Museum of Transport. The aircraft along with many other historic artifacts was destroyed in 1944 during an Allied bombing raid on the city.

The Japanese also captured and tested two Hurricane IIB Trops, BE208 and BM900. These were both captured during the fall of Singapore.

The Italians used one of their captured examples in a propaganda film. Two Hurricane MkIs, built by Zmaj under licence in Yugoslavia, had been captured at Zemus airfield near Belgrade in 1941. These were tested then stored at Guidonia along with other captured aircraft. One Hurricane was later used in Roberto Rossellini's period film Un Pilota Ritorna (A Pilot Returns) with a Bristol Blenheim MkIV. ∎

Words: Tim Callaway and Julian Humphries

One of the few Hurricanes to be supplied to America. This MkIIA, Z2963, was evaluated by the NACA. **Editor's collection**

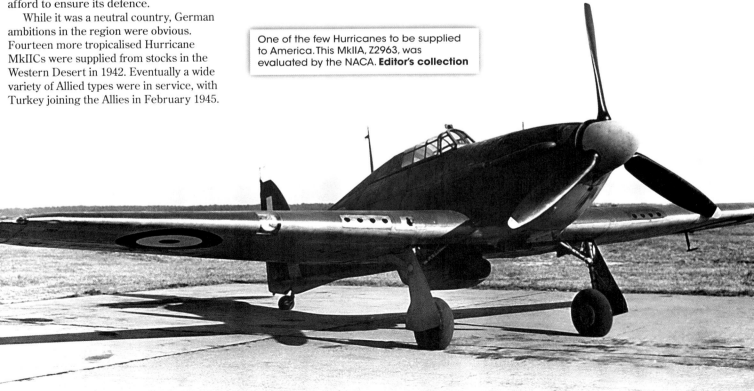

FINEST HOUR ART

HAWKER HURRICANE

HURRICANE FORCE

FLYING CAN OPENERS

P38 LIGHTNING

MARGE

YIPPEE

F4U CORSAIRS

'DEATH RATTLERS'
F4U-4 VOUGHT CORSAIR-WS18 OF VMF-323 CAPTAIN DENNIS C. HALLQUIST - USS SICILY 1951

DEATH RATTLERS

'THE CHECKERBOARDERS'
F4U-4B VOUGHT CORSAIR WR5 OF VMA-312 -CAPTAIN PHILLIP C. DELONG USS BATAAN 1951

THE CHECKERBOARDERS

'THE POLKA-DOTS'
F4U-4B VOUGHT CORSAIR MR 16 OF VMR 332 - USS POINT CRUZ 1953

THE POLKA-DOTS

HARRIERS

IRAQI FREEDOM
BAE HARRIER II GR.7 ZD408/37 OF NO.20(R) SQUADRON.
AHMED AL JABER AIR BASE, KUWAIT - 2003

IRAQI FREEDOM

FLEEING HAWKS
SEA HARRIER FRS.1 - NO 800 NAVAL AIR SQUADRON - FALKLANDS TASK FORCE 1982

FLEEING HAWKS

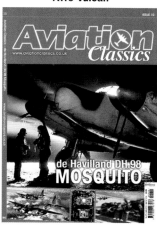

Survivors

The end of service and the Hurricane today

The Hurricane left RAF service very quickly after the end of the Second World War, the last ones seeing service in the Balkans and Palestine with 6 Squadron before they were retired in January 1947. They were replaced by another aircraft from the Hawker stable, the Tempest, and most of them were unceremoniously scrapped, a sad end to a legend. However, a number still fly or are in museums today, often with incredible stories of chance that led to their survival.

Hurricane MkXII BG974, registered N96RW, of the Lone Star Flight Museum at Galveston, Texas, USA. **Luigino Caliaro**

THE LAST OPERATIONS

As the war drew to a close, so did the career of Hawker's most famous fighter. The Hurricane production line ended in July 1944 after 14,533 examples had been built. Even though production had ceased with the MksII, IV and V, it was not until the end of the year that the few surviving MkIs were belatedly declared obsolete, such was the longevity of the Hurricane and its supposedly mediocre performance.

Despite the construction of new aircraft ending, shipments of the type still went overseas after this time, Hurricanes continued to be delivered from existing stocks to Russia for example. Hurricane MkIIs and IVs were still in use all over the Far East, and although predominately employed on ground attack duties, still made the occasional air to air engagement. Flying Officer Chandra Verma of 6 Squadron Indian Air Force shot down a Japanese Nakajima Ki-43 Oscar on February 15, 1944.

Hurricanes still performed many second line duties in Europe during and after the D-Day landings. 1687 Flight used several MkIIs with long range tanks to deliver high priority mail and documents to the Allied forces in France, while others were employed in calibration flights for radar and anti aircraft purposes.

Hurricane MkIIC PZ865 of the Battle of Britain Memorial Flight. **Luigino Caliaro**

HURRICANES STILL PERFORMED MANY SECOND LINE DUTIES IN EUROPE DURING AND AFTER THE D-DAY LANDINGS

The Royal Navy was still operating the Sea Hurricane MkIIC in the fighter role from light carriers in the Bay of Biscay and North Atlantic. On May 26, 1944, Sub Lieutenant Burgham of 835 Naval Air Squadron shot down one of the four engined, long ranged Junkers Ju 290s that entered service late in the war. Later that same day, Sub Lieutenant Mearns and his wing man Sub Lieutenant Wallis engaged a pair of Ju 290s, sending one of the big maritime reconnaissance bombers crashing into the sea. This marked the Hurricane's final aerial victory of the Second World War.

The 'Flying Can Openers', 6 Squadron, commanded by Squadron Leader Slade-Betts, continued to use Hurricane MkIVs right up until the end of the war, operating over the Balkans. This was the last RAF front line unit to operate the type. Postwar, its aircraft were painted overall in silver, with a broad anti-dazzle strip extending from the base of the windshield to the rear of the propeller spinner.

The JV squadron code and individual aircraft identity letter was applied to the fuselage sides in the normal fashion but in prominent black lettering. The squadron also operated briefly from Palestine during the troubled transitional days of the Mandate that eventually saw the creation of the state of Israel.

The tired machines of 6 Squadron were eventually handed over in exchange for Hawker Tempest MkVIs at Nicosia in Cyprus on January 15, 1947. About 60 MkIV Hurricanes had been stored to support this single squadron, which along with around 220 MkIICs also in storage were destined for export to Portugal and Iraq. Once they had outlived their usefulness, the remaining retired Hurricanes were unceremoniously reduced to scrap. Just a few were preserved for the nation, but the rest were simply cut up and melted down.

SURVIVOR STORIES

The final aircraft, a Hurricane MkIIC, PZ865, was completed at the Hawker Aircraft Ltd factory at Langley. It was test flown on July 22 by none other than 'George' Bullman, the man who had flown the first Hurricane back in 1935. This particular aircraft did not see service with the RAF, instead it was purchased from the Air Ministry by Hawker, and in tribute to Churchill's famous 1940 speech it carried the inscription 'the last of the many!' in yellow lettering on either side of the cockpit. After a brief period of storage the aircraft was demilitarised and fitted with a Merlin 22 engine with Spitfire style separate exhaust stubs. It led a useful life as a company communications hack bearing the civil registration G-AMAU.

At some time in late 1940s the drab wartime camouflage was replaced with an attractive royal blue paint scheme, the registration and inscription were picked out in gold and three parallel stripes from the engine bulkhead to the tail further enhanced the appearance of the aircraft. In 1950, PZ865 was entered into the King's Cup Air Race by the Queen's sister HRH Princess Margaret and the pilot was the famous Battle of Britain ace Group Captain Peter Townsend who had served as an aide to the King.

The faster aircraft were heavily handicapped as the slower types were despatched first at intervals based on their respective performance, Townsend with his aircraft bearing the number 41 was among the last to take off. He tore through the field and as he approached the finish line he could see Edward Day's white Miles Magister at very low level diving for the finish line. The Hurricane was beaten into second place by the narrowest of margins in one of the closest and most exciting races in the event's history. In 1960, PZ865 reverted to its wartime colour scheme and was used as a chase plane for the innovative vertical take off Hawker P.1127 which would later evolve via the Kestrel into the highly successful Harrier. The Hurricane was ideal in this role as its broad speed range matched the low to medium speeds of the trials aircraft as it ➤

Hurricane MkII LF738 on display at the RAF Museum, Cosford, Shropshire, UK

Hurricane MkII LF751 painted as BN230, FT-A, of 43 Squadron RAF and on display at the Hurricane and Spitfire Memorial Museum at the former RAF Manston, Kent, UK. LF751 was the basis of a composite including parts from MkII Z3687 and MkIIC PG593.

Hurricane MkIIA AB832 on display at the Indian Air Force Museum, Palam Air Force Station, New Delhi, India.

Hurricane MkIIA Z2389 under restoration to taxiable condition at the Brooklands Museum, Weybridge, Surrey, UK.

Hurricane MkIIA Z3055 restored to static display condition at the Malta Aviation Museum, Takali airfield, Malta (it was ditched off the coast of Malta on July 9, 1941).

Hurricane MkIIB AP740 on display at the Vadim Zadorozhny Museum of Technology, Krasnogorsky, near Moscow, Russia.

Hurricane MkIIB Z2315 is displayed in 111 Squadron RAF markings at the Imperial War Museum, Duxford, Cambridgeshire, UK (a former Russian operated aircraft).

Hurricane MkIIC BM959 is a war memorial at Revda, 200 miles from Murmansk, Russia.

Hurricane MkIIC LD619 is on display at South African National Museum of Military History, Saxonwold, Gauteng, Johannesburg, South Africa.

Hurricane MkIIC LF658 previously displayed as LF345 at the Musee Royal De l'Armee, Brussels, Belgium.

Hurricane MkIIC LF686 is on display at the Steven F. Udvar-Hazy Center of the National Air and Space Museum, Smithsonian Institution, Washington D.C., USA.

Hurricane MkIV KX829 is on display at Millennium Discovery Centre, Birmingham, UK (painted as P3395 as flown by Flight Lieutenant Arthur Clowes DFM of 1 Squadron RAF).

Hurricane MkIVRP LD975 is on display at the Yugoslav Aeronautical Museum, Belgrade Airport, Serbia.

Hurricane MkXII 5390 is on display, painted as Z3174, XR-B, at the National Museum of the US Air Force, Dayton, Ohio, USA.

Hurricane MkXII 5418 is on display, but reportedly fully operational, at the Reynolds-Alberta Museum, Wetaskiwin, Alberta, Canada.

Hurricane MkXII 5461 reconstructed around original partial nose section is on display at the Commonwealth Air Training Plan Museum, Brandon, Manitoba, Canada (Painted as YO-J of 401 Squadron RCAF).

Hurricane MkXII 5584 is on display at the National Aeronautical Collection, Ottawa, Ontario, Canada.

Peter Teichman's immaculate Hurricane MkIIB BE505, seen in formation with Peter Vacher's Hurricane MkI R4118. **Darren Harbar via Peter Teichman**

explored the transition from the hover into level flight. After being displayed at numerous air shows during the 1960s, often in the hands of the famous fighter pilot and test pilot Bill Bedford, PZ865 starred in the epic Battle of Britain film alongside two other airworthy Hurricanes. The aircraft was overhauled at RAF Coltishall, before being handed over by Hawker Siddeley to the Battle of Britain Memorial Flight (BBMF) in 1972, where it has been superbly maintained and expertly displayed ever since.

Another Hurricane MkIIC, LF363, is believed to be the last of the breed to have been taken on to RAF strength, having been delivered from a maintenance unit on January 28, 1944. This aircraft was issued to 63 Squadron and eventually served with 309 (Polish) and 26 Squadrons before the cessation of hostilities. Unlike many Hurricanes, LF363 was not scrapped but served on various station flights. Between 1945 and 1959 this aircraft had the honour of leading the annual Battle of Britain flypast over London.

It also appeared in the films Angels One Five, Reach for the Sky (the story of Group Captain Douglas Bader's life) and Battle of Britain as well as the television series The War in the Air. In 1957, LF363 was delivered to the BBMF's forerunner, the RAF Historic Flight at Biggin Hill. During a transit flight on September 11, 1991, from its home base at RAF Coningsby to the Channel Islands, LF363's engine developed a serious fault.

With the aircraft losing power and belching smoke, the pilot declared an emergency and diverted to RAF Wittering, where the engine cut out completely as he approached the runway. Fortunately the pilot survived the crash but sustained minor burns and a broken ankle. The Hurricane however was completely burnt out.

The wreckage was stored while funds were procured to restore this valuable aircraft and work commenced in 1994 at Audley End in the hands of the highly specialist and expert engineering firm Historic Flying Ltd. LF363 rejoined the flight in 1998 and has delighted the public in

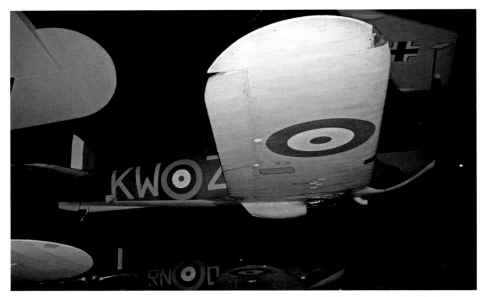

The rare fabric wing of the Science Museum's Hurricane MkI L1592 is clearly visible, but difficult to photograph. **Editor**

Warm summer days, mown grass and the best of British, it can only be Shuttleworth. Here Sea Hurricane Mk IB Z7015 is landing at Old Warden, Bedfordshire, UK. **Constance Redgrave**

Hurricane MkI P2617 on display in 607 Squadron markings at the RAF Museum Hendon, London, UK. **Editor**

several famous and highly representative wartime colour schemes including Douglas Bader's MkI LE-D.

Hurricane MkXIIa 5711 (G-HURI) was built in 1942 by the Canadian Car and Foundry, joining the Royal Canadian Air Force in 1943. It is believed to have served with 123 Squadron at Debert before going to 127 and 129 Squadrons at Dartmouth and thence to 1 Operational Training Unit at Bagotville. Retired and put up for disposal by the RCAF in 1947, it was purchased by a syndicate in Saskatchwan, before being restored by Paul Mercer in 1985, making its first post-restoration flight in 1989.

The Historic Aircraft Collection acquired the Hurricane in 2002 and brought it to Duxford. In September 2005, the Hurricane, now painted as Z5140, a MkIIB of 126 Squadron, became the first Hurricane to return to the Mediterranean island of Malta since the Second World War. It flew there together with Spitfire BM597 as part of the 'Merlins Over Malta' project. Since then it has been a regular display aircraft at Duxford and other air shows.

Hangar 11 is a private collection of superbly maintained wartime aircraft based at the former Battle of Britain fighter airfield of North Weald just north of London. The collection includes a very rare Hurricane MkIIB, one of the 1451 aircraft built in Canada by the Canadian Car and Foundry.

This Hurricane joined the Royal Canadian Air Force and served as a home based fighter for the duration of the war.

Sold off to private owners at the war's end, many of the Hurricanes in Canada ended their days as spare parts supplies for agricultural machinery in the vast farms of the prairies. This particular aircraft remained substantially intact, and was rediscovered by Tony Ditheridge in the 1990s. Restoration work began in 2005 and was completed in January 2009, with this rare Hurricane ➤

Hurricane MkIIC LF363 of the Battle of Britain Memorial Flight. **Luigino Caliaro**

LOST AND EXCAVATED AIRCRAFT

Hurricane I (excavated remains) – L1599 – US-C at Thameside Aviation Museum, East Tilbury, Essex, UK.
Hurricane I (excavated remains) – P3234 TP-E – at Thameside Aviation Museum, East Tilbury, Essex, UK.
Hurricane I (excavated remains) – P3518 – at Thameside Aviation Museum, East Tilbury, Essex, UK.
Hurricane I (excavated remains) – V6685 – at Thameside Aviation Museum, East Tilbury, Essex, UK.
Hurricane I (excavated remains) – P3966 – at Thameside Aviation Museum, East Tilbury, Essex, UK.
Hurricane X (excavated remains) – AM280 – at Thameside Aviation Museum, East Tilbury, Essex, UK.
Hurricane I (excavated remains) – P2725 TM-B – was on temporary exhibition at the Imperial War Museum, London, UK.
Hurricane I (excavated remains) – V6995 – North East Aircraft Museum, Old Washington Road, Sunderland, UK.
Hurricane BD731 reported recovered from Russia and now at Wings Museum, Balcombe, near Crawley, West Sussex, UK.
Hurricane I (excavated remains, part reconstructed) – P3179 – at Tangmere Military Aviation Museum, Chichester, West Sussex, UK.
Hurricane I (excavated remains) – V7233 LV-K – was reported at Tangmere Military Aviation Museum, Chichester, West Sussex, UK.
Hurricane I (excavated remains) – L1685 – at Musee du Souvenir Militaire de Thierache at Martigny, France.
Hurricane V6846 was at Patna, Bihar, India. Reported as derelict.
Hurricane IIB Z2769 whereabouts uncertain, possibly moved to the US from Russia.

STORED OR UNDER RESTORATION

Hurricane AM274, registered N274JW, using parts from three ex-Russian Hurricanes, is being restored by John Norman at JNE Aircraft Restoration Services, Burlington, Washington, USA.
Hurricane MkI P3311 is to be restored to flying condition by Warbird Recovery at Broomfield, Colorado, USA.
Hurricane I P3717, registered G-HITT, is composite based on a former Russian aircraft being restored at Hawker Restorations Limited, Moat Farm, Church Road, Milden, Suffolk, UK.
Hurricane MkI P3554 is with The Air Defence Collection, Shrewton, Salisbury, Wiltshire, UK.
Hurricane MkI L1639 formerly of 85 Squadron RAF from the Battle of France is now with the Cambridge Bomber and Fighter Society, Little Gransden Airfield, Cambridgeshire, UK. ➤

Hurricane MkI N2394 of the Finnish Air Force, serial number HC-452, is at the Aviation Museum of Central Finland, Tikkakoski, Finland.

Hurricane MkI P2902, registered G-ROBT, a recovered wreck that crashed May 31, 1940, near Dunkirk, is with Hawker Restorations Limited, Moat Farm, Church Road, Milden, Suffolk, UK.

Hurricane MkI V7350, cockpit only, is at the Brenzett Aeronautical Museum, Romney Marsh, Kent, UK.

Hurricane MkI V7497, registered G-HRLI, a recovered wreck that crashed September 28, 1940, while operating with 501 Squadron RAF, is now with Hawker Restorations Limited, Moat Farm, Church Road, Milden, Suffolk, UK.

Hurricane MkII Z2330 is a restoration project believed to be in Burlington, Washington, USA.

Hurricane MkIIA Z2768 is a restoration project with the Fighter Factory, Virginia Beach Airport & Museum, Virginia Beach, Virginia, USA.

Hurricane MkIIB Z5227 is an ex-Russian Air Force aircraft and a stored restoration project believed to be in Minnesota, USA.

Hurricane MkIIB BH238 is the wreck of a former Russian aircraft now with Airframe Assemblies, Sandown, Ryde, Isle of Wight, UK.

Hurricane MkIIB Z5207, registered G-BYDL and a former Russian aircraft, is now with Classic Aero Engineering, Thruxton, Hampshire, UK.

Hurricane MkIV KZ191, last operated by the Israeli Defence Force, is now in a private collection in Berkshire, UK.

Hurricane MkXII, G-RLEF, is stored off site with Classic Aero Engineering, Thruxton, Hampshire, UK.

Hurricane MkXII 5389, FN-M, is stored in an unrestored state at the Aerospace Museum, Calgary, Alberta, Canada.

Hurricane MkXII 5447, AF-W, registered C-GGAJ, is being returned to airworthy condition at Vintage Wings of Canada, Gatineau, Quebec, Canada.

Hurricane MkXII 5461, YD-J, is being rebuilt at the Commonwealth Air Training Plan Museum, Brandon, Manitoba, Canada.

Hurricane MkXII 5400 is in store awaiting restoration at the Fantasy of Flight Museum, Polk City, Florida, USA.

Hurricane MkXII 5487, registered G-CBOE is with Classic Aero Engineering, Thruxton, Hampshire, UK.

Hurricane MkIIC 5625 is being restored to flying condition by Moore Aviation Restoration and The Tiger Boys at Campbellville, Toronto, Ontario, Canada.

Aside from these aircraft listed, there are reports of various parts of other Hurricanes in storage in the US, and of course, a wide range of full size replica aircraft on display as gate guardians at RAF stations, museums and other facilities.

rolled out in its fighter-bomber configuration resplendent in the markings of BE505, a Manston based MkIIB operated by 174 (Mauritius) Squadron in 1942.

Its first flight took place from North Weald on January 27, 2009. Since then the Hangar 11 Hurricane has become a firm favourite at airshows, representing a rare version of the aircraft, complete with dummy bombs that are mounted on the wing pylons when on static display.

The Shuttleworth Collection, based at Old Warden Aerodrome near Biggleswade in Bedfordshire, is a national treasure. It contains a large number of rare vintage vehicles and aircraft, including the only flying Sea Hurricane in the world. Hurricane Z7015 was built by Canadian Car and Foundry at its Fort William, Ontario, plant during 1940 as a MkI. After flight testing, Z7015 was shipped to the UK, where, on June 27, 1941, it was converted to Sea Hurricane MkIb standard.

After a short flying career, including time with 759 and 880 Naval Air Squadrons of the Fleet Air Arm, the aircraft was delivered to Loughborough College as an engineering instructional airframe. After several partial attempts, restoration started in earnest in February 1986 by the Shuttleworth team. This led to the first flight of the world's only Sea Hurricane MkIb on September 16, 1995, in the hands of Andy Sephton. Although the aircraft mainly flies as part of the Old Warden air displays, it is a regular visitor to Duxford and other shows.

As I mentioned earlier, the construction machinery to manufacture the long tubes for the fuselage and spars was scrapped when production ended, which is why there are fewer Hurricanes than Spitfires still flying or in museums today. However, modern restoration companies have developed methods of manufacturing the necessary tubes, so we may yet see a number of Hurricanes return to the skies in the near future.

Other parts are also hard to come by, but occasionally a new airframe is discovered in some far flung corner of the world and restored to flying or display standard. You can

Hurricane MkXII Z5140 of the Historic Aircraft Collection in flight at Duxford, Cambridgeshire, UK. **Julian Humphries**

still see Hurricanes fly at many air displays across the world, as there are air forces and enthusiasts who maintain them in Britain, the US and New Zealand. There is something both unusual and really rather charming, in fact stirring, about a Hurricane in the air.

Its wide track undercarriage, tall fuselage and deep engine note lend it a presence other fighters of the time lack. It gives the impression that the stories about its reliability and sheer dogged toughness are all true, and probably understated. In short, the Hurricane is a real character, welcome and refreshing in any air show line-up, doing its own thing its own way, with scant regard to modernity and a refusal to grow old. If you get a chance to see one, don't miss it, its always a real treat.

It has to be one of my favourite aircraft of all time. Many observers felt it obsolete at the time of the Battle of Britain, yet it thundered on, first as a fighter bomber, then as the first rocket armed fighter, but always tough, reliable and able to operate from the kind of places nothing else could. I think that is why it has endeared itself to me so much, it really is the little fighter that could, and indeed, did.

The list of aircraft here is as complete as we can make it, but as ever, there may be aircraft we have missed or which have moved to new owners. If you know of any, please do let us know and we will publish the details on the Aviation Classics website. ■
Words: Tim Callaway

Hurricane MkII LF738 on display at the RAF Museum, Cosford, Shropshire. **Clive Rowley**

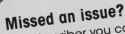

Saab

A Saab Viggen and Gripen break formation, showing the profiles of two of the best know designs from the innovative Swedish aircraft manufacturer. **Luigino Caliaro**

From the first deliveries of the Saab 17 bomber and reconnaissance aircraft in 1942, Saab (Svenska Aeroplan Aktiebolaget) was to become the major supplier of military aircraft to the Swedish Air Force and remains so to this day.

Its innovative approach to aircraft design has kept the company at the cutting edge of aviation from its first jet fighter, the J29, which set world speed records in 1954.

The fighter and fighter bomber line developed into the J32 Lansen, through the double delta of the J35 Draken and the hugely powerful canard J37 Viggen to today's highly manoeuvrable and successful J39 Gripen. Aside from the Swedish air force, these unique aircraft have also been sold to several other countries.

The company has also been successful in the civil market, producing the Saab 340 and 2000 twin turboprop airliners. The Saab 340 has also been produced in a military Airborne Early Warning and Control version, equipped with a powerful radar mounted over the cabin.

This year marks the 75th anniversary of the Swedish aerospace giant, so the next issue of Aviation Classics is dedicated to telling the full story of the company, its innovators and its aircraft.